HEADHUNTING IN
THE SOLOMON ISLANDS
AROUND THE CORAL SEA

THE MACMILLAN COMPANY
NEW YORK · BOSTON · CHICAGO · DALLAS
ATLANTA · SAN FRANCISCO

MACMILLAN AND CO., LIMITED
LONDON · BOMBAY · CALCUTTA · MADRAS
MELBOURNE

THE MACMILLAN COMPANY
OF CANADA, LIMITED
TORONTO

HEADHUNTING IN
THE SOLOMON ISLANDS

AROUND THE CORAL SEA

by

CAROLINE MYTINGER

ILLUSTRATED

NEW YORK

THE MACMILLAN COMPANY

1942

Copyright, 1942, by
CAROLINE MYTINGER

———

———

22819

PRINTED AND BOUND IN THE U. S. A. BY
KINGSPORT PRESS, INC., KINGSPORT, TENN.

TO MY MOTHER
ORLES MACDOWELL

ACKNOWLEDGMENTS

I approach the expression of my indebtedness with due reverence and perhaps a little too much imagination. For one thing, to thank a great number of people for help in doing something seems to imply the performance of a big job in a rather large way. It's vaguely immodest. Yet I cannot reduce the size of my gratitude. It took a lot of people to do this job of painting Melanesians; and, whatever the work amounts to, there was no one person who gave help without whom we could have done as much as we did. The help was not always material. There was, for example, the "squaw man" whose real name we never knew. He was a frayed Irishman married to a Maori woman in the back country of New Zealand, and all he did for us was to row us across a lake—which saved about four miles of a forty-mile walk in pursuit of a tattooed Maori man. But he had evidently got the idea, going across the lake, that we were not walking those forty miles just for fun—only because we were out of funds and could not afford the bus. So on the far side of the lake he dug down into his pocket and brought up three shillings which he offered to us, apologizing for the amount by saying that at least it would buy us a spot of tea some time when we needed it. And if we felt indebted we should just pass it on some time to someone else who needed a few shillings. The knowledge that such human goodness is abroad carried us along almost as much as the less abstract help we received. And it still keeps us from coming unstuck in a world of hates between nations and peoples and individuals. Omission of the names of such persons as the squaw man is unavoidable—there were legions of them; but we are none the less grateful.

I do not need to dwell on my own indebtedness to Margaret Warner. We are both deeply obligated to Walter Boyle, the American Consul at Auckland, and his wife; to W. W. Thorpe of the Australian Museum of Sydney, who had a cellar full of very instructive skulls and pocketfuls of letters of introduction to the "right people" in the islands; to Miss Olive Haynes and Mrs. Rose Nichol, who gave a special brand of aid by being explorers themselves; to Mrs. H. Colwill, who scoured New Zealand and found the last tattooed Maori warrior for us; to Captain William Voy, Mr. and Mrs. Vivian Hodges, Ronald A. Robinson, Mrs. Hamilton Carrie, Harold A. Markham and the Reverend John R. Goldie of the British Solomon Islands, who gave us both bed and benediction; and to Judge F. B. Phillips who, among other things, retrieved for us a year's paintings from tumbling Rabaul.

I am indebted to persons and institutions who, on our bedraggled return to the United States with the results of our four years' work, reassured us as to the worth of that effort. The interest of Dr. Margaret Mead caused the Melanesian portraits to be exhibited by the American Museum of Natural History in New York. And I am grateful to this institution for permission to reproduce here their excellent photographs of my paintings. For later exhibitions of the portraits I am indebted to the Brooklyn Museum, the Los Angeles Museum of History, Science and Art (then under the direction of William Alanson Bryan), the Santa Barbara Museum of Natural History, to which the collection was introduced by Miss Margaret Irwin of that institution, the Legion of Honor of San Francisco, the E. B. Crocker Art Gallery of Sacramento, the Seattle Art Museum, and the

Junior League of Tacoma (Mrs. Albert Hooker and Mrs. Charles Ingram being personally responsible).

For subsequent research in confirming data in this book I am grateful for the help of the Burlingame Public Library, which, under the direction of Miss Irene Smith, is one of the most courteous and efficient small libraries in the West.

Anyone who does not like the result of all this work by so many people as it is reduced in "Headhunting in the Solomon Islands: Around the Coral Sea," may notify Harry Noyes Pratt of the E. B. Crocker Art Gallery in Sacramento. He struggled through the pounds of original manuscript and took the responsibility of advising me to send a few ounces to the Publisher, and I am grateful to him for taking a load from my shoulders. A woman's destiny, they say, is not fulfilled until she holds in her arms her own little book; and it was just plain worry about whether that was true that pushed the writing on to the end. But it was Mr. Pratt who saw the manuscript through to the Publisher.

CAROLINE MYTINGER

August 18, 1942

HEADHUNTING IN
THE SOLOMON ISLANDS
AROUND THE CORAL SEA

1

One day the Expedition set out, quite simply, to paint the portrait of a race of primitive negroids living in the Southwest Pacific. I say "quite simply" because we were unencumbered by the usual equipment of expeditions: by endowment funds, by precedents, doubts, supplies, an expedition yacht or airplane, by even the blessings or belief of our friends and families, who said we couldn't do it. We especially lacked that "body of persons" listed for expeditions by the dictionary. We were a staff of two rather young women: myself, the portrait painter, and Margaret Warner, the bedeviled handyman, who was expected to cope with situations like God—if machinery was lacking, then by levitation. Her expedition equipment was a ukulele.

Yet we were an expedition; we had a purpose. And while the reader may be expected to lose sight of it, as we ourselves often did in the batter of our adventures, precedent requires me to give a sane excuse for having launched us into them.

The purpose was to make a pictorial record of one of those groups of "backward human beings who are fast vanishing from this earth before the advances of civilization." The prospective models themselves were a little less pompous than that sentence. They were the "black" headhunting cannibals, called Melanesians, who inhabit the islands bordering the Coral Sea northeast of Australia. Their territory begins on the mainland of New Guinea in the north and extends through the Solomon Islands clear to New Caledonia in the south. One of the original reasons for our having chosen to paint this particular group of "vanishing primitives" was the compactness and accessibility of their country—one of the few realistic considerations of our plans, I might mention. For to paint a complete portrait of a race its members cannot be spread from one Pole to the other as are, for instance, our nearer-to-home "vanishing primitives," the Indians.

To do a thorough job of race-painting the plan is somewhat like this: first, to paint examples of typical full-blood natives; next, to paint types illustrating the elements that contributed to form the race—all races being composite, Hitler notwithstanding. The Melanesians, for example, are an ancient mixture of indigenous Negroids and invading Mongoloids (presumably from the Indies islands west of New Guinea). Finally, there are the subraces to paint, descendants of full-blood natives who strayed beyond the borders and interbred with an alien stock long enough ago to have formed a distinct new type, but one which still has physical features identifying it with the mother race.

The Melanesians had been particularly thoughtful of the expedition in respect to creating scattered subraces. There are evidences of only two migrations out of the territory: one to the Fiji Islands where the mixture had been with Polynesian stock and evolved a predominantly Negroid type; and the other to the New Zealand islands where, again, the contact was with Polynesians, but here evolved a wholly Polynesian-appearing man.

The itinerary of our expedition should have been determined by this geographical distribution of the race, but even before the launching we had thrown out the New Zealand unit as being too far off the route for our financial resources. I don't know why we should have used this feeble excuse; we were almost penniless to start with. It was probably just an excuse; the itinerary on our chart looked neater without that long dart down toward the South Pole. Otherwise everything seemed pretty shipshape. We planned to paint Polynesians in Hawaii, Fiji Islanders in the Fiji Islands, then nip straight across westward to the New Hebrides for our full-blood Melanesian models.

To illustrate the ancient Negroid element we had our choice of two modern groups. In the western Solomon Islands are some especially dark-skinned Melanesians who were offered to us as a possible remnant of the islands' indigenous inhabitants. And then there were the Papuans of New Guinea, another race, also very dark, and undoubtedly "original settlers" compared with the Melanesians who even today have got only a foothold along the eastern end of the big island. Both groups were in our stride (on the chart) and that was the way we intended to paint them.

Then, as no one seemed quite certain where the Mongoloid ancestors of the Melanesians had started from, except that they were probably Indonesian "mariners," we had our choice of all of the Dutch Indies in which to get models to illustrate this element of our race.

It was as simple as that, our plan and purpose.

Its very simplicity shows, perhaps, just how mature we were when we set off on our project. Scope is the one thing we had plenty of. But possibly, too, those disbelieving friends had a case when they said no female outfit such as ours could go alone to paint headhunters and come back with their own heads. No man had done it. No man had yet tried, we replied. How would we move about, without an expedition yacht? Where would we stay? And what would we do for *money!*

When we sailed out of Golden Gate that foggy March day of the launching all we took with us was our holy purpose, four hundred dollars and some change, good health, and Time. I say "all"; surely that was enough. And probably the lack of funds seemed least important. For we also carried, under the heading Equipment, a battered old cigarette tin which had magical properties for producing gold. It contained the drawing materials which were to pay our way to Melanesia—and back. The broken stubs of charcoal and wads of dirty eraser in it had already created portrait drawings which had paid our way over a good part of the United States; those drawings had bought our present passage to Hawaii, and accumulated the four hundred dollars with which we were launching the expedition. This fund was not intended to take us to Melanesia—it was more a reserve fund "to ship the bodies home." We expected the cigarette tin to keep right on lopping off heads so long as there were white residents in the South Pacific. For so long as there were still Europeans with heads to draw and purses to pay for the likeness, there must be portrait commissions. We hoped.

And we considered ourselves amply equipped by experience to cope with the struggles of those owners of the white heads. For the partnership of the expedition staff was not a new one. Margaret had been playing Hendricka to my Rembrandt ever since I chose the highroad making portraits. Together over these broad United States we had followed portrait commissions from city to hamlet and from coast to coast, Margaret always coping with situations efficiently in the manner she was expected to do on the headhunt. In the many studios, she picked up and handed and put away, and entertained portrait sitters, singing them soothing lullabies with her ukulele or reading to them, playing games with children, and generally keeping everyone awake in the pose and interested in paying for the finished portrait. (There were many savages among our sitters.) In between times she kept house, mended clothing and the car, caught my tears of despair over a bad piece of work, and then went abroad and by some metaphysical system known only to Margaret attracted new portrait commissions. But it was her enduring patience and merriness that best qualified her as studio cat, and would likely come in handy when dealing with real savages.

All this time we were reading anthropology, everything written about human beings that was available for borrowing from public and university libraries. It was not a highbrow choice; reliable accounts of peoples are actually the most exciting literature there is, stranger than fiction. And so out of it grew from the beginning the plan to paint primitives. The world's primitives were vanishing, every book wailed, so what could be more exciting for a painter than to make a pictorial record of some of these peoples before they vanished forever?

Unexpectedly the one thing with which we sailed from San Francisco, and which we had underestimated, was Time. We had a lifetime ahead of us. And we needed it. For it is only expeditions with fat bank accounts behind them that can nip straight to their objective, buy off obstacles, and come blazing home to a public not yet cooled off. Instead of our expedition nipping straight from Hawaii to the Fiji Islands, thence straight to the New Hebrides in a few months, it took us over a year to earn our way with portrait commissions to the heart of Melanesia. And it was by a route far afield of that we planned. In Honolulu, being still on home territory, we had a colossal success with paying portraits, and we painted Hawaiians as well. But they were not the Polynesians we had come for. They were various combinations and degrees of Hawaiian-Japanese-American-Portuguese-Filipino-Chinese-Germans. For the Polynesian-Hawaiian has already almost vanished, mown down by the Four Horsemen of crossbreeding, white men's diseases and vices, and the weakening of race virility which overtake primitives when white men move in.

We consequently looked forward to the Fiji Islands with a special hope, for here in some of the near-by Polynesian groups we might get our Polynesian head, as well as the sub-Melanesian Fiji Islanders probably living right in Suva. But alas, nipping out of Suva was the only nimble stretch we had in this hunt. We traveled to Suva submerged in steerage, and not until the day before arrival when we came up for air did we discover that the steamer was carrying an entire first- and second-class list of bowlers—the kind who roll balls on the green—all bound for the Fiji Islands. There was an annual bowling meet being held in Suva and not only was our shipload of bowlers being dumped in the little mid-ocean town, but bowlers from all over the Pacific were arriving in similar ship lots. Suva had no bed accommodations for little headhunting expeditions and we were forced to get back on the steamer and go on down to New Zealand near the South Pole after all.

Now we had to earn enough to get back up to the Equator. And this was a lot because the only route to Melanesia now was via Sydney. Also the prevailing British attitude toward portraiture was a little different from that back in the dear old United States. It was not the wildfire epidemic that followed introduction of our first portrait in a town at home. In Auckland we made a drawing of a member of the American consul's family and though that was given plenty of "refeened" publicity at the Thursday "at homes," the portrait commissions came in only after cautious and prolonged consideration. And our prices had to be cut almost in half, for New Zealand was still in the depression following the First World War.

However, finding ourselves in New Zealand, although unwillingly, we could now capture heads of the Maoris, who are remotely related to the Melanesians. We had been feeling guilty right along of omitting them from our schedule. And in the end we not only overcame local shyness toward portraits among those who could pay for them, but searched out the last living tattooed Maori warrior, ran him down, and took his head three months before he passed the way of the doomed primitives. Also our pleased customers in Auckland gave us letters of introduction to possible patrons in Sydney, which was important because we had no idea how to crash a portrait clientele in the Australian metropolis. It was not likely that the American consul there would be another fatherly Georgian like the one who had passed us on into the bosom of his family in Auckland.

Sydney was generous to the expedition—for Britishers. When they did not order portraits they fed us, which was a good second best, for we were hungry. They did commission enough portraits, however, to pay our local expenses and buy our passage to the Solomon Islands, though they contributed beyond that less than a hundred dollars to our meagre "body" fund. This was fairly serious, because once we reached the islands there was only one settlement of town size, Rabaul in New Guinea, which would be a familiar market for portrait work; and we could not count too much on the scattered planters of the group who were the only white residents. (Portrait work has many features of the disease epidemic; it has to spread from one customer to the next, and if potential patrons are too widely separated the epidemic travels slowly or not at all.) And when we set sail for Tulagi in the Solomon Islands, Rabaul was still almost a thousand miles beyond, and in another group.

Yet when we boarded the *Mataram* for Tulagi we did not regret our sojourn near the South Pole. We should be just about even when we arrived back up at the Equator, just about normally anxious over finances, and though we had missed out on the Fiji heads we had those of Maoris. But we did have to admit at last that being on an expedition that was earning its own way was much more like being on a Winnie-the-Pooh "Expotition." Anything could happen.

2

When Margaret and I entered the dining room of the *Mataram* our first sensation was one of pleased surprise. For here, behold, was the usual unexpected, something we had not thought of at all. It was a whole covey of white heads for the Expotition—almost a town of them. Neatly trapped, too, on the ship for over a week and unable to escape from any epidemic that started. There were about thirty passengers present and, we knew from the passenger list, about twenty more hiding somewhere, probably trying to survive the transition from Sydney Harbor to the open sea churned to a froth by a record gale of the winter. All the passengers were "white and over twenty-one" and all, with a half-dozen exceptions, were bound for home in the islands. Apparently all we had to do was start the epidemic.

The technique was simple. Margaret would ask someone to pose for me "just for fun," then everyone else, seeing what a remarkable likeness came out of the cigarette tin, would scramble for a sitting. Toward the end of the trip if there were any laggards they would be rounded in if only by shipboard ennui. And the charcoal masterpieces would cost them three guineas a head—for Art had to be charged for in guineas, not pounds, in this British society of "clawsses" where even so little as a shilling difference distinguishes the lowly "trade" from professional goods.

We only waited to pass Brisbane, where the steamer would take on more victims, and to get out of the storm when those missing twenty would have recovered their health and the ship would be steady enough for me to do a charcoal portrait.

All might have gone off as hoped if it had not been for two peculiarities of this journey. One of them was accidental: knowledge of the "Malaita affair," which reduced the entire ship to such a state of suppressed fever that anyone trying to sit still for a drawing would probably have exploded. (I shall have to return to that later because I can't tell two stories at once.) The other was just the normal peculiarity of the island steamer. The planter returning from his holiday in the South is no subject for a portrait, either financially, spiritually, or physically. He is a broken man. He may go South after the three-year period between vacations so ill or weary from the tropical heat that he can hardly stand on his feet; but after his recuperation in the cool bars of Sydney he can barely sit up. The return trip to the islands is a cruel easing back to reality from fantasy. You can't draw that—and get three guineas for it.

There were only five women on board besides ourselves. Three of them were rare tourists for the round trip, brave enough to be tempting the malaria-bearing anopheles mosquitoes of the islands, but without the extra courage to be attacked by ourselves for their heads with any success. The other two women were the wives of planters. The elder was returning from a Sydney hospital where she had gone to be treated for blackwater fever. Blackwater, we learned with some interest, is a frequent result of malaria—usually after numerous attacks—and more often than not it is fatal. This convalescent did not look as if she had recovered; she looked more like a medical school cadaver which has been in the "tank" too long. Her skin had the odd hue of chop suey tea and was so thin that one could trace the blood vessels and muscles around her eyes. Still, she said she felt "quite fit," but even supposing, as we did, that she had not long to live and that her family would be grateful to find a picture of her after she had gone, she made a subject too much like the broken planters to be asked to pose for that important "speculative" portrait.

The other planter's wife was a new chum (new comer), compared with the survivor of blackwater fever. She not only still had her health, she even had a new baby, and a fresh enough viewpoint to give us our best preparation for the country we were entering. Down at the bottom of the stairs in the passageway of the cabin deck, the line had thoughtfully provided a big table and electric iron for its women passengers, and it was here, performing the commonplace chore of ironing baby clothes and cotton underwear, that the two island wives unbuttoned their stiff British upper lips. Women working together can reach some simple truths which are kept guarded when they are idle.

Among other things we learned about the trials of having a family in the islands. It was not likely that this was going to be one of the hazards of our headhunting expedition, but the account revealed, incidentally, certain features which did interest us. All white babies, for instance, had to be delivered in the South because of the danger of septic poisoning when labor takes place in the islands—the hospital at Tulagi notwithstanding. (We wondered how native women escaped.) And the expectant woman must, further, go South early in her pregnancy because of numerous complications during such a period due to malaria and other island afflictions. Then it is necessary for the mother and child to remain under medical observation anywhere up to months after the delivery because malaria is sometimes passed on prenatally to the infant, and frequently babies are born with an enlarged spleen and other affected glands which are also consequences of malaria.

Having a family or, in other words, conducting a normal adult life, seemed to be quite a liability to the white islander. Our young mother, in any case, was no subject for one of our three-guinea masterpieces; she had just finished eight expensive months in the South having her "little sausage" and getting him started safely for his first dangerous year ahead in the islands.[1] And he still could not be breast-fed because this was another way of transmitting malaria.

Malaria, always malaria—that is, when we were not discussing the Malaita affair. Was it inevitable that *we* get malaria and end up looking like a specimen in alcohol! Then, how to treat it? Already we had found there were numerous schools of thought among the initiated. Outstanding was the dashing treat-it-like-a-cold group, a member of which we had met in Sydney. He was a gold miner down from New Guinea on holiday and was therefore in a state of fantasy; but it was he who dissuaded us from taking the antimalaria injections. He said they gave you blackwater fever, right off, without having to go through several attacks of malaria! But we were easy to dissuade because the injections were expensive and we still had more of our American health than Australian pound notes. However, on the miner's advice we laid in about a bushel of quinine capsules for treatment after we had got it. It seemed to be a foregone conclusion here that we were going to get it. Also of this opinion was the old-timer on board, whose remedy was also quinine, but it had to be in *tablet* form. When we got our "go" the quinine had to act quickly and the old-timer knew that capsules took too long to dissolve and be effective. We obtained this information before we reached Brisbane, so we persuaded a chemist there to exchange our bushel of capsules for about

[1] White children who survive the first two years without fresh milk and vitamins are presumed to have weathered the dangerous period. After that they have about five years of normal development before the heat and food deficiencies begin to tell.

two bushels of *tablet* quinine. The old-timer also believed in the whisky cure and for the entire journey was a staggering example of his own best remedy.

Then there were the preventive school and the if-you're-going-to-get-it-you're-going-to-get-it fatalists. The former advocated five grains of quinine daily, starting at least ten days before going into the anopheles country. We began taking daily quinine. And never having had malaria, we then thought it preferable. I wondered how I was going to paint pictures with a skull full of dripping water and butterflies.

Of the you're-going-to-get-it-anyway faction was a young Australian on board by the name, so help me, of Vivian Nankervis. (You'll remember him later, if only by the name.) He was a real new chum, on his first trip to the islands to fill a job as assistant overseer on a coconut plantation on Guadal-canar,* a born Empire Builder about to achieve his destiny. Undoubtedly he would get malaria but he was far too mas-culine to do anything to prevent it. It wouldn't hurt him anyway. You knew that; he was too buoyant, too completely alive to be sick even when he was sick. In other words he was twenty-six years old, over six feet tall, and had the muscles of a boxer. And he was beautiful, even with a name like Vivian; moreover, he had never been ill a day in his life. But before we had got very far from Australia he was as dizzy, without taking quinine, as we were with it. For he had seen the blue of Margaret's eyes.

The quinine-butterfly, no-quinine-malaria issue came to a head after we had made a drawing of the Captain. For he was the only detached and uninhibited model we could find in all those seventy-odd heads on board. This drawing was just something to work on, with no idea of profit, for the cir-cumstances were such that no profit seemed possible. Yet un-wittingly, bread was never cast on more profitable waters than when we gave this drawing to the Captain, for the

* More commonly called Guadalcanal.

Solomons run of the Coral Sea was the skipper's own, and according to his whim we would sink or swim.

We worked in the Captain's stateroom; rather, he posed inside, while I sat outside on deck with my drawing board on a chair. There wasn't room for all of us inside. And as usual I addressed my little prayer to the enchanted cigarette tin as I opened it to begin work. A mere formality, respect for its record as a flying carpet. Margaret, armed with her ukulele, took up her usual station opposite the model to keep his head attracted in the same direction. (To keep the head tipped the same way the model always has to cross the same leg over the other, if he starts the pose with them crossed.) It was impossible not to watch Margaret when she was making music. She enjoyed herself so. And her fingers, trained on the violin, flew up and down the fret board while the other hand whizzed across the strings so fast that the technique alone held sitters spellbound. But the music was good. Margaret is the only player I have ever known who could make a ukulele sound like a musical instrument, and her repertoire ranged from everything to keep dear old ladies awake to the sort of thing that made a captain's foot wag.

Later on we knew this was a wagging foot with a special meaning. For the Captain was plump and Scotch, and when he laughed it was a disturbance which began deep inside his middle somewhere and worked out to the surface like a subterranean upheaval. Nothing happened until it reached the surface. Then there was a violent vibrating of his starched white suit, but with no change of expression on a round pink face. The mouth remained slightly agape to emit bursts of air, but through all of Margaret's slightly bawdy chanties the expression was dourly Scotch. This was the way we made history; the Captain sitting quivering through his hemisphere at Margaret and glowering at me occasionally. But the cigarette tin performed with its usual objectivity. For one thing it gave the Captain a neck. He had one, but it didn't show when he was sitting down; and then we also let him wear his cap. One thing the tin would not do was to draw hair where none grew, and the Captain hadn't any on the top of his head. We knew full well that the only portion of his face he would recognize anyway was that part he shaved, so what he refused to look at in the mirror would be hidden by the cap in the picture. It was very becoming, too, especially with the neck.

"Rest!" I called weakly. I was so dizzy from the combination of still-rough sea and quinine that I could see nudes descending staircases. "So you're taking quinine to keep from getting sick!" roared the Captain. There was always a storm he had to talk above. "Why, you'll get quinine poisoning and lose all your teeth before a mosquito bites you." He began crumpling his laundry. "Just keep your bowels open," he bawled, "drink all the best scotch that's offered you, and you'll still be healthy enough to enjoy your weddings by the time I've got you married off." More vibrating. It was the Captain's claim, not without substance, that he had brought many a virgin to the islands but had never returned one South.

"Now let's see what you've done to me," he said on the final rest. I dodged back, suffering as a portraitist always does, no matter how sure he is of his work, when the sitter views his picture for the first time. I usually dodged right out of the room leaving Margaret to take the brunt of it, and listened around the corner for criticisms unrestrained by my presence. Now there was no corner, so I braced myself. The Captain would either bawl, "My sainted aunt, who's *that!*" and begin to shake, or he would probably grumble that he looked just like that, which is somehow not a compliment either. But we had never drawn a Scotch captain before. This one just looked, glowering naturally, and didn't say anything.

We waited, not being sure whether we even dared offer him the drawing as a present. Finally he left off looking and busied himself mixing what he said was a Mataram Special which he served to us in cocktail glasses, not taking one himself. "That admits you to my faminil," he said, and he was glowering blacker than ever.

Some idea of this family is illustrated in the reasons for the Captain not taking a cocktail himself. We heard the story one day when, nearing the islands, the Captain came up to us as we were hanging over the rail trying to get a photograph of a whale (probably a dolphin) not far off. "Want to see my plantation?" he asked. He pointed off to the west and there, sure enough, were three full-grown coconut palms apparently growing right out of the sea. There was no visible land under them and no other islands anywhere in sight. Under the palms, of course, was a reef which was hidden by the high tide. And the way the palms got there is the story of the Captain's abstinence while on duty. Several years ago his ship piled up on this reef on its way down from the islands. The steamer was loaded with copra and some whole coconuts, and in the wreck some of the coconuts floated onto the reef, took root, and through the years grew into these three bearing palms. Hence, the Captain's "plantation."

When the wreck occurred the Captain was off duty and his second officer was in charge, so it was not his fault. But when a steamer is smashed up the Master is held responsible and he automatically "resigns"; his career as a seagoing captain is then at an end. But this gruff skipper was so beloved by his faminil—all the white residents of the islands whom he had ferried back and forth in his years on the run—that they got up a petition which every last man and woman signed asking that he be retained as their captain. And the line had given in to what was tantamount to a demand. However, lest anyone attribute the wreck on the reef to a Scot's natural affection for scotch, he never afterwards drank anything while on duty, not even his own mild Mataram Specials.

So this was the much-beloved Jove of the islands whose portrait we had drawn "just for something to work on," and who now admitted us to his family with a Mataram Special. When a cocktail is served at the unveiling of a portrait it is usually the artist who is toasted, whether he deserves it or not; but with our model empty-handed and mute about his picture we had to do ourselves the honor. So we toasted the Scots inclusively, the Captain being a Voy and ourselves of the clan MacDowell. "And may we always meet on the high seas." "That's the only place we will meet," said the Voy. "We can't make a living in the Highlands—artists starve." And his eyes under the beetling brows seemed suddenly very gentle. We had seen that look before.

For the world is gentle with artists. We had encountered the fact endlessly on our long journey to Melanesia. And it was something better than just the traditional attitude toward an impractical fellow. We saw the faces of strangers change to sudden interest when we said we were an artist party. Then, we needed help; it was assumed (almost correctly) that we were destitute. Without flattery to myself—for the predisposition toward the artist does not hinge on the quality of his art, nor any charm he may exude as a personality—I believe that encounter with an artist brings out in advance all the "humanness" in human beings, which is not extended to all kinds. Nothing else in the world could have got the penniless Expotition so far as the Solomon Islands.

The Voy was bawling at us—ashamed of having looked human. "Now then, get along and wash your filthy hands for dinner. You look like a chimney sweep." We got along. At the top of the steps we jumped at another bellow. "And be sure to put your stockings on. I'll have no lasses on my ship

half dressed." "We can't," we called back. "We haven't any."
It was true; we had run "ladders" in our last pair weeks ago.

Down in our cabin we resumed the malaria-quinine debate.
The final word of the Voy, that one about getting quinine
poisoning and losing all our teeth, was all I needed in the
way of an excuse to discontinue the preventive. Besides,
would I not get more work done by being sick only part
of the time than by being giddy all of the time? With so
many opinions we had to settle the matter for ourselves, and
we thereupon decided to settle it for all expeditions to come
by becoming experimental guinea pigs. Margaret would continue her daily doses, and I would drop them. (There is a
full report of the results later on in this story.)

3

All the elements present on the *Mataram* which should have combined to make the journey a profitable one for us—the seventy-odd white heads, the world's sweet benevolence, and a fellow Scot for captain whose portrait everyone else, at least, admired—all these were reduced to exactly zero (even without the natural handicaps already mentioned) by the shock of the Malaita affair. The only way I seem able to get started on it is first to introduce the natives of Malaita as we knew them (from books) when we innocently boarded the *Mataram*. It is an unspectacular way of beginning an incident which threatened to make a farce of our entire venture into Melanesia, but at least it gives the reader an even start with what came to be known as the Expotition.

The Malaitamen are Melanesians, like the rest of the Solomon Islanders, and as such, of course, were potential models for our collection. In preparation for painting them we had learned that there was some slight difference in type between them and the neighboring islanders; they were more aggressive and up-and-coming, and consequently were the best labor for the coconut plantations in the Group. The difference was probably due to a remote infiltration of Polynesian blood. Most of the interior of Malaita—though the island is in the eastern Solomons and next door to the seat of government—was still unexplored and outside government control. However, it was estimated that there were between sixty and a hundred thousand natives on the island, with several hundreds more scattered throughout the Group on plantations.

That was all. Nothing we had read had prepared us in any way for what we were to hear, first-hand, about these natives on the second day of our journey in their direction. A week before, Malaitamen in the mountain village of Sinarango had murdered an entire government party!

A murder at Sinarango would not ordinarily have concerned us in the least. Sinarango is in the interior of Malaita where we had not the slightest need or wish to go. And a single murder would not have excited anyone else very much; not even the island administration, nor the white planters, nor especially the southern newspapers. Murders of individual white men still continue cheerfully throughout Melanesia— though with far less frequency and respect for etiquette than in the white men's own countries. It was the magnitude of this job which staggered everyone; nothing so wholesale had happened in years anywhere in the South Seas. When the news finally got through to the southern papers—we did not see a printed word about it until we were tucked on the *Mataram* with our precious dollars in the pocket of the steamship line, which *could* have warned us—the usually conservative press referred to it as a "massacre" and an "uprising"; the Solomon Islands were "in a state of war."

Meantime the islands ahead of us appeared actually to be in a state of war. The Australian cruiser *Adelaide* was on her way to the group, and a volunteer army of planters had organized (there being no standing army except the native constabulary—ironically, Malaitamen) and was only awaiting the arrival of the *Adelaide* for orders. Following us was the *Adelaide's* coaler, and on board the *Mataram* was a naval officer who had missed the cruiser by being on holiday and was on his way to join her. His presence gave us all something to bite on—but where, in the name of San Luca, patron saint of artists, your Expotition-to-paint-natives fitted into this scene of battle not even the all-provident Captain Voy could guess. Nothing like this had happened to him in his twenty-five years of going to the islands.

There was a curious atmosphere on board the *Mataram*, rather hard to describe because those who expressed it were British and not American. We got our impression more from what we felt than what we heard. Where Americans would have been yapping and speculating endlessly, as we do about our own and other people's wars, these Britishers clamped down their long upper lips over false teeth, and waited. They "had the wind up" all the same. They hung over the radio bulletins and at meals made brief, crisp comments which had the sound of questions, and they conveyed something extra by staring in silence at one another after each remark. They seemed, outwardly, not to know what was going on ahead.

The idea of an uprising of Malaitamen was not new to these islanders; rumors of such a move had been circulating through the Group for years, and one of the things which kept it alive was that the white men could see how easy it would be to get rid of every last European in the land in one brief blow. Malaitans were scattered all through the islands; the house-boys were Malaitans, the boat boys were Malaitans, and the labor lines on the plantations were made up almost entirely of these sharp "black fellows." There were anywhere from fifty to eighty boys on each tract under a single overseer, never more than two white men. And the plantations were widely distant from one another, sometimes a matter of two or three hours by launch—and that launch, paradoxically, in the hands of a Malaitan boat boy, was the only means of escape from unexpected trouble.

Without ever having met a Malaitaman we could see that they had no love for their employers. There were numerous tales, pried out of the Voy, of individual conflicts, trickery, and organized practices to bedevil—all of which I shall have to illustrate later by one of our own experiences. But on the whole, all the characteristics of special energy and enterprise which made the Malaitans the preferred labor, also made them the worst troublemakers even in normal times. What they might do at this abnormal time, inspired by their relatives at Sinarango, was anybody's guess.

As we drew nearer the Solomon Islands the reports that came over the wireless became increasingly exciting. We now heard that the planters and missionaries of Malaita had evacuated the island; women even from the other islands were coming into Tulagi for safety. Extra arms and ammunition were being sent by the government to the outlying plantations, while every last man able to leave his tract in the hands of an assistant had now joined the volunteer troop. Then, H.M.S. ADELAIDE LYING OFF EAST COAST MALAITA, and finally, GOVERNMENT LAUNCH RENANDI CONVERTED TO TRANSPORT VOLUNTEER OUTFIT AWAITING ARRIVAL MATARAM BEFORE PROCEEDING TO MALAITA.

We were to arrive that night—ourselves the most belated, but at the same time most excited, brace of headhunters ever bent on raid in the South Seas.

4

It was night, the purple-blue of a moonless night in the tropics. As Tulagi located itself in the dark, we felt that incomparable thrill of coming into a strange port at night, not knowing what the day will uncover. Now there was the dark lump of an island, twinkling like a Christmas tree with lights all over it, and on the level bottom side a massing of light. This gradually became lanterns bobbing in the dark water, and then we could see the ghost-white shapes of little boats, scores of them. Finally figures, then whistles and shouts and cries everywhere, on the ship and all over the water, and that most stirring sound of the islands, the long hallooing *"Sail-o-o, sail-o-o-o,"* when a vessel is sighted. The *Mataram*, with its engines silent and the ship steady for the first time since Brisbane, moved majestically toward the land, drawing the little white boats toward it like a maypole its dancers. Then there was the rumble of the anchor chain and the clanking of the accommodation ladder going down. Passengers rushed to the head of it, boats bumped woodily below. We breathed the odor of land in a sudden waft of warm breeze. It was sweet like the steam of jam-in-the-kettle. Running feet clattered up the ladder and there were shouts, cries, and laughter. We eddied off to one side and presently found ourselves grabbed from behind. It was the young "missus" of Ruavatu (the one with the new baby) screaming an introduction to her tall young husband. "I'm going *home*," she shrilled, as if she hadn't been expecting to. "When the *Mataram* comes around to Guadalcanar, stop off." And she was gone. What did she

23

mean: stop off for tea? White of her, but a little far to go
for a spot of tea if we were to stay at the hotel at Tulagi.
Those must be the Empire Builders, those men in khaki, rushing past as if there were a fire down at the bar. Then there
must be another fire down on the unloading deck; a swarm
of dark, naked figures was piling on board, yipping like
Comanches. The scene had all the earmarks of an uprising—
and by the way, where *was* the Malaita war?

We turned from watching the deck below to find ourselves
absolutely alone. The racket was still all around us but there
was not a soul to be seen.

We were just going to see if there actually was an uprising
getting under way below, when a steward appeared carrying
a little gramophone. Following him was another man with a
stack of records. Calmly the first man wound the machine,
started "Yes, Sir, That's My Baby," and then departed leaving the subordinate on duty by the machine. Next came the
Voy. He had his starched white jacket off, and around his
neck hung a bath towel worn athletic-fashion. A blue rubber
kitchen apron was tied over his ample façade. "Where is the
Malaita war?" we asked first. "The war?" he shouted. "Oh,
yes, did you try the bar?" He was vibrating, but now like a
mound of jelly instead of a pile of laundry. "Just wait a
minute; the war will be here—meantime, may I have this
dance?" And without removing either apron or towel he
whirled me off.

We had not made the width of the deck before I understood the reason for the rubber apron. Without it I should
have been lathered by the Voy globe. As it was I was
lathered only by his hands. It had not seemed a warm night
until this moment, but now we dripped, separately and together. Fountains of perspiration started from my scalp and
began splashing off hair and chin. On the second lap it was
sweat pouring in rivers down my chest and back to gush out

down my legs and soak the linen slippers my feet were already swelling out of. The Voy stank; there is no sweeter word for it. Every now and then he dropped me to mop the soaked towel under his chin and around his neck; then he wiped his hands, took me up again, and away we waltzed, panting and spraying.

This was the formal opening, this workout with the Captain, of the regular "steamer night" dance—war or no war. I had barely got wet all over when the deck began filling up with those gentlemen in khaki. I saw Margaret splashing past with her face smothered in the chest of the tall Nankervis, and even the seat of her dress was wet. On the next lap her glistening face was momentarily visible and it wore an expression of acute anguish. She was now in the clutches of a gentleman in shorts and he was spinning her like a top, standing on her feet to do it. No other biped males in the world can do the things an Australian does when inspired by the rhythm of dance music. And it was my turn immediately. We were two girls to an army, for these hard-kicking, hard-sweating, beer-powered partners were none other than the volunteer army. We fought only half of them; the rest stayed in the bar catching up on the iced beer they had missed by the six weeks' absence of the steamer. But they could tell us little about the Malaita threat that we had not already heard over the ship radio, and we had to "fight-em, good fella" to get that little. No one would be *serious* about the war. I suppose most wars are like this; the nearer one gets to them the less romantic they are. This one even began to take on a Gilbert and Sullivan daffiness as the evening wore on. For instance, the planters, in dead seriousness then, had organized because the administrator was too slow in asking Fiji for military help in running down the murderers,[1] but he had retaliated like the

---

[1] All native disturbances in the South Seas must be reported to the Fiji Island Administration of Native Affairs, and the authorities are reluctant

Puntab of Ook. The planters as they appeared in Tulagi full of revenge were set drilling eight hours a day under the hot sun with the intention of sweating out of them the idea of being a volunteer army. They had stuck it out and in the end got regular military status with army pay, rations, and an officer in command. But one of the irregular rations they had demanded and obtained was a quart of good whisky per week per man to be taken as *medicine* for malaria. Everyone took it as a preventive, naturally, and today had been ration day, so the Malaita war was a hi-de-hi and a yo-ho-ho, and they would be back on their tracts in a week with the scalps of the murdering swine on their bayonets. "How about overseers with Malaitans on their plantations?" I asked a heaving partner. He swung his head like a horse's tail to splash off the drips and then answered lucidly, "Oh, him—he look-em strong fella too much long boy." Interpreted that means, watching —watching the boys good and hard.

So it went. I got back to Margaret and the Voy toward midnight when the deck suddenly cleared. Nankervis had disappeared and Margaret was hanging onto the rail, one slipper off, examining its shredded toe. The *Renandi*, the government transport, had pulled in toward the *Mataram* and its deck was crowded with our late wrestling partners. "Nankervis said he was going to join the army. Is he down there?" I asked Margaret. "I don't know," she started to answer; "he—" And the *Renandi* cut in with a clanging of bells. The *Mataram* responded, waking the dead of the spirit land with a fog-horn blast. Instantly whistles, bells, conch shells, and shouts started up all over the dark water, and then the *Renandi* got under

to report such incidents because these reflect on the efficiency of the administrator. The position of governor is a political appointment which can be renewed, apparently indefinitely, by a good record and, naturally, by the right friends in Australian offices. An administrator makes a bad record who permits the natives to murder more than one white man at a time. For the planters to have organized their own army was a "scandal."

way and headed out to sea Malaita-bound. Down on the loading deck of the *Mataram* we saw a row of black naked backs leaning over the rail, their heads turned toward the departing transport. There was not a sound out of them. But on our deck the gramophone, running down, was whining a hoary *"I've got rhyth-m-m. YOU'VE got rhyth-m-m-mmm . . ."* Then it stopped. The lights of the Ook battleship blinked out around the dark end of the island.

"Well!" we said, surprised. The vast unvarying blue above us was lazily winking star eyes down on a quieted island whose Christmas tree lights had vanished. "Now, that's that," admitted the Voy, "and what are you two planning to do?" We thought we would move to the hotel in the morning, and thus get one more night's lodging and a free breakfast from the *Mataram.* "You'll not stay there long," said the Voy; "hotel's full of wild animals. But if you're set on it, you'll have to do your moving tonight. The *Mataram* won't be here in the morning. We move over to Guvutu tonight, Su-u on Malaita the next day, Berande on Guadalcanar—" "Did you say the steamer was going to Malaita?" we interrupted. "Is it going there *anyway?*" "We are picking up copra at Su-u like we've always done." It was a smug Britisher talking.

"Then we're going to Malaita," we announced. As we turned to go to our cabin I thought I just caught the beginning of a Voy earthquake. I even looked back to be sure, but he had his jacket on now and it wasn't buttoned, so it was not tight enough to show rumpling.

5

The next forenoon, calling at Guvutu on the way to Malaita, we had what I think is the commonest form of narrow escape from murder in these "cannibal isles."

When I woke that first morning in the Solomon Islands it was out of a comatose state bordering on death. It took me at least fifteen minutes to discover I was alive. There were, meantime, some confusing thoughts about savages executing a man. They had smeared him with coconut oil, tied him to a stake in the sun, and watched while the ants finished him off. I could plainly smell the sweet, thick odor of coconut oil and feel the ants and terrific heat, even hear the drum thumping and yips of delighted savages. That was something we had read about the method of execution on Ongtong Java—and I had reached the point of being able to move. My fingers were swollen, banana-sized, by the exercise and heat of last night's gaiety.

When I got my eyes open I saw that the round hot shaft of sunlight drilling into the cabin was a mass of buzzing insects. Not mosquitoes, but copra bugs, the constant attendants of copra loading. The cabin was full of them, and heat, and the odor of coconut pulp being taken aboard the steamer. Margaret, still asleep, was flaying about in the throes of her own nightmare, her face twitching off the "ants" and wet with perspiration.

But now, wide awake, I could still hear the dream savages whooping it up outside. I staggered dizzily to the porthole, grasped it to help my head outside, and promptly ungrasped.

The metal frame was burning-hot. And the glare of the scene beyond blinded me for minutes. The first thing I could see of the Solomon Islands was the gray corrugated-iron side of a huge warehouse. The heat was writhing off its iron roof so that the top fronds of some coconut palms sticking up behind looked as if they were out of focus. The sky above was the blank white of pure glare. Everything that was happening—all the clamor, the drum thumping, the blood-curdling yelps and running—was in the foreground between the warehouse and the loading deck. There was a large black hole where the cover was off the hold, and another large black hole in the doorway of the warehouse, and between these two was speeding a double line of human-sized brown

beetles. Those who galloped out of the black opening in the warehouse were bent almost double under huge hundred-and-fifty-pound sacks of copra—more than the carrier weighed himself. As each beetle bumped up the gangplank, he swung his sack to the deck and with a wild yelp from a cavernous mouth straightened up and became human. Then he thrashed back down the wooden plank, thumping his big flat feet in time with each other. By closing my eyes I could again hear the savages' drums.

So there were our Melanesian models, the heads we had come across the world for.

I could see almost all of every one of them for they were naked except for a strip of calico *lap-lap* rolled up around the loins, but there were no individuals, no personalities. There was a double stream of spindly figures with big faces, each head made bigger by an enormous mound of tightly kinked hair on top of it, a rippling line of skin drenched in sweat and coconut oil to the richness of henna-colored satin. As these figures sped past, the sunlight played over their sharp muscles exactly as it does over the coat of a chestnut race horse. No white-skinned runners ever looked so dazzling. We had heard a lot about the laziness of these "black swine" on the trip up, but I had never seen men of any color work so fast. I had never before seen a mass of naked men working either fast or slow. These first Melanesians were surely unlike any other aggregate of men in the world.[1]

I had put a bathrobe on the hot sill of the porthole and had my head as far out as I could get it, chin hooked over the edge. I probably couldn't have stood, what with the heat

[1] Some of this "enthusiasm" for work is a feature of only steamer loading. The ship must travel on schedule no matter what the size of the shipment of copra at each plantation, but the larger the shipment the greater the speed and excitement, for this is the one time when all the indentured boys work together. Besides, it is "steamer time," as exciting a time for the native as it is for the white man.

and excitement, if I had not been hooked on something. "Down there—you!" bawled a familiar voice. "Haven't I told you not to go out without a sun helmet on!" I just nodded. The Voy might have to be cautious because his brain was almost bare, but I had almost as much hair as a native. And we had never read of a South Sea Islander having sunstroke.

It was an old issue, this pith topee matter. Margaret had started it in Sydney when we laid in a few supplies for the islands. I said I would *not* look like a lady tourist on a camel and refused to get one. (Besides, real ones were expensive.) But Margaret rather fancied the idea and the one she got was just about as chic as a caterpillar tank. The brim was almost an inch thick and curved down all around, the back longer than the front as a theoretical protection to the spine at the neck. When Margaret had her beautiful hat on, the only way you could tell which way she was pointed was by looking at her feet; but if you got down on the floor and looked up you could see her pleased face cast in a striking arsenic light from the green lining of the brim. This is a color chosen to discourage infrared rays and man alike.[2] There was no angle to which the hat could be worn that would make it becoming to even a beautiful girl like Margaret. Yet, when my excuse for not owning this kind of headpiece was that we both could not afford such a monument, the Voy *gave* me one. And we later saw him playing tennis in his bald head right out in the (almost) noonday sun! But that was later.

"Get your hat on or take your head in," the voice bawled down. "Haven't you heard the breakfast gong? And make it nippy; I've a savage I want you to meet." We made it nippy. The "savage" turned out to be the manager of Guvutu, on board for breakfast, and the first part of the meal was de-

[2] Nerve-destroying infrared rays are numerous along the Equator, while the invigorating ultraviolet are scanty because of the extreme density of the atmosphere, which the latter ray is apparently too short to penetrate.

voted to the island diversion of putting the wind up in the
new chums. The two old-timers started on sunstroke, covered
malaria and blackwater, yaws and island sore (which are
different but look the same—either might be syphilis),
mosquitoes, alligators, bachelors, and hookworm, finally getting to the cannibals and headhunters, at which they ended on
the inevitable—the Malaitans—and became serious. Something
had actually happened since we arrived the night before, or
at least news of it had just got down from the west. A planter
had been run off his tract by his boys. The man had got away
on his launch but had not yet arrived at Tulagi. Nothing but
those bare details had reached this end of the Group. There
was a wireless station up west at Rendova, but Tulagi had
been unable to get any information there. "Interesting," said
the Voy. "Very," said the manager, while we went away,
tingling, to get our gear together for the morning's work.

The steamer was to be loading all morning and the Guvutu
manager had offered us a model from his labor line who, he
said (with a glance at the Voy), would make a nice savage
picture. We were to go up to his residence to work and the
boy would be sent to us just as soon as he had removed some
of the scale of the years from his hide. So we started off for
the house—after I had been bawled back for the cork tank, a
piece destined to be the *casus belli* between the clans.

So this was a Solomon Island. We could see little of it because the long winding path which led to the residence was
bordered by bushes and, above them, all we could see were
the crisscrossed fronds of coconut palms. The path was dazzling white coral sand, patterned with swaying blue frond
shadows from waving branches above us. It made one seasick, what with the heat. But the face of the hedge was even
less soothing. It was an almost solid bank of citron-yellow
croton alternating with hibiscus green, on which were wads

of shrieking, scarlet blossoms. It must have been a quarter of a mile before we got out of that suffocating tunnel.

At the end of it we came to the plantation house. But this can pass unsung because it was as near like a house in a temperate climate as the homesick exiles could make it. Here we found the cool-palmed "missus" of Guvutu entertaining Malaita refugees as house guests. It was only nine o'clock but they were having tea—not iced tea, but good, strong, piping-hot English tea. "Oh, you *must* have tea," said our hostess. "You must have lots of liquids. See, you've lost a quart of your own liquid just coming up from the wharf. You'll find yourself losing weight if you're planning to stay very long. And stuff yourself with food; more than you want." We took the tea, and then fell to talking about Malaita.

The two visitors—one was the wife of the missionary at Su-u, the port we were headed for—were only too happy to tell us what heathens the Malaitans were. She and her husband had spent fifteen years working for the salvation of those lost souls on Malaita, and now look at them: run off their island. "But did anything actually happen? Did any native actually attack you?" we asked hopefully. The answer was lost in a burst from all three women. The Malaitamen were insolent, untrustworthy, filthy, stupid, lazy, cunning, ungrate-ful, and about everything else you can think of. All this time two Malaitan houseboys, spotless in blue-bordered sarongs (called *lap-lap* here), with even the monogram of the house appliquéed on the opening flap, were shimmering noiselessly about serving tea like a couple of Jeeveses. There was not a hair out of place in the perfectly round black ball of their coiffures, and each had a red hibiscus blossom stuck in the very top center of his mop. Their hands were clean, and beautiful. The fingers were the long, tapering bony spatulates of the esthete—or what we like to think is the esthete. (Most of the beauty lovers I have met had club thumbs.) The fingernails were unusually long, though cut to the end of the finger, and they were a pale-lilac color (because there is no pigment under the nail). And these delicate hands were handling the fragile china with the elegance of a Ming poet.

Still in our ears was the racket of condemnation, and in our gullets the boiling tea of "civilized" conviction. By eleven o'clock even we were willing to believe that the natives were untrustworthy, because no model had appeared. Margaret staggered when we got up to leave. "You're taking quinine, aren't you?" said our hostess. "Well, you'll both feel better when your blood thins a bit. Take it easy for a while." She was like a mother seeing her children off to boarding school; a dear. Then we began the smothering trip back through the hedged tunnel. The sun was on top now and the frond shadows on the path were motionless; they looked inlaid on the white coral. We sauntered; there was no need to hurry so long as we could hear the distant racket of the loading at the steamer. The air had the thick odor of fresh blood and I went along sniffing blossoms to locate it; no perfume to the hibiscus, and that of the usually pungent frangipani and gardenia was faint. They all had ants in them. I stooped to smell a dead gardenia and felt a rush of hot molasses into my unventilated skull. What if those big-mouthed Malaitans on the ship and the fifty working on this plantation, and those bony-fingered houseboys—what if those hundred or so natives should suddenly drop their sacks and tea trays and take over? What would we do? What . . . ? I stood still to listen. There was not a sound. The *Mataram* must have finished loading; it was silence as complete as a moonless night on a desert. "We'll have to hustle . . ." Margaret stopped speaking, and her jaw slowly sagged. As it was sagging the world was filled with the most harrowing sound we had ever heard. It was human voices, a mob howl shrieking one long piercing note. Afterwards I remembered and could still feel acutely the way my scalp had pulled up, raising every pore and hair, and stayed there while the freezing scream continued. It was only a second or two, perhaps longer, then it died away leaving us with our ears pulled back—and an even less pleasing sound coming to them. This was the crunch-crunch of running feet on the path ahead of us.

If from imagination I should try to paint a picture of a savage bent on slaughter I could not create anything so convincing as the snorting, dripping apparition that suddenly bounded into view around a turn in the path ahead of us. Its base was native all right, and he was clearly as startled by running onto us as we were by him, for he stopped short, heaving and staring. His huge mouth was hanging open and the wide nostrils flared above a long white nose bone. The whites of his black eyes were glinting wildly in a big-boned face smeared with white paint. The whole vision was flapping with branches of yellow croton stuck in arm bands and leg bands and somewhere in the back of him. But it was the bundle of five-foot barbed spears in the hand of this creature which made him the most unpromising fellow I had ever met.

I suppose the adrenal glands can stand just so much and then they give up. When I had taken in about a quarter of this picture the sweat began to spurt. I did not run as I had planned if this horror should come to us. In the face of my Maker, I leaned over and unswallowed hot tea and biscuits! And in the face of *her* Maker, Margaret stood by.

But so did the savage. When I could raise my head again he was still standing in the place where he had stopped. He was still glinting, still vibrating and panting. But now he was *scratching his head*, and it was with the point of one of the vicious-looking spears. This was reassuring enough because anyone dead set on a massacre cannot itch. But the lack of any other action was not. The native remained in the middle of the path. We had the choice of retreating, crawling under the hedge to get out, or walking calmly around him, and then having him behind us. It was the *Mataram* which decided everything for us. It gave a resounding blast—indication that someone on board was alive enough to make a tootle. At the sound of it all three of us leaped into the air, and as the bloodthirsty savage landed conveniently to one side of the path, the Expotition made a dash for it.

We ran and the cannibal ran after us whooping all the way to the water front!

And he was still maintaining a respectful distance behind us when we came in sight of the *Mataram* with, of all unfortunate things, the Voy, very much alive, standing on the bridge watching for us. Even at a distance we could see the obnoxious man shaking. And he was still shaking when we got to the dining room. "Oh, you intrepid headhunters!" he bawled happily. "Only an American would run for exercise in a country like this." He knew very well why we had been running; we had been making material for one of those island yarns which never die. "Did you ever hear that one about those two American girls . . . ?"

The unusual thing about this yarn was that none of it was plotted to give the new chums the wind up. Our savage pursuer was merely the model promised us, but no one had ordered him to dress up like a whooping Iroquois. He had been told to clean up for a "pic-a-ture" and he had done his native best which had taken him two hours. But beyond this, the reason he could be spared from work was that he never did much work. He was an old, indentured boy, slightly daft, who was kept on simply because his life in the village was pathetic. The villages haven't much use for half-wits. Before the government outlawed homicide they were even disposed of as soon as their weakness showed itself in youth. Undoubtedly, dressing up in dance paint and leaves had stirred the fellow up, but he would have looked crazy asleep, with his big hanging lips. Awake, with those glittering eyes . . .

The harrowing howl we had heard had an even more commonplace explanation. This was the daffiness of the normal Melanesian kind. Whenever steamer loading is finished, the loaders are permitted just one magnificent bellow of relief. Another time we heard it we were on the wharf when the last of the gang ran down the plank, and it was infinitely more harrowing at close quarters. The big, dark faces split wide open, revealing pink tonsils, tongues, and rows of strong teeth, and the hysterical piercing yell that went up fairly corrugated the skin. No one could exaggerate the effect of that mob howl given without mirth. Just go down in the cellar and scream as hard as you can in dead seriousness with a mirror held up in front of you and you will get the effect even though your skin be as the lily.

The moral of this chapter is that it does not necessarily take a savage to kill off an author in the "cannibal isles." The combination of heat, yarns for new chums, unfamiliar natives, and a little imagination can do a fine journalistic job. And with the added impetus of the Malaita excitement we died just as bloody a death as the best authors.

The *Mataram* was tucking things in to get on to Malaita when one of the pretty Guvutu houseboys came panting on board with a "paper talk-talk" for us. It was a note from the Missus asking us to "stop on" at Guvutu. She offered, as an inducement, the whole line of native boys as models! Delighted, we hurried to the Voy to ask him to hold up the sailing until we got off. "Skip it," he said briefly, and with no more explanation we trustingly skipped what certainly seemed to be an oasis in the wilderness.

6

Malaita ahead!

With the early morning sun behind it the island was a long slender strip of solid behind a stretch of water so dazzling with sunbursts that the land itself seemed colorless. It was an abstractionist's marinescape. Both ends of the hundred-mile island were left unfinished, dissolved in hot vapor the colorless note of sky and water. The portion dead ahead of us was flat gray from jagged skyline, sharp against a glaring sky, to level shore. There was no height to those unexplored mountain tops, no nearness to the white surf below, which looked like teeth clenched on the lower lip of ocean, a barrier to outsiders who would penetrate the mysteries of the island. A bundle of billowing clouds, those signal flags of hot land in an ocean, hung above the horizon for a while; then the day's sun began its work. The clouds grew smaller and smaller, and then just weren't there, like the Cheshire grin.

But with the sun now striking the western watershed, the land became even more abstract. Lighted crests of ridges appeared in the flat gray, but there was still no perspective. The streaks of light did not create valleys. And even as we drew nearer, nowhere in the shadow could we see those signs of habitation that would have indicated the presence of a hundred thousand "murdering swine." There were no breaks in the solid tone of foliage that would have meant village clearings, no variation from the faint gray-green of the mass to show gardens, land under cultivation. There was no

column of smoke, not even the cut of a river which gives life
to the most nostalgic scene. The earth was hidden under
foliage, and in the blaze of morning the pupils of our eyes
were shut down to their finest focus to see even the palm
trees, feathering the shore like a mustache above the teeth
of the surf.

Su-u, what there was of it, was under those palms at the
beach. And there was more to it than to most of the steamer's
ports of call with the dignity of a name. There was a huge
corrugated-iron warehouse, several little iron outhouses, the
planter's own European house up on piles, and farther down
the beach hidden from view the missionaries' house and a
native village. The missionaries and planter's wife were refugees in Guvutu and Tulagi, and the planter himself, the
remaining white man, was staying on his launch nights for
safety. From what? Business was going on as usual this day.
The beach before the warehouse was shimmering with those
satin loaders again, and a huge lighter loaded with sacks of
copra plied between beach and steamer.

The near-by village was our objective for the morning
and we went ashore immediately armed with our work gear—
that gear now become colored crayon pencils and heavy tan
meat-wrapping paper instead of oil paints and canvas. It was
an outfit lighter to carry than paints, and the studies could be
rolled up immediately and carried with us until we found a
haven where they could be copied in oil and made into picture compositions. The Su-u planter went ashore with us.
We had had breakfast with him, but no conversation went
with it. The man was Scotch, too, but not the cut of the
Voy; he was half as thick, for one thing, and twice as dour,
and he was as mad as hell at the Sinarangoans. This somehow
seemed to include American headhunting expeditions, for we
made the trip to the beach in absolute silence. We had

wanted to ask him if he could spare an interpreter to go with us to the village, but it would have taken castor oil to open a conversation with this gentleman. Therefore on shore we loaded ourselves up with our gear and were preparing to start down the hot beach to tackle the unknown without help when our companion spoke. And in speaking he suddenly became something like a knight in shining armor. "Just a minute . . ." he growled. We waited. "You want a model for a picture?" We did. Then how would a bushboy do? A bush Malaitaman—was it possible? a native from the interior? There was one locked up in one of the outhouses waiting to be taken over to the Tulagi jail to await trial for the Sinarango murders. The police had been out scouring this side of the island for natives who might have scattered after the murders, and they had brought the bushboy in the night before. Was the man actually from Sinarango? one of the "murdering swine?" Well, he was from the Sinarango district, and he had no explanation for being so far from home. Murderer or not, he was enough for us just being a genuine bush Malaitan.

I do not know exactly what we expected to see in this bushboy model, but there was a vague background. There is an old belief among the coast Malaitans that the bushmen of the mountainous interior are "monkey" men, covered with hair and having long tails. But since no Melanesian has ever seen a monkey, there being none in these islands, the appellation would seem to be one supplied by white men to fit a description. However, if the monkey story proves anything it is how much a mystery the bushmen are to even the natives who live on the coast. The missionary-ethnologist, the Reverend Mr. Brown, mentions having met naturally light-haired bushmen who were unquestionably full-blood natives, not half-castes. And our own knowledge of their "unreliability" as expressed in the recent murders made the hairy, long-tailed, light-haired bushman about to be handed over to us a lively picture.

We waited for him to be brought up, standing in the shaded north doorway of the copra warehouse which was to be our studio. Loaders were galloping in and out with sacks of copra and we had our first close-hand look at that striking native energy. These salt-water (coast) natives looked a little less stringy than they had at a distance. They were taller than either of us, their faces looked grotesquely big, and their muscles under the burdens of copra sacks bulged like those of a boxer. (Only healthy natives can be recruited and the planters try to get the men in best condition.) We were a little awed by their yipping closeness. Yet even they had not prepared us for the police boys who presently appeared with our model. The precious bushman was somewhere in the midst of them and all we saw coming toward us was a crowd of tall, great-muscled brown men. These police were the cream of the salt-water natives, picked for their size, their fearlessness and youth. Cocky is what they were with their uniform caps balanced high on top of big black pompadours, leather belts pulled up tight enough to hold up something more weighty than the scanty lap-laps they wore. Police boys are the only natives permitted to have rifles and the first thing we noted was that these guards were unarmed. Was it possible that, being Malaitamen, they too had been relieved of their rifles because of the wind up over a general uprising? That idea was comic later. The police were unarmed for a different reason: they didn't need rifles to guard this bushman.

There he stood, the "murdering swine." He was a little brown gnome, almost a head shorter than any of his hooting captors, and he was as hairless and unmuscular as a maiden. We bulged with joy remembering that this puny little man had thumbed his nose at one of the most powerful nations on earth; it was for him and his fellows that the Australian navy had been called out; it was these little fellows whom a whole Gilbert and Sullivan army had left its work and property to run down. Pathetic brown man—no matter how tough in his own bush.

However murderous the bushman was by nature, there was no evidence of it in his face now. When the crowd of tall police boys parted he had stumbled forward, regained his balance awkwardly, and then stood staring at us like a wild doe with the whites of his eyes showing above the iris. What new horror were these two white creatures before him? He had probably never seen white women before, but we are certain our gender would not have interested him if he had known it. There was a tall rooster tail feather in the very top of the center of his ocher-colored hair and it was trembling as if electric currents were going through it. Also trembling was his monkey tail. For he actually had a long "tail." It was a narrow strip of some soft fiber cloth, which was bound around his hips, drawn between his legs, and hung down in back in a long roll to his ankles. Swinging behind a fleeing figure of the same color it could very easily be mistaken for a monkey tail.

Margaret offered the bewildered little man a cigarette thinking a smoke would quiet his evident fear. The bushman took it, fumbled it between his fingers for a minute and then just held it. The police bullies were hooting because the stupid bushboy did not know this form of precious tobacco—for which they would have turned handsprings. We lit cigarettes ourselves to demonstrate, but when we flicked the cigarette lighter toward the boy he ducked at the sudden flame in Margaret's hand. Howls from the police boys.

The contempt for bush people is a traditional one with the coast natives, probably because the ancestors of the latter had once run the ancestors of the former up into their mountain retreat, which is the human history of most of these islands. The salt-water people are cosmopolitan—"savvy," "flash," "sport"—and these lads of the constabulary with their authority were insufferable toward their captive. The hardest thing for a native to endure (which in the village is even a means of enforcing conventional behavior) is being laughed at, and the police kept up a continuous fire of gargling, yipping laughter at their defenseless victim. This was the only time I purposely used our advantage as lordly Whites. "All right now, *bushboys*," I glared at the strutting police, "let up." They did not know what I meant by "let up," but the "bushboy" had a nice effect; it withered them to silence. Margaret took the little gnome by the arm, led him over to the place where I wanted him to sit, and pushed him to the floor. He subsided onto the spot and never moved from it until Margaret again pulled him up by the arm for a rest. "Better keep your hands off them," said the supercargo who had stopped to watch. Then to our questioning look, "Wogs," he said ominously, "dysentery, yaws, anything—wogs all over them. You'll catch 'em."

I was sitting on the floor to work, peeking around the side of the drawing board at the model, and the boy—for he was little more than that, though all male natives are called boy—never took his wild eyes from the edge of the board where my head was popping in and out like a clock cuckoo. He could not possibly have known what I was up to, but he clearly expected something frightful to happen at any minute.

His was interesting for a human head, the Negroid "long." The hair was fairly close-cropped and the skull behind the ears was narrow and bulged high in back, which made the neck look thin and the wide cheekbones and jaws too big for a normal face. This disproportion was not nearly so evident in the heads of the salt-water police boys who formed our audience because of their concealing monumental coiffures.

We were pleased to see these savvy lads squirm when I looked at them for comparison. They knew all about camera pic-a-tures and loved posing for them, but this business of being stared at for a picture was a new fashion. It made them step back and look silly when any one was a target for my mean picture-making look.

None of the police boys wore ornaments around their heads, though they did have the inevitable woven grass bands above their elbows and below the knees; but all of them had a single hole of varying size in the lobe of the ear, and there was a hole through the septum of the nose to receive a nose bone. But the bushboy had numerous perforations in his ears and nose which must have been very painful to come by. Those of the ears ran up the rims and held little plugs of white coral, and the ones in the nose ran across the tip from one nostril to the other and were filled with pegs of wood which looked like allspice.[1]

The pants pocket of the native all through the Solomon Islands is the foot-long, plaited dilly bag, which the coast native wears chevronwise across his body from one shoulder; but the little bushman had his hanging down his back from his neck. And if he was the usual native he had in it all the things he held dear in this world: betel-nut makings, the ornamented lime box and spatulate, perhaps part of a fathom length of wampum (strung coral disks) and certainly garden tobacco.[2] Then there must be a wooden comb for scratching,

[1] Holes are pierced in the flesh with a sharp-pointed shell and then stuffed with "grass" to keep them from healing together, the incisions usually being made when the subject is a child, and the number and location being determined by the traditional custom of the village. Even the savvy boys seldom improve on this when they leave the village, though they do occasionally add a sophisticated bit of tattooing to their clan emblems, their name in irregular upside-down letters on chest or arm.

[2] Savvy natives smoke stick (trade) tobacco in clay pipes, but the "fashion belong village" is a long bamboo tube. A wad of rolled tobacco leaf is stuck in a small hole at one end of the tube and the smoke is drawn into the tube by sucking on the opposite end. When the pipe is

and a pair of bivalve shells for pulling out whiskers. And if shaving mirrors had worked their way up into the mountains to this boy's district—they are passed up from the coast by trading between friendly tribes—then there was surely one in our model's bag, for we never later met a Melanesian man who did not own one. Only we had reason, when the picture was completed, to doubt whether this boy had ever seen his face.

I got up to examine the ocher-colored hair of the model and he let me poke down in it to his scalp without ducking. There was a thin fan of hair extending out above one ear, stiff enough to have been wire. The fan was real hair but the color was synthetic. The legend of light-haired Negroids vanished before our savvy knowledge of Hollywood blondes. This hair had been bleached.

That fan of hair and the "cock-a-rocka" tail feather were contradictorily explained to us later by different authorities who saw the picture. One said the fan was a symbol of an ethical murder, and another said the cock-a-rocka feather was it. Whichever it was, it was a despised "fashion belong bush." Both authorities were savvy salt-water boys who said the bushman had to kill a man before he could wear these emblems of courage. The villages would laugh into exile the man who could not win them by killing someone—anyone.

The most marked difference between our model and his hecklers was his complexion, which was shades lighter than that of any other native in the vicinity. One could reasonably suppose that the mountain people were of an older stock which had Polynesian blood, but it is our guess that the fairness was due to environment. Later when we got our taste of the interior of the bush we saw that these mountain people lived in a permanent twilight through which came al-

full, the hand is clapped over the end and the pipe passed from one man to the next, each one drawing only one draught of smoke from it.

most no sunlight to tan their hides. And that black natives do tan is a fact. The total absence of ultraviolet rays, not abundant even in full sunlight, and the notoriously deficient diet of the "wild" native could easily explain the stunted stature of our model, even his slightly effeminate features. Another characteristic due entirely to environment was the closely cropped hair, for the bush native does not need the colossal wad of wool on top of his head that the coast native wears to protect his brain from the sun. Occupation could explain the unmuscular torso of the model. His legs were well developed because it was up hill and down dale for him to get his living from the sparse wildlife of the island. The coast people get their living mostly in canoes when they are not working for the white man, and either occupation is arm work. Hence the muscular torsos and spindly legs.

Not until we saw women, coast and bush women, whose occupation and environment (in the sunny gardens) were the same, could we know definitely whether there was a difference in type between the two peoples.

This first Melanesian picture proved to be uneventful, rare as the model was. I had finished the head of the boy completely when the pose came to a brisk end with the murder scream of the loaders down on the beach, indicating that their job was finished and the *Mataram* about to go. Promptly the loaders came galloping and yipping up to the warehouse studio to examine what they had caught only glimpses of during the morning. Margaret shooed the still wild-eyed model to his feet and brought him around to see his portrait where the police boys were hooting with delight. They were not admiring the portrait, by any means; they were laughing at the model for being both himself and the pic-a-ture, but principally for his being a stupid bushboy and not knowing himself. The model was just dumb. He stood there in the din looking in the direction the other natives were pointing, at his portrait, and there was not the slightest sign of recognition in his face. It was as if he had never seen his own face, and if he noted the cock-a-rocka feather he probably thought it was another like his own, not a "likeness." For three hours the boy had not said a word, nor changed his expression from one of utter bewilderment—one of the best models for sustained pose we ever had—and even now when we gave him the stick tobacco (which he did plainly recognize) as a present there was no sound from those monkey-pursed lips, no relief in the worried forehead. The police boys, now in full possession again, gave the boy a push, surrounded him, and off they strutted down the glaring beach. The last we saw of the bedeviled little Malaitaman was his long monkey tail swinging along in a forest of stringy saltwater legs.

7

That long dangling tail was our last sight of the bushman model but it was not the last thought of him. He became a haunting spirit which rose up, trembling and wild-eyed, whenever we were about to be won over by "civilization." Was the bewildered little gnome one of those captives who died in the Tulagi jail even before the Sinarango culprits came to trial? Over a hundred natives were rounded up, but it took the combined forces of volunteer army and navy working in from opposite coasts three weeks to bring in those prisoners. The natives scattered from the villages and the white avengers burned those villages, destroyed gardens, and left the entire mountain district "greatly chastened." It must have left it incalculably shocked, for to destroy the food of even an enemy is inconceivable to a primitive in this poor country. Seven of the prisoners died in jail while still awaiting their trial, from homesickness, fear, and just distress of penned freemen. Of the remaining captives six were found to be the actual instigators of the murders, and these were hanged by the neck until dead. Those indentured Malaitans fortunate enough to be working in Tulagi at the time were "requested" to witness the executions. But being salt-water boys they probably failed to see the government's point. They may even have been highly amused by the comically jerking legs of the hanging bushmen, ridiculous even in death.[1]

[1] Strangulation has not been unknown in Melanesia, but the victims have always been infants who were put to death for ethical reasons. The first-born of a native couple was buried in sand because it was known that evil spirits possessed such a one, and if allowed to live it

Of the remainder of the Malaitan prisoners several were given lengthy jail sentences—a moderated form of death sentence—and the rest were returned to their mountains properly subdued. A suddenly paternal government provided them with enough rice to keep them from starving to death until their ruined gardens could be brought into bearing again, and then peace once more spread over the land.

Only, *had* it? What was the cause behind this wholesale murder? and had it been removed with the "chastisement"? Why should a whole village of gnomes like our model have risen up and slaughtered an entire government party? Was it just "the savage lust to kill," or something reasonable which even we might understand?

The government party that was wiped out had been on duty attempting to collect taxes from the Sinarangoans. Every village in Melanesia under government control pays a head tax of about two dollars and a half's worth of coconuts annually upon every able-bodied male between the ages of sixteen and thirty-six. The only men exempt are natives in the constabulary, the fathers of large families, and village headmen appointed by the government—often over the heads

would grow up sickly or stupid. Perhaps behind this lay the same reason for infanticide and other ritualistic homicides practiced in most of these small isolated islands where overpopulation would have meant disaster centuries ago. But anything like strangulation by hanging is a form of death no simple savage could ever have thought up. Being unimaginatively direct, his method is to stab, spear, or club his victim to death, and then lop off his head, tongue, or penis, the purpose being to retain for himself the courage known to be imbedded in these members. And that is that. Only the civilized mind can appreciate the exquisite value of torture: slowly strangling hope and the will to live by confining the offender against society; watching him frantically claw for freedom through the trial for his life (why are the courts jammed with spectators if not to enjoy this agony?); then imposing the death sentence and giving him maybe several months in which to contemplate his end; finally, with great ceremony, strangling him by "humane means." It took the higher intelligence of Polynesian blood in the primitive Ongtong Javanese to think of anything so satisfying as the coconut-oil-ant execution.

of hereditary chiefs. And with one exception (Port Moresby, Papua) the natives have no voice in the administration of their affairs. "Taxation without representation" is what we called it. On the other hand, the mothers of large families are given a bonus, five shillings a year for four children, and another shilling for each additional child. Unless the lagging birth rate is thus stimulated, the native population decreases and the source of plantation labor dwindles in proportion. And without cheap native labor it would be unprofitable for any nation to hold these islands.

The native taxes pay for medical treatment by a "lik-lik" doctor ("little bit" doctor—a man, white or sometimes native, trained only in first aid and routine dressings) which doesn't make sense if illnesses are caused by malevolent spirits. The other "benefit" of being under government control is military protection, when needed, against raiding enemies. If there is anything else these taxes pay for besides the courts which punish the natives for disobeying the government taboos, we never heard of it. In fact the taxes bring in such a small revenue that they can be regarded only as a gesture: a reminder to the individual of his obligations to an entirely, to him, mythical king. They also "encourage" the natives to work on plantations where they are personally exempt, the employers paying the taxes.

Looking at it from the native viewpoint—as if there should be any other!—these taxes seem to pay only for the privilege of being deprived of liberties. The taboos of the government are even so numerous and obscure to the native that a wall of secrecy has grown up as a futile effort at self-protection—one, incidentally, which was to be the Expotition's greatest stumbling block in understanding our native models. The villagers do not know what the government is going to disapprove of and punish next. It is better to tell nothing to the white men, explain nothing, and offer nothing;

just say "Yes" to every question—that, at least, will keep the man in a good humor.

The first taboo is, naturally, against raiding, and individual homicides, whether ethical or attending a feud. And who enjoys a feud more than a feudist? Raiding is a form of sport, something going on in an otherwise dull world. Abortions are also illegal, though this usually can affect only the sorceress who sells the hocus-pocus and abortifacient—when she can be caught. No one is going to report a figure so much appreciated. This comes under the heading "black" magic as against "white" (innocent), and all kinds of black magic are punishable. In villages not yet under government control the magic of the sorcerers is the only existing effective means of enforcing law and order. There are no policemen, no courts, no way of punishing bad men, and for centuries fear of those black spirits under the command of the sorcerers has kept these people from annihilating one another, as we ourselves might easily do in an unpoliced world. But the government outlaws black magic because it is "terrorization." And terroristic also are many of the practices of the men's secret societies, about which the whole social structure of the village revolves. The hazing of the young novitiates and the waylaying of women and children and nonmembers in the bush by the clubs' patron spirits, who try to scare them out of a year's growth—such little pranks have to be discontinued.

In private life, no man who pays taxes is permitted more than one wife, no matter how many he can afford, nor how many unwilling spinsters the observance of this law creates—not to mention the moral issue resulting from the presence of the leftovers (one, incidentally, we haven't solved ourselves in monogamy). Then, in the village, the numerous dogs which are kept for hunting and sometimes eaten when game is scarcer than usual, whose teeth are afterwards used for currency and personal decoration—most of these dogs must go;

only two dogs to each hunter. The domestic pigs, which had ranged at large for centuries and scavenged the villages clean, must be kept tethered or in stockades, for their foraging in neighbors' gardens starts a good number of the feuds. So on and on down to each tax-paying native giving a certain amount of his time to the guv'men. For on top of obeying all these new taboos and paying taxes, the village men are required to make and keep clear bush paths by which the government may approach to enforce those laws and remove the tax coconuts! Often these paths lead to villages with which the path-hewers have been warring for generations.

Then how is it that a people reputedly so tough and so far outnumbering the whites can have been induced, without wholesale bloodshed, to relinquish their freedom? The process is known as "peaceful penetration"—a most exquisite piece of machinery such as could have been devised only by God-sent Empire Builders. Inoffensive missionaries are the real trail blazers, sometimes preceding even the Empire Builders. Encouraged by the island administrations they make their honestly peaceable calls on villages which have never before had any contact with white men—then later comes the patrol officer.

The guv'men man is a nice fellow, lavish with presents of tobacco, calico lap-lap, and the much-needed axes, and if some chief seems to think he smells badly, the patrol officer simply flatters a rival sorcerer by appointing him headman (with a pretty cap and belt) over the head of the one who won't play. This cap and belt do the work. It is then the duty of the new headman to see that the natives have ready the tax coconuts for the patrol officer when he returns the following year to collect them. The officer departs, doling out a little more tobacco to any noisy grumblers, and the next year he returns, collects the taxes, lays down a few primary taboos, and adds a threat of jail to any delinquents if they fail to pay up the next year. It all takes time but good Empire Builders are patient. The following year a few truculent villagers have to be made an "example" of by being taken down to jail at the coast government station. And from then on "control" is complete, and the operations of "peaceful penetration" proceed on up higher into the mountains.

At other times these primitives seem to think and react peculiarly like normal human beings. Particularly in the interior of Malaita, newly visited villages often told a government patrol officer to go to hell; if he poked his offensive head in the clearing the following year or any year after, it would be promptly bludgeoned. This is what the Sinarangoans told the government man on his first call there, and when he turned up the following year—the year of the Expotition—that was what they did. They let the patrol officer come into the clearing with his lik-lik doctor and police boys, and they let him set up his table. They then lined up (each man frisked for rocks by the police) with their taxes, each man holding a bunch of nuts tied together by their husks. When the officer bent his head to enter the first tax payment in his book, he received those taxes on the back of the head. Instantly the natives behind fell on the surprised police boys with their coconuts; women ran from the huts with clubs and spears, and before the police could use their rifles the job was done. Only one of the party escaped, a wounded police boy; he somehow got to the coast and reported the butchery, but he did not live to see the sweet revenge a white man can take. He died of his wounds before his bush brothers swung.

This, then, was the background of the subjects before us. The villages where we could work would naturally be under government control, would have submitted to the tax, willingly or not, and could be expected to receive us as Whites according to the spirit left in them.

8

"Could this possibly be the notorious lady anopheles mosquito with malaria wogs in her beak?" I held my arm out to our host; there was a tiny insect on the wrist buried to its eyebrows in my hide. While we watched, the flat body swelled with blood to the shape of a ball, and still the insect stood on his head. "Well, I wouldn't be sure about its sex, but it's a dinkie-die anopheles, righto!" "Early for him to be out, isn't it?" I asked, trying to sound calm. "Don't they come only after dark?" "Not on Guadalcanar," our host laughed; "no union hours here." It was still within a half hour of sundown—five-thirty, to be precise—and we watched the sunset spectacle in the eastern sky from the veranda of Berande, where we had been unceremoniously dropped by the Voy that morning. He had simply announced that we had been invited to Ruavatu, not to tea, but to *stop*. Translated, that means to stay. We were advised to take advantage of the invitation because Ruavatu had a "bawth." The Berande launch was to take us down to Ruavatu in the morning and the *Mataram* would pop in on its next trip up from Sydney to see if we wanted to be picked up. Everything seemed to have been arranged for us behind closed doors. And we were unresisting: we were more: we were swollen with gratitude for such luck.

And here at Berande, by a peculiar coincidence, was none other than the young Nankervis, not away rebuilding the Empire on Malaita, but digging into his new job as assistant to our host. No one could have been more delirious at having missed being a hero, for here was Margaret again, practically dropped in his lap by the miracle of that lap being at Berande. Yet even Nankervis was not so happy to see us as were the Berande bugs, and probably few other plantations in the Group were better equipped to introduce us to these new associates.

Berande is a famous old tract. During the time of Jack London it was owned by an American with a countess for missus, reported variously to have been Russian, Spanish, and bogus. The house was then a "palace" filled with European treasures; there were blooded race horses, champagne week ends, and an endless stream of guests. In fact, Berande was so hospitable that any launch attempting to pass without stopping was fired on from the veranda. Then, so the story goes, the countess ran away with a recruiter and the American shot himself. Berande was taken over by one of the big copra shipping companies and now, forty years after the era of glamor, we sat on lame chairs on its unscreened veranda fighting every biting thing except alligators.

Dinner, when we had finished our scotch and warm water "sundowners," might be compared to the old-fashioned hazing of a college fraternity. Berande was a bachelor household and the "mastah" had been in the islands long enough merely to exist wearily between his holidays South. The houseboys— and there seemed to be an army of them—were not the shimmering, embroidered lads of missus-managed Guvutu. With the exception of the "cookie" they were village Malaitamen brought in raw from the plantation to prepare and serve the banquet for guests. The dinner table, consequently, was rather interesting. Something suspiciously like a sheet had been used for cloth, and spread over it was an array which looked as if it had been taken from a delicatessen shelf. There were half-used bottles of catchup, chili and Worcestershire sauces, curry, pickles, mustard, onions, salad dressing, vinegar, several kinds of jam, and some things we did not recognize; all the seasoners and appetizers with which the desperate islanders drench their tinned food in an effort to give it flavor. There was everything there that the Mastah had ever asked for at the table, for the cookie was running no chance of having his head sliced off for forgetting anything. There were dozens of knives and forks and every size of spoon and dish, all in the wildest disorder. And as the room was unscreened and a blazing lamp stood in the middle of the table, the entire banquet board was under a cloud of insects by the time we got to it. They swarmed to meet us, snarling in our hair; they dashed at our teeth when we bared them in polite chatter; they expired in the jams or, mortally scorched, finished their death agony on our plates.

But these insects, at least, we could *see*. It was the invisible hordes of mosquitoes in the dark under the table, and those working down our thinly clad backs that absorbed our attention. I was sitting on a cane chair and, so help me, they were stabbing up from below. To make the situation acute our hosts had set a very formal key—we were Miss This and they Mr. That—not an atmosphere sympathetic to easing things as a cow does on a tree. But our tensely polite company could not fail to see that what interested us more than culture was what was happening under the table. We were alternately stamping our feet as if we were at a football game and ducking down to scratch our legs with one hand while trying to rescue a bat from the soup with the other. The soup was too hot for a bat anyway; it was too hot for an Expotition; and besides it had had a lot of Malaitan thumbs in it. One had just been taken out as my plate was set before me, and it was not the dainty lavender thumb of a Guvutu Jeeves. The fingernail on it was an inch long from root to tip. And all up the dark, bare arms of the waiter belonging to the thumb, all over his naked chest and down the front of his white lap-lap, were soup and other kinds of food. There was flour in his hair and sweat on his brown wild-eyed face. When he served the burning-hot dishes he stood off about four feet and held the dish down under the edge of the table as if it were a football held for a kick.

Between the dozens of courses there were long mysterious waits. Something terrific was going on beyond the door from whence issued these half-naked boys. They were probably throwing our food at one another. There was a crashing of china, a battery of kettles and cutlery, and a continuous yipping and thumping of bare feet on bare wood floor that shook the whole house on its ancient piles. Through the useless screen door between the dining room and what hell lay beyond, a cloud of smoke smelling of wood and food drifted in, and every time a waiter fled through the door it screamed in rusty agony and flapped shut with a bang.

Over the uproar our host was trying to get our attention above the table by shouting that his aunt was an artist, she painted china—and in the middle of the word his face got suddenly purple and he boomed, *"Boy!"* Boys catapulted through the screen door: "Yas, Mastah?" *"Goddam,"* said the Mastah in an apopleptic rage, "fetch-em pickaninny palm leaf. Quick time." The boys jammed in the door, so quick was their time in escaping. And they were back in a jiffy with a small round frond, one of the thousand varieties of palm in the land. "All right," said the Mastah, "now fight-em mosquito 'long table strong fella." The boy with the frond stood with his big mouth hanging open, the wild-horse light of bewilderment in his eyes. *"Goddam,* fight-em!" and the Mastah grabbed the frond and gave the air a vicious swipe with it. The boy took the frond and proceeded around the wall of the room swiping the air. " 'Long *table!"* bawled the poor man. The boy closed in, slapping our back hair. We ducked, trying not to get hysterical, but the Mastah had snorted to his feet; he now had the palm frond and was crouching around the table flapping it at the dark shadow underneath. Crouching after him was the boy soberly flapping his arm in imitation but without a palm frond. After one round the Mastah handed his frond to the boy, roared, "All-a-same!" and rose with a veined scarlet face. As he re-seated himself at the table he wiped off the perspiration with his napkin, spat out a bat, and said evenly, "You shouldn't scratch your bare legs; you'll have a crop of island sores if you do."

We survived the hazing of the dinner, but just barely, because sleep, an embarrassing, drugged stupor, smote us almost before we reached the blessed concealing darkness of the veranda. Nankervis was hell-bent on dancing, and the Mastah brought out a stack of gramophone records which looked as if Dali had painted them. The years of heat had softened the rubber disks and they were stiffened into shapes like cold pancakes. They were, nevertheless, put on the rusty gramophone and between secret dozes we dutifully rose and let ourselves be guided over the rough wood floor. But between sleepwalks even the now-frantic anopheles could not keep us awake.

Then at last to bed.

This was when we started waking up—for this first night on shore in the islands was to be full of contradictions. The guest room was in actual fact a spare room, filled with trunks and every odd and end except furniture. But there was our bed standing in the exact center of the room, looking like a hearse covered by mosquito netting. It must have been a survival of the countess's era, but minus the glamor of her day. The mosquito net was gray with age and looked as if it had undergone machine-gun fire. Many of the larger rents had been drawn together and tied into rosettes with string, and we gathered a few more together with hairpins; but there were still numerous gaps for the delighted hordes of anopheles, which had now claimed us for their own. And inside the net the bed smelled of the tomb, dank and moldy with the years of undried moisture. The mosquitoes followed us in. The first half hour we spent romping around the coop, slapping the nimble little fellows, and the next we spent hairpinning the remaining rents, until there was neither entrance nor mosquito to be seen—though we could still hear the roar of the frustrated outside the net. Then at last we felt safe in blowing out the lamp.

That was just the beginning of the night. For the bed filled up with a new itch. This was the bite of the sand fly, famous for having the most efficient sucking system of any insect in existence, and for being able to get through anything more porous than alligator hide. They, further, have a neat disappearing act. They are all over you sucking up your life blood and then are nowhere to be seen after they are slapped. Our bites raised large welts in an instant, which we scratched.

When dawn came I was surprised to see Margaret standing over by the door, *not* admiring the sunrise. I did not think I had been asleep, but there she was out of bed and absorbed in what she was doing, which was *cutting swollen mosquitoes off her arm with the manicure scissors!* This is what one night in the islands had done to a lass too gentle to squash the poisonous spiders that threatened to drop down our necks in Hawaii.

By eight o'clock we were beginning to understand why the Voy had guided us past other hosts because Ruavatu had a "bawth." It took me a quarter of an hour to find Berande's. Our hosts were already off on the tract and we were left to the mercy of two wild-eyed houseboys, none too kindly disposed toward us anyway. Every houseboy in the employ of a bachelor lives in dread of his acquiring a missus, for we are well known to talk-talk-talk-talk strong fella too much. There was no bathtub in the house, and as the houseboys refused to understand either bath or "bawth," I began a search, leaving Margaret happily shearing off mosquitoes. Around the veranda, outside the house proper, were other little one-roomed houses complete with roofs. One of these was the "house cook" where our breakfast bread

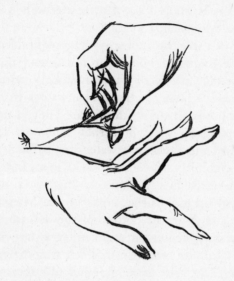

was being burnt over a wood fire in a stove; and I finally found a black cubby hole, about the size of an upright coffin which I identified as the bath by the evidence of a wet floor with a fragment of soap on it. There was nothing else; no tub, no basin, pipes, nor towels. *"Boy!"* I screamed toward the house cook in a good imitation of the Mastah's voice. A boy came thumping out, shuddering at sight of me. *"Water!"* I bawled. "Missus wantemboyhimhefixemwash-wash?" he asked, with a sort of death rattle deflection. I caught the final "wash" and said, "Yes." The boy tore for his life and immediately there were watery sounds coming from the house cook. These finally ceased and I sat down on the veranda steps to view as a resident this island world. There was a double train of ants going up and down the steps. If I had known it they were making off with our clothes by the mouthful. The house was not far back from the beach and between my steps and the horizon there was nothing but a strip of dazzling sand, a strip of dazzling surf, and a strip of dazzling ocean. I might have been on a desert island in mid-sea for there was not a spear of tropical green to be seen anywhere ahead, though far down the shore on each side the coconut palms of the plantation feathered out to frame the sides of the picture. The water is the highway of the islands, and island residences are built as near the side of the road as the tide will permit—and how familiar this barren vista of sand, sea, and water was to become to us in this luxuriant land!

When the bath finally came it was water in a bucket hoisted to a crossbeam of the "coffin" by a pulley. There was a string hanging from the bottom of the pail which I pulled, after closing myself in gloom and hanging my robe and towel on the doorknob for lack of nail. The string did not break as many a subsequent valve chain did; instead it released a freshet of steaming water on my surprised hide—for bath water must boil to prevent fever chills. I sprang back into a wall of nails, onto something squashy, and fled sweating in a drenched bathrobe. Margaret and I met our host on our way down to take a safe bath in the Coral Sea. "Swimming's taboo here," he warned, "dangerous undertow." So in this tropical paradise we went down and got sand-blasted on the safe side of the breakers, thinking fondly of the bawths to be had at Ruavatu, all unaware that baths are an island menace.

9

Perhaps it is the things one leaves behind on land which make the first journey in an island launch such a holy experience for the new chum. Now, with all the heathenish sand flies and mosquitoes on the other side of the surf we can strip our hides in cool shorts and sleeveless jumpers—an intolerable exposure on shore despite the movie version of what the well-dressed man wears in the tropics. And on the little launch one can abandon maidenly modesty. There is a Malaitan boy on board but he is aft at the tiller, and the Mastah has gone into his own coma over some magazines we have brought along. In the shadow of the sail we lie on our backs on the forward hatch, a position which pulls the ribs up and allows the soul to expand. Further to assist soul expansion the artist pulls up one leg and hooks the opposite foot over the knee of the bent leg; this forms in the crotch a dark triangle frame of legs through which to watch the passing pictures. But the picture does not change often. Guadalcanar is an island almost as long as Malaita and twice as fat, and in the full sunlight of midday it looks almost like a continent. There are few of those South Sea coral islets through Indispensable Straits and none along the east coast of Guadalcanar. The shore is an almost straight stretch unbroken either by peninsulas or by river estuaries. But with the tide going out we know when we are passing a hidden river, for a wide semicircle of yellow water fans out into the clean ocean water. And the outline is so sharply marked—as if the two waters were different elements—that in the space of two feet the water is opaque on one side and transparent on the other.

We sail close inshore before a fine following wind, with the ocean ahead a gently dancing expanse of diamonds—no color to it, no blue anywhere, with the sun on top. The jib boom in our leg frame soars up and up as the boat lifts on a swell, straight up past the shimmering horizon into the sky, then ever so slowly pokes down into the glittering sea. And up again. Flying fish spray out with the foam before the prow, their iridescent wings motionless, tails flipping violently as they hit the water to take off again. There is the sweet creaking of the mainsail boom tugging at the mast and those little tunes taut ropes sing; and all the while the gentle gushing sound that water makes when it is running with the boat. The wind is blood temperature and in this flawless moment we feel as if we love and are loved very deeply.

This is just about the moment for something to happen.

On a launch trip it is almost always a squall. The sky may have been spotless a minute ago, but suddenly there is a curdling ahead, always dead ahead. It may start on the horizon, or over the mountains of the island, or it just materializes in the middle; but no matter where, once started, it comes fast. And the clouds are not the pretty cumulus ones seen while safely on land; they are a glowering black mass filled with rain. The sun shining on them casts a long block of shadow down on land or ocean which tears toward us at the rate of knots. Almost instantly there is the hesitating flut-flut of the sails as the wind changes. "Looks for a wet," observes the Mastah, who takes over the tiller while the boat boy begins clearing the deck for a hurricane, furling the sails and removing the cover of the engine.

This business of addressing the engine is largely formality. Everyone knows the engine cannot be started, not at least in the usual way. Island launch motors refuse to start for various reasons; oftenest the boat boy has forgotten to see whether the tank has any gasoline; sometimes spark plugs are dirty or a piece of wire has been borrowed for some other purpose. Frequently, it is just the weariness of age, or hurt feelings from a lack of understanding. For the Malaitan boat boy can polish boat brass by the hour and still never live to know what makes the wheels go round.

But whatever the trouble, the motor sturdily refuses to start by mere spinning of the flywheel. First the boy spins himself out, then the Mastah takes over, always in a rage as if it did not happen every time he used the launch. Both spinners have choked the engine liberally, with the result that if there is any gasoline at all the engine is gagging for air. Meantime the black, cold shadow of the clouds envelops us and we are in a torrent. If the engine had any idea of giving in, it changes its mind in this wet onslaught. Squalls have the liquid content of cloudbursts, and this one drums down on us, drenching wiring, spark plugs, and all on board with the fury of a fire hose. Yet, on all sides beyond our own private block of solid water, the sun is beaming down with a sort of remote innocence. Whitecaps tear toward us, and with the anchor still up waiting for the engine to get started, we drift helplessly backward before a fierce, cold wind. Then the Mastah, drenched and sizzling and chilled, begins jerking in the first paroxysms of a "go" of fever.

On this typical launch trip to Ruavatu we towed behind us a dinghy conveying a wicker rocker, a case of beer, and a crate of live chickens for our hostess at Ruavatu. Also the Expotition supply case was in the boat. I am such a scientific packer that few average strong men can lift the trunks I pack, and it had been all that four boys could do to get the big case over the surf and into the dinghy, where it had stayed. It was a cheap tin trunk, the best we dared afford, which we had got in Sydney, and the synthetic leather handles were already gone; the lock would not stay shut, and the whole business had to be held together with a thick harness strap. We were relieved when the Mastah decided not to try transferring it from the bobbing dinghy to the dancing launch. In it were all our drawing materials, films, both exposed and new, photographic chemicals, even a portable typewriter, and a tiny "Peter Pan" gramophone—and the quinine, of course, our only medical supplies. But most precious was the portfolio of all the studies we had made from Sydney on, the Malaita bushman included. This was no case to receive rough treatment. Therefore, imagine our sensation—which you cannot—when we found the dinghy, supply case, chickens and all, *gone!*

The last we had seen of the dinghy was when the stalled launch floated past it. Then the launch, pulled around by the dinghy's tagging weight, had pointed back toward Berande and headed straight in toward a line of surf over some reefs. From then on our attention had been devoted to the imminence of the hereafter. The anchor was still up for no reason I could fathom until I asked, when I found that there was no bottom for it to catch onto in this "foul ground" until we got uncomfortably near the reef. The useless engine boy was set to work at the prow paddling with the dinghy oar to head us out to sea, and I took the tiller, so we floated sideways toward death and destruction on the reef. Still the Mastah did not hoist a sail when even the small jib would have taken us out to safety in this hurricane. Planters on launches are always like this; perhaps because they have escaped so often, and the ones who haven't aren't jeopardizing the lives of Expotitions. But this time, without Margaret's not-too-welcome help, I wonder if the Mastah would not have given in and used the sail. Sheltered under a tarpaulin the two of them hurriedly dried spark plugs on their still-dry crotches, and then Margaret blew out the gas line. It must have had sand or water in it even before the deluge, because the minute it was connected again and the flywheel spun, the engine chuckled and snorted into action. Just on the brink, too, when we were getting into the swells before the surf. But even then we did not miss the dinghy. Heading out to sea and back into the teeth of the racing whitecaps, we had plenty to engage our attention; Margaret and I were down in the hatch to get out of the cold wind; and we had probably gone a mile before we heard the bellow of astonishment from the Mastah. Followed a scorching barrage of pidgin English addressed to the boy for not securing the dinghy tightly enough. My first morbid thought was that the boat had floated into the reef surf and was naturally at the bottom of the sea by this time. The launch, nevertheless, headed back toward Berande to search, and now with the sea and gale behind us we passed the scene of our late escape in a jiffy. Nothing floating on the water there, not even between the shore and reef surf. We kept on, cruising inshore as near as we dared, and must have gone two miles when we heard the incongruous shout of "*Sail-o*" from the boy. Out to sea, on the border of the cloud area, but silhouetted against a beaming ocean beyond, was the dinghy. All we could do

was laugh hysterically. The rocker was rocking violently and the drenched chickens had their long thin necks stretched up, waving them back and forth to counterbalance the bobbing boat. And as we drew nearer we could see the shining wet top of our beloved supply case.

One usually finishes a launch trip after dark; this is in order that the landing over the surf will not lose any zest in contrast to the trip itself. It was therefore black night when we sighted the beautiful lights of the Ruavatu residence. It was no longer raining but the clouds were low, and along the horizon to the south was a pale-green remnant of twilight. Our boat boy posed himself against it, a purple-black profile with a big mound of hair on top and a curling rose conch shell to his lips. He blew a long mooing blast on the shell which raised the hair on our chilled skin. Another blast and then we saw swinging lanterns coming down the beach from the lights of the house. "Sail-o-o," came the cry over the wind. We dropped anchor well out from shore, for the water was fiercely rough behind the surf. And now lay before us the business of getting on land.

We went one at a time, and my turn came first. While Margaret and the Mastah held the ropes at each end of the wrestling dinghy (in which the boy was already at the oars), I leaped from the comparative safety of the launch deck into the dark and landed by sheer luck in the dinghy, on my chest on top of the crate of chickens. The boat swung into a bottomless pit of black, then the foam of a whitecap washed overboard as the boy pulled us around in the trough and, rowing furiously, headed straight for the precipice of surf. Dimly I saw black heads and arms bobbing around in the far side of it, and then suddenly the breaker dropped with a roar, and we with it. Hands grabbed the sides of the dinghy to prevent it from being sucked out in the strong ebb flow.

It dragged the dark figures a little way, but somehow the rocking chair was out, and I was on it—just as a wall of foam bore down behind us. I shall never know how those chair boys manage to keep their feet, how they can carry the monumental white men between them through the surf and do not drop them. Yet they never do, even intentionally. These boys not only kept their feet, they ran with my ten stone between them in a fiercely pounding waterfall, on sucking sand, up to solid land. And they did not throw me on my face on the beach as I deserved, for I had been clutching the precious hair of one of them through the entire trip.

Then, since these people are British, one says just as formal a how-do-you-do to one's hosts as if one's seat were dry.

The bewildered chickens came out of the surf next, then the case of beer, and finally Margaret followed by the Mastah on his own feet. Rather, he was on all fours, not being a Malaita salt-water boy. When we saw him in the light of the veranda he was jerking like a man with epilepsy and his face was the color of a flamingo. This was a "dinkie-die go of fever, righto-o-o."

But the Mastah's suffering was nothing compared to ours when a few hours later we went to get our toilet case from the stacked luggage on the veranda. The supply case had been dropped in the surf!

10

For the first week at Ruavatu we did nothing but try to salvage drawing materials and nurse our other supplies back to health. The supply trunk must have stayed in the ocean for some time because even after the contents were taken out there was about a foot of water in the bottom of it. The drawings, first of all—poor pulpy sheets of paper now, reminding one of the temporal quality of art—were spread out to dry all over the sand before the house, weighted down with rocks to keep them from blowing away. The unused drawing paper, a huge roll of it, was unrolled about a quarter of a mile down the beach above tide line, and this was also weighted with stones, so that the wind could tear it—though the idea was to dry it in the hot sun. But the hot sun of the tropics does not dry; it merely steams and buckles paper. Scores of fiddler crabs and other forms of wild life took shelter under its shade, dug caves, and created families. The first night we left the pictures and paper out overnight, reassured by our hosts that there would be no rain; Ruavatu was going through a drought and not even the launch trip squalls touched it to fill the water tank which drained from the corrugated-iron roof. In the morning we found havoc. Some nocturnal insects or animals had eaten holes in both drawings and unused paper. The paper, being meat-wrapping stock, had a little oil in it (which took the crayon better than rough stock), but curiously the oil-hungry beasts had not touched the crayons of the drawings. Still the paper was eaten away behind them and when we picked up the Malaita bushboy great freckles dropped out of his face.

All of the studies were promptly put in the portfolio where they never did dry; nor did the drawing paper. Working on it was like drawing on damp, corrugated cloth; erasures rolled up the surface, or ground the error deeper, and any spirited attack with the crayon simply dug holes. Those hundreds of crayon pencils, being waterproof wax, should not have been damaged, but the wood of pencils is made of two sections glued together, and these all came unglued. We restuck them, bandaged them with twine, and hoped—in vain—that the sun would dry the glue. Charcoal, red chalk, erasers, and thumbtacks we roasted in the oven until done. The rubber erasers got overdone, but when cooled they worked better than when they were damp.

Sydney had been unable to supply us with the films that come in metal tubes and we had been obliged to take ordinary tinfoil-wrapped rolls which, of course, were ruined, as were all of the exposed films. And photographic paper and chemicals, even those in tins, were too damp to be safe—in case we ever again owned a film that had to be developed and printed, which did not seem likely. About the only objects we restored to their original use were the typewriter and dinky gramophone, which were soaked in tubs of kerosene. They emerged gummed but still kicking.

I needn't go on; everything we were to use, the very core of the Expotition, had been in that supply case, and the only thing we did not groan over was the mush of quinine. We saved this anyway, Margaret planning to take her doses by the spoonful, or even by the chip if it ever dried.

When the full extent of the damage had been realized we tightened our belts, held our heads, and wrote out a long, expensive radiogram to an art supply firm in Sydney requesting a waterproof oil painting outfit, no matter how heavy it was to carry. But sending a radiogram in the Solomon Islands is not a simple matter even if you have the gold it costs. The wireless station is at Tulagi and Tulagi was thirty miles away. Also Ruavatu had no launch. This was on account of the Malaita war, for ordinarily the plantation shared the launch of a neighbor whose tract adjoined ours; he had gone off to scorch Malaita in the volunteer army, then sent the launch, in charge of a boss boy, off on a recruiting trip. The radio talk-talk therefore had to be given to a runner who theoretically tore off with it for Berande. The Mastah there would then take it to Tulagi on his next trip and when the *Mataram* returned in six weeks the art supplies would be on it. Meantime I had the prospect of working with materials which gave me about the same sense of security as a woodchopper would have chopping with an axe with a loose head. I might kill myself at it.

And this is probably what would have happened if I had been permitted to work at all; which I was not.

There were two native settlements near Ruavatu, one right on the west border of the tract, which was a French Catholic school for native girls, and the other, a village, about three miles east of us on the coast. And it was this village we chose as the objective of our first attack.

Most salt-water villages are "owned"—bought with gifts of tobacco and calico—by some mission; a few villages even have their own "house lotu," or Church of Jesus, pronounced "Zhezhus" through the teeth. The village for which we were bound belonged to a New Zealand mission society—which I will not name lest I get sued—and had not only a house lotu but a native parson in charge. It was no settlement for a painter of primitives to choose for models, but it was something to start on, and ordinarily the presence of neither church nor parson changes the even tenor of heathen ways.

But these were not ordinary times. The very vibrations of the Expotition's approach always seemed to create an extraordinary time.

So now when we arrived at the village after a hot three-mile walk down the beach we found the clearing running in circles. Scores of little yellow dogs with wrinkled foreheads and long ears tore to meet us, screaming an unwelcome, and then scuttled away still screaming with their behinds curled under them.[1] The milling villagers, men, women and children, paid not the slightest attention to us, even though they could not have missed the canine announcement of our arrival. Afterwards we realized that they had been "dressed to kill." The women, otherwise naked, wore their bunching grass skirts, but over them were gathered petticoats of calico with the fringe of brown grass sticking out beneath. There was not even a naked pickaninny. The toddling girl children were in grass petticoats and the little boys in calico lap-laps like those of the men. Some of the men even wore white shirts or chemises, and all the cloth was spotlessly clean. It would be hard to say what everyone was so busy about; the villagers were just going from here to there, darting in and out of the bamboo huts, jabbering and laughing, children yipping, and scuttling out of our path like the dogs, as we advanced.

Only one person did not gallop off on some urgent business as we approached, and he was unmistakably the "luluai," the government-appointed headman of the village. And his costume reached a climax of sartorial confusion. On top of his close-cropped woolly hair was the badge of his office, the uniform cap; below that he was parson in a black surplice, and he stood on bare native feet with splayed toes, and with

[1] These ribby little dogs must be the least common denominator of all the breeds in the world, for we had seen the same cut of mongrel in the wild dogs of Haiti.

the white scars of old yaws up his ankles. Also in his eyes was the wild white light of an excited primitive. Without waiting to hear what we had come for he broke into a flood of pidgin English from which we later extracted one sound fact. The *Ark of God* was due at the village. This is a schooner belonging to the mission society, which makes the rounds of the South Sea Islands cheering on the good work at its stations and taking promising converts South to train them for the cloth. It sails only once a year, and yet, by a grim coincidence, it had to pick this very time to upset our village. The excitement at the prospect of its annual visit could have been produced by no other stimulus; we never again saw a village in such an uproar. Until its departure there was not the slightest chance of getting a model here, nor even anyone to listen to us.

The idea of a mission school model was even less tasty than a village convert, but we retreated from the village, planning to attack the French Catholic station after lunch. We planned, however, without considering the peculiarities of the island schedule and our status as guests, and therein lay the snag. The island world, both white and native, literally folds up for two hours through the midday. Everyone goes to bed and if the new chum cares to begin his decline by staying up he does so on a deserted island. It would have been not only rude but useless for us to go to the station, for even the missionaries take the siesta. Then, after the rest there is tea which murders another hour of daylight for the artist. One need not drink the bitter boiling stuff, but he can get no one else to do anything until he has been "refreshed." And for some reason our Missus thought we should get a better reception at the station if she or the Mastah took us over to introduce us. The idea of having to be introduced to anyone in this reputedly informal country staggered us, but we were willing to learn the ways. However, we must first wait.

There was the infant in the house who was a tyrant for schedule, and the Missus took the entire care of him herself. This left about half an hour in the day for mission-station calling. And the Mastah could not go with us because it was a rule even in normal times that the Missus never be left alone. In desperation we offered to carry the "little sausage" in a mosquito net if the Missus would take him with us, and then discovered he was having a rash of prickly heat which clothing would aggravate.[2] However, the problem of how to make a call in the Solomon Islands was solved just in time to keep me from having a rash myself, of burst blood vessels.

The entire household and even some of the plantation migrated in a body to the mission station.

On Saturday afternoon after siesta the carriage was brought to the door. It was an ancient spring wagon, hitched to an even more antiquated-looking horse. The horse seemed to be sleepwalking and was led up by a brave plantation boy holding the bridle near the head, while another boy, walking at a safe distance, held the end of the reins. Following, also at a safe distance, were five more plantation boys. On the head of the horse was a branch of leaves almost covering his face, and under the leaves was a shocking island sore with a pustu-

[2] This precious new infant was like an incubator baby in that it was never taken out of its heavily netted crib except to be bathed, and this rite took place in a nursery house built especially for him. The house had double screening with a space of about two feet between the outer and inner screen walls, a double roof, and like the residence was built up on piles with metal plate tops to prevent ants entering. On top of this the nursery was sprayed daily with "Buzzoff" to discourage sand flies and mosquitoes even sniffing at the outer screen. There were double doors at the entrance and one examined himself for insect passengers in the vestibule between. Though there were three servants in the household, they were never allowed to enter the nursery nor to touch anything belonging to the child, there being too much danger of infection from their hands—dysentery, hookworm, and all the rest. The only time even we went into this sanctum was to make a drawing of the child, and I had to work peeking under the net at it. And with all the caution the baby was a "little sausage" in fact, as happy and healthy, save for the rash, as any infant in a temperate climate.

late diameter of three inches. We looked in curiosity. So this was an island sore, the same kind humans got, both white and native. There were great bottle flies on it and a cloud of them buzzing around the leaves. The horse flicked his head and all of the boys scattered, including the one holding the end of the reins. Were they afraid of this tired old nag? They were; no big animal higher than an alligator or wallaby was known in these islands until the planters imported horses and cattle, and the horses without sufficient exercise gave the boys a merry time getting them caught and saddled. And this was no antiquated nag that was hitched to the spring wagon. It was a young horse beaten down by the unnourishing fodder and *malaria!*

When the horse was sound asleep again the Ruavatu heir, complete with thrice-netted crib, was brought out and put on the back of the wagon with a tarpaulin for awning. The Mastah and Missus ascended to the high seat, we hitched on behind (but got off soon), the three houseboys lined up on one side, the bottles flies overhead, and the five plantation boys brought up the rear. We looked like a frieze as we got under way. The native escort was magnificent. The purpose of their company was to push the van out of the sand when the horse failed (which it did most of the trip); but also this was a rare chance for them to ogle the mission girls. The plantation boys were never permitted to set foot over the mission-station borders, except when on duty with the Mastah. Even then they were not too welcome. And these lads were making the most of the opportunity. They had hibiscus blossoms in their hair, colored leaves in their arm and leg bands, and all of the flash jewelry was out: glass bead chokers and bracelets, fancy leather belts, and a swipe of lime in the black hair. (The houseboys used flour.) The boys following us sounded almost delirious.

The way led through the plantation, and it is only will

power which keeps me from describing it now, for we saw nothing so beautiful after we had crossed over to the mission settlement. The school clearing was shaded by tall coconut palms, but there was not a green thing anywhere on the ground between the weary weather-beaten frame buildings. The compound was lively with natives, all girls too, but they were covered from throat to the ugliest part of their thin calves with white beltless mu-mus (Mother Hubbards). If the purpose of the garments was modesty, it missed. Nothing could be more inspiring to the evil-minded than those two sharp points of breasts poking out the front of the mu-mu; and our boys seemed to be about normally evil-minded. They made such a clatter that they had to be sent out of the clearing, but they retreated only far enough to be still seen and heard quite plainly.

This call took a painful hour and a half and had a painful finale. The mission station could provide us with no models; none for the present anyway. The first hazard was the absence of the padre, the only person on the station who could speak English. He was away calling on villages and would not be back for three weeks—if we understood the sisters. For the two sisters could speak only French, while we could speak only English with a bad French accent. Yet we got as far as artistes with them and seemed on the point of getting models until they discovered we wanted them au naturel—without the mu-mu. Seeing their shock we would have retreated and taken a girl in a racoon coat, but there was no way of unscrambling our first request. We were all sweating like waterbags with leaks in them and the sisters, in their faded black challis robes, were so fragrant we had to breath through our mouths. In the end we parted the most esteemed friends and went off wanting to dice those pale thin saints. They could do nothing for us until the padre returned.

11

Whatever happens in the island world, if it happens on land, usually comes into the plantation house by the back door via the houseboys, who get the news out of the air while it is still hot. Anything coming by water the planter gets first. He keeps his binoculars on the veranda and at the first sing of *Sail-o* he is out examining the horizon for the sail, and knows long before it comes close whose sail it is. Therefore, we must have known, even before the excited villagers, when the *Ark of God* was over the edge of our stuffy world. And Margaret and I were off at the rate of knots for the village.

We had a great deal of curiosity about this schooner because it had been in Auckland when we were there, and we had pulled every string, up to the surplice of the archbishop, to get passage on her for the islands. But the *Ark of God* carried only professional Christians and we were almost professional heathens. Now our haste to get to it was partly to see what we had missed, but more to engage the aid of the Noah on board in behalf of the Expotition. He would be a man of influence with the villagers, and would understand what we wanted of them and so be able to explain to them in their own language the complicated business of posing-pictures-payment. And by being our interpreter he would lend us prestige, which it seemed we were going to need to get attention.

All this went off precisely as hoped for.

The villagers were already out on the water in their canoes

as the *Ark of God* sailed slowly in. It was a dream of a galleon which would have made a perfect expedition yacht—alas. We stormed into the surf and hopped a ride in a canoe filled with villagers, which was just putting out from shore, and the *Ark's* accommodation ladder was barely down when we were on board. Being the only white visitors we received first attention, and it was gallant attention even to blistering tea served by the scrubbed black Christian crew. We shook hands with a new native parson being delivered to his post, and examined a portfolio of excellent drawings made by a native convert who was being taken to Auckland for religious training. The Noah made us a present of arm bands and plaited baskets he had picked up in the islands, and then, after explaining everything we wanted to the village luluai— who understood everything and promised us the village—he sent us ashore in the schooner's dinghy. Its native oarsmen carried us over the surf on their locked hands—we clutching their necks. In all ways we had had a successful extremely clubby visit—to our undoing.

We then returned to Ruavatu and while waiting for the *Ark* to depart and the village to return to normal, we made a drawing of Ruavatu's precious "little sausage." And only incidental to the story, we also made two sloppy corrugated-paper portraits of our hosts. All of which was piling up trouble.

The week that succeeded the departure of the *Ark* was curiously blank after the excitement of the preceding one. Ruavatu might have been a reef in mid-ocean for any traffic that crossed our sand-sea-and-sky vista. Ordinarily the store launch from Tulagi would have been by, making the rounds huckster-fashion to deliver stores and pick up orders. But even this sail had not appeared. The Mastah supposed it was because the store launch was now serving the planter army on Malaita, but we had learned the reason for its absence while on the *Mataram*. There had been a wharf hands' strike in Sydney when the *Mataram* sailed, and the steamer had come up with only mail and government cargo. There was no gasoline for private launches, so those launches in use were probably being conservative. But there were also few stores to be delivered. Ruavatu was short on tinned butter and tea, and we had so little kerosene that we lived by candlelight after dark; and used those candles sparingly.

So fragile is this lifeline of the white islanders that a strike fifteen hundred miles away could endanger it. (A blockade, as in wartime, could completely isolate these islands immediately.)

We felt guilty at being present to help drain the dwindling supplies of the plantation, but we were helpless. This was no place where we could send ourselves a telegram urging our return home immediately. There was no possible relief for our hosts before the return of the *Mataram*. Meantime, the situation was being made more acute by the continued drought. We saw the black blocks of squalls passing out to sea, but not a drop of rain fell on the corrugated-iron roof of Ruavatu. The gauge on the water tank behind the house showed a quarter full, and that remaining unpolluted water had to be reserved solely for cooking, drinking, and the baby's baths. So no "bawths" in this rare island household with a hot-and-cold system.

There was a river running through the plantation in which we might have swum, except for a few peculiarities about it. We asked if there were any alligators (properly crocodiles) in it and were told that there were a few but the sharks might be more bothersome. The tides along Guadalcanar were high and ran up the river carrying sharks with them, which then got trapped by the sand bar that ran across the mouth of the stream in low tide. When the tide was out, the river was a deep-brown color with rotting logs, and alive with wriggling things in the backwaters. Further, it ran down past native villages inland and unless he was well plugged a swimmer ran the chance of swallowing a mouthful of dysentery. But it was our "wounds" which prevented our experimenting with sharks and wogs and alligators. The wounds were the promised crop of island sores that had resulted from our scratching bites. Wherever the skin had been scratched open a tiny round infected spot had appeared. These did not hurt but they would not heal, and even with a twice-daily treatment and bandaging they continued to spread wider and deeper until we were taking them very seriously as a nuisance.

The alligators had to be taken seriously, too, because the precious hens brought down from Berande, which were intended to provide us with fresh eggs and eventually fresh meat, disappeared in a batch one night. From then on we never visited the toilet at night without a pious prayer. It was built on the end of a little pier jutting over the river, and though we always took a lantern or a "kerosene-belong-Jesus" flashlight, there was a presence about the location which made constipation an ever present threat. And that presence was not just the mosquitoes which bit up from below nor the centipedes we occasionally found on the seat in the regulation search. What was under the seat God only knew.

Being an artist, a breed famous for its dislike for washing, we could get along moderately well on spit-baths, and at meals we could refuse with admirable stoicism the remaining soft rancid-tasting tinned butter; and when the comparative coolness of night lowered our blood temperature we could even forgive the missionaries for holding up our work. But it did not seem possible that we could continue to live with sanity in the increasing heat of the days. There was not a breath of wind night or day. The fronds of the palms hung limp and motionless in the airless steam, and even the surf seemed to hush under the weight of that slugging sun. Actually the thermometer on the veranda never went above eighty-six but it was an eighty-six bath temperature. Our vital body juices oozed away by the quart; the whole household was tense in the unrelieved siege. The houseboys wrangled with one another in the house cook, and brought their battles into the dining room by dropping dishes and banging things. The Missus was sizzling pidgin English and the Mastah finished up the last of the beer and said he expected an earthquake. Margaret and I even had a few cool words about a missing nailfile, one she was always using as a screwdriver to tighen up the pegs of her ukulele. We might be deserters but, come Monday, we were out of this; we were going to the village.

Friday came first and with it the drought broke; the first torrent of the wet season beat down on a celebrating household. Cold rain, oceans of it, thrashed in wild waves on the ovenlike iron roof. It ran the gauge of the water tank up another quarter in an hour. Margaret and I tore out into it fully dressed and held our mouths up and wide open so that the cold streams fell straight down our throats from heaven. Then we stood in the waterfall that fell from a crotch in the roof. We stripped and stood naked in it, and washed our hair while the wind screamed through the plantation and the palms whipped about with their skirts over their heads. Nuts thudded to the ground by the hundred and battered on the iron roofs like cannonballs. The surf reached a superlative in sound effects and from the labor quarters came the shrill cries of the rejoicing Malaitamen. It was a wild and wonderful night.

We slept that night in beds as wet as if they had been sprayed by an atomizer, but it was cool, almost cold, and we could breathe again without hanging our tongues out.

The next morning everyone in the household except the baby and ourselves had malaria. And by midmorning the storm of the night before was rising from the earth in visible clouds. By noon the heat was worse than before. The houseboys took up their dish-breaking where they had left off, the Missus took to her bed with fever, and Margaret and I resumed the nailfile matter.

The baby was crying.

A crying baby might not seem worth mentioning on a headhunting expedition, but the bawls of this one were to put the final plug in our efforts to be headhunters at Ruavatu. The first unusual thing about it was that the Ruavatu "sausage" was not a howler by nature. Yet he had begun bawling with the storm and by Saturday night had left off only long enough to take in wind for new blasts. He had a slight temperature and the evidence of dysentery, and the Missus was beside herself because dysentery in an infant could mean any disease. We were thirty miles from a doctor, and without a launch we might as well have been three hundred. A child seriously ill could die before a runner with a paper talk-talk could get to Berande, before the Berande launch could get to Ruavatu and take the child to Tulagi.

Yet the runner was sent off, and we waited outside the nursery house feeling more unnecessary than ever as guests.

Then came Monday morning.

So far our attitude had been that of intensely sympathetic but detached spectators at a crisis, and now, lo and behold, we discovered ourselves principals.

About ten o'clock there was a shout of Sail-o down the plantation and in a jiffy the Mastah had identified the "sail," not as the Berande launch, but the Renandi, the government launch which we all supposed was off at Malaita. However, this was a launch and a way of getting the baby to the hospital and we were all down on the beach as the Renandi headed straight in toward Ruavatu. But to our horror, when it was within shouting distance, instead of dropping anchor, it continued to cruise straight ahead half speed parallel with the shore. As we all took off down the beach following the launch I remembered the Berande countess and her habit of potting at launches when they refused to stop. The Mastah was shouting in an agonizing way above the surf. "I say, hold on," he bawled, "aren't you stopping?" Three white men stood along the deck, one cupping his hands. "Got any sickness there?" he shouted. "What's up?" screamed the Missus. "*Measles!*" came the answer. "Epidemic . . . brought . . . by the *Ark*. On our way down to the village to quarantine."

I felt as if we were drowning. Our clubby visit on the *Ark;* we had shaken hands with its passengers; we had brought away the baskets and arm bands, clutched the necks of those boys who had brought us ashore. And then gone straight to the baby's crib and spent the next three days breathing on it in half-hour periods making its picture. There had been no baths to wash away our sins. And now the baby had a temperature. My next no-less-harrowing thought was that the temperature everyone else had which they thought was malaria was actually measles.

The doctor from the *Renandi* looked very serious when he heard we had actually spent an hour on board the *Ark of God*. Measles in this country is not the pleasant holiday from school it is at home. It is a serious disease, as serious as smallpox in a crowded city. Even more so, for in cities there are hospitals and umpty-ump doctors to every patient, watertight quarantines and all the medicine that's needed. Here in the islands there were only two real doctors in the whole Group, and never enough lik-lik doctors to handle even the routine sore-dressings of the natives. Whole villages had been wiped out in the past by measles epidemics because the natives have no conception of quarantine. Any epidemic, therefore, spreads like a bush fire. The natives die like flies because they have no immunity, and white men, debilitated by malaria, have a special receptivity to the virus. Margaret and I, with our veins still filled with healthy American blood, felt almost guilty at not having a temperature.

But the incubation period of measles is ten to fourteen days, and only nine had passed since we were on the *Ark*. If we had got measles or brought it back to Ruavatu it was too early to show on any of us, even the baby. And so, until the full time had passed, the doctor could do nothing. He was obliged to go down the coast to the villages that the *Ark* had visited—every place it had called at in the islands was stricken—and quickly quarantine them, leaving a police boy and lik-lik doctor to enforce the quarantine and treat cases as they developed. He would return on the third day following and take the baby over to the hospital anyway. Meantime Ruavatu itself was under watertight quarantine.

The suspense of the next few days, our shame at even existing, our inarticulate sympathy for the desperate mother, and our misery with the continuous screams of the infant in our ears, should be dragged out for another chapter if the reader is to suffer as we did. But no measles appeared at Ruavatu, by what miracle even the *Renandi* doctor could not guess. Perhaps Margaret and I had had measles as children— we couldn't remember—perhaps we were not carriers or had not been near enough to the baby to transmit any *Ark of God* wogs we had on us. This baby provided the anticlimax of the whole dreadful business. The doctor, instead of taking the infant to the hospital, decided to stay over to the fourteenth day to keep us all under observation. He remarked as if by way of explaining his neglect of the natives that they would die in any event. It was not callousness; there was a sort of weary hopelessness in his voice. Anyway, before the final deadline this excellent doctor of measles epidemics, black-water fever, amoebic dysentery, leprosy, venereal diseases, shark and alligator bites, was taking the bawling infant's temperature and exploring about for the white spots on the gums that are a symptom of measles. And then he happened to notice something else on its lower gum. There, so help me, apparently just emerging, were two teeth!

It was an ironic twist of fate that the *Ark of God*, whose only mission was to save souls, should have been the means of making so many of them immortal. In the epidemic it distributed, thirty-five natives died in our village alone, leaving a population of eighty in a settlement which had once contained three hundred natives. This last figure was the population before the influenza epidemic of the First World War which killed natives by the hundreds all through the South Seas. The population of villages in Melanesia is usually nowhere near so large as three hundred, but the program of the government, cheered on by the missions, is to collocate friendly tribes. (The village east of us had been a combination of three villages moved together.) This concentration naturally simplifies the work of control and soul saving, but it also simplifies that of epidemics.

So the anthropologists' lament for the "vanishing Primitives" was no longer a statement in a book for us. Thirty-five of our models had vanished before we obtained their portraits, and the survivors, for the time being, were segregated beyond approach. The white man's diseases had joined religion to stymie our work.

12

It was not until we were idling in the measles doldrums at Ruavatu that the real reasons behind this expedition to Melanesia came to us. Deeper than the lofty wish to record for posterity a vanishing race, was an old yearning to get enough shredded coconut to eat. I know exactly when that yearning started. It was simultaneously with a suspicion that all was not aboveboard in this life, when, at the age of eight, I discovered, after weeks of frenzied search, that they were keeping the cake-icing coconut in a coffee tin in the pantry. My disillusionment almost coincided with the discovery by those in power over me that my mouth was stuffed with coconut. So that what might have been the satisfaction of my yearning at an early age was terminated by my being swung out of the pantry by the neck, spraying coconut. Thus the yearning became a subconscious urge, which finally blossomed into this expedition to paint Primitives in Melanesia. It was no accident that these Primitives lived in the very birthplace of shredded coconut.

Second to the shredded coconut urge was another good reason for having fought our way these hundreds of miles to the Solomon Islands. It was a secret yearning of many Americans in this driven span; the wish to relax, to be beautifully ambitionless and amount to nothing—but with an excuse that the Puritans would approve of. Isolated on some tropical islet one would be forced to lie on the soft warm sand where he need exert himself only to open his mouth and let the necessary vitamins drop in from an abundant tree above one.

And here we were on a tropical island forced to live the dream life.

Then there was another matter we had to look into in this ideal location. This was to get numb on betel nut and thus satisfy a curiosity as to why the world is divided into four great vice areas. From the United States to eastern Europe the natives swear by grain alcohol as a means of forgetting reality. From the west coast of the Americas to about the date line in the Pacific escape is achieved by means of the raw juices of a variety of pepper root, called kava. The betel-nut area extends from Melanesia to India and identifies these users as one big cultural unit distinct from the Oceanic kava sots. And the Mongoloids distinguish themselves by going in for narcotics. Wine and kava we had already experimented with, and now we had the betel-nut "jag" to experience before sending in our report to the Royal Society.

So, with three good excuses, we set out down the beach one morning, supplied with betel-nut makings and no worth-while ambitions, other than to contemplate the leaves of grass like Walt Whitman. We advanced toward this "soft warm sand" of the island picture we had formed from books, clad in sandflyproof breeches, mosquitoproof woolen socks, shirts buttoned up to the throat and down to the wrist, cork tanks over our precious brains, dark glasses over our eyes, and every remaining inch of exposed skin smeared with pungent "Buzzoff." We couldn't find a spot along the beach where there was any Walt Whitman grass, but the place we chose to sit was shaded by a very picturesque tree and there were several safaris of ants going from here to there all around us which we could contemplate. We went right to work getting numb on our betel nut.

The nuts were about the color and shape of small limes, and the leaves, from the same tree, were heart-shaped and had curling stems like vine leaves. The only other ingredient was the lime, which is coral rock, burned and crushed to a white powder. The outfit belonged to one of the plantation boys and the lime was kept dry in a decorated gourd which had a stopper of raffia-covered wood with a fine boar's tusk as a handle. The spatulate for ladling out the powder was a long ebony-black stick with a paddle-shaped end and a beautifully carved handle—a vice set as elegant, of its kind, as any Regency snuffbox.

We had been told there was no need to sterilize any of these betel-nut makings for dysentery, and the minute we got them in our mouths we understood why. They almost exploded. First (as instructed) we stuffed a leaf inside the lower lip in front of the teeth, and on top of this went a quarter-section of betel nut, the pack then liberally sprinkled with lime. It was a quid the size of a golf ball and to keep it in our mouths we had to hold the lip up with our hand.

As anyone knows who has had a dentist's hands in his mouth, the very fact that one is supposed not to swallow them immediately sets up a freshet of saliva. Our golf-ball quids started a deluge which flowed onto the lime and began fizzing and foaming like Seidlitz powders. The agitation spurted more saliva and the deluge became a maelstrom. We were supposed to hold the torrent because it is the action of the wet lime on the nut and leaf that extracts their corrupting juices. So, all but strangling, we held our mouths shut.

We could hear the stuff foaming inside our heads and the taste was puckery, the sensation on the membranes of the mouth about like a peroxide mouthwash. This was still only the lime, however, and I am sorry to report that we could not hold on long enough to get any other reaction. We began spitting very conservatively at first, hoping to save the situation, but the more we spat the more there was. The saliva ducts were stimulated to a frenzy of giving. At the end of a half hour we were not even spitting pink—the ideal is a cadmium red—and we felt far from numb anywhere except the actual spot the quid was scorching. The local sensation, in fact, was exactly that of raw alcohol held in the mouth, which, we decided, was too painful a way of "forgetting" to bother with. The removal of the quid, however, did not stop the deluge. We puckered and spat for twenty-four hours afterwards and couldn't taste our food. Finally Margaret sloughed a long string of membrane from her lower lip which had been eaten loose by the lime; and if the experiment decided anything it is that the habitual betel-nut chewers of the world must be almost as desperate and hardy as we were during Prohibition.

But to continue with the contemplative life: the experiment just proved to us that an American has to be a little sick to get the best out of doing nothing. Contemplating the industrious crawling things around us made us itch, while in the foliage above us a squawking battle for existence was going on between some fruit pigeons who sprayed us with their leavings. There is too much going on in this life to sit and watch. All it took to tear us away from the dream was the din of a harried existence back in the plantation. At the first yips we were off like old fire horses.

The coconut plantation, copra producing, is the soul and hide and end of European occupation of these native islands. It is Big Business, with all the organization and ruthlessness of any competitive big business. Most of the plantations are under the control of one or the other of two enormous English copra producing-shipping-and-manufacturing companies, which function all through the South Sea Islands. They lease the land (from the governments, there being no freehold land), hire managers, own all the ships (which are also the only passenger steamers), control the London market price of copra, and finally, as subsidiary companies, manufacture most of the products in which coconut oil is used. Yet behind all this highly commercialized industry there is still the plantation, containing enough beauty and human interest to satisfy any artist.

The native coconut palms that lean gracefully out into the wind all along the shores of the islands are propagated by nuts that fall to the ground any which way and take root. And though a little trite, the native palms are very picturesque. But a graceful lean to a plantation palm is a sign of bad planting. The tree trunk has to be exactly straight, and this is achieved by placing the nut in the ground at just the right angle. The rows of trees must be precisely thirty feet apart, so that the same amount of sun reaches the ground everywhere through the tract. All this orderliness would seem to delete any beauty, but it is the very orderliness that makes the plantation so beautiful. The impression inside the stand is that of a vast cathedral. There are acres and acres of aisles as far as the eye can see in every direction; great columns of cool, gray trunks, ringed to a rich texture where the old fronds have fallen off, all towering evenly to fifty or sixty feet from the ground. Thin ropelike roots above the earth form an ornamented base to each pillar, and at the top is a rich capital of clustered taupe-colored nuts with flags of henna-brown fiber. From there the great strong arms of the fronds sweep out to meet those of neighboring trees, forming a groined vault ceiling with interstices of criss-crossed leaflets. With the white sky piercing through, the effect is of intricately designed leaded glass.

Then there is the soft footfall of holy places, for the entire temple is carpeted evenly with clover or sensitive plant (which helps keep down tall weeds). The sensitive plant un-rolls a gray rug ahead of one, for even the vibrations of one's approach are enough to wilt these hypersensitive leaves. And in the shaded light we at last see some of the rich color Gauguin found in his tropics. The spiny shadows of the palm fronds are violet on the gray pillars, deeply blue on the green carpet. There is perspective not to be seen out in full sun-light; there is loftiness and distance, yet one feels sheltered— which is the comfort of churches. At night there are even the lamps of the faithful. Fallen palm fronds are gathered into piles and burned, and these pyres are everywhere down the long avenues, lighting the surrounding pillars and ceiling in an eerie orange glow and filling the roof with smoke. When the moon is full, sending down its white shafts of light through the fronds and smoke, the rays look like those coming from heaven in the old church pictures of the Nativity. The late-afternoon sun illumines the whole cathe-dral with sharp fingers of light which beam out from the shafts so that even the shadows gleam. Those X-ray planes of superimposed patterns make a "modern" masterpiece, but even so, the picture is one easier to describe than paint.

Armies of millions and millions of ants travel up and down the columns unceasingly, great white cockatoos with lemon-yellow combs squawk savagely among the fronds, battalions of little yellow butterflies flitter along in ball formation, and sometimes, rarely, flying at bird height, is a blue jewel of a butterfly almost bird size.[1] But it is not until one rides out through the plantation just after sunrise that one sees the handiwork of the hidden insect life. The spiders, which must have worked all night, have stretched gigantic webs from one pillar to the next, catching the points on low-hanging fronds. The night's dew is still on them and, fanning out in the dawn's breeze, they glitter in the oblique rays of the early morning sun. Curtain after curtain of these strung diamonds turns the cathedral into a fantastic fairyland.

Riding into the webs at a canter one has his cork lid tipped off, his nose pulled to one side, and his face drenched. The fiber of the webs is so tough that some natives use it as a ligature to stop the hemorrhage of a wound. I once used a strand to bind my hair to keep it from falling in my eyes when I was working, but we had to use turpentine to get it out after I had been smearing it into my hair for three hours of creative ecstasy. It was like wet chewing gum. No wonder one sees whole schools of the little yellow butterflies fluttering, hopelessly glued, in the diamond curtains. It is from the spider webs that the natives collect their yellow pigment.

From five o'clock in the evening until seven-thirty the next morning the plantation is all serene beauty; but at the howl of seven-thirty the copra barons take over and the cathedral becomes something like a circus tent. Things were well under control at Ruavatu and as the boys started off.

[1] This particular species of kingfisher blue butterfly is not found anywhere else in the world. Also very rare is a yellow and blue variety like one we found a boy in Papua wearing in his hair. Collectors pay as much as two pounds to any native bringing in this species undamaged. We painted the boy and his decoration, bought the butterfly for a shilling, but the ants had left nothing but a shell and the wings by the time we found out what a treasure we had. The little yellow butterflies supply the natives with the pigment used to dye the grass for their plaited arm bands.

from their quarters for the day there was only a polite little scream of about a second. This was improved on, however, the farther the boys got from the quarters and Mastah. Most of the line were coconut pickers and they spread out down the avenues in groups of four and five boys, each carrying three empty sacks which they were required to fill in the day with nuts picked up from the ground. The younger boys made a game of it, forming in a wide circle and bowling the nuts toward one boy who filled the sacks. The idea was to keep him jumping and break his legs if he weren't nippy enough—something that seemed a possibility because the nuts are as big as a football and weigh as much as a bowling ball. The game was enriched by the liveliest yelping and hopping, but by the end of the day when each boy had carried his three heavy bags to the distant copra shed, there was no energy left for speed. There was just one fine yip when the last sack fell on the pile.

Outside the drying shed the earth had been cleared of weeds and grass, and in this purple-shaded space the air milled with jabber, flying machetes, white coconut meat, and copra bugs. And there was that sweet odor of the drying copra, and the nostalgic fragrance of burning wood, which swept one the thousands of miles to home and an open fire in the hearth. There is not much that is familiar in these islands, but the wood smoke of the drying shed was always at the plantation to lend that much of the land reality. Here, at the shed, coconuts began to turn into copra—the "o" of which, incidentally, is pronounced not as in cobra, but as in copper. Several boys sat around on the ground, their legs forked out in front of them. One hand held a big nut, pointed end on the ground between the legs, the other hand held an awesome machete at least eighteen inches long. And the way the boys wielded those cutlasses to whack the heavy husks off the nuts was a nice illustration of what they might do, sufficiently inspired, with a white neck. Two whacks and a gouge and the small inner nut was out, one more whack and the nut was in half, the milk running out on the ground. A gouge and a flip, a gouge and a flip, and the white coconut meat was flying from the hard shell onto a great pile. All day long the brown arms whacked and gouged and flipped, the tongues clacked endlessly, the insane copra bugs, never seeming to alight on anything, filled the air with their flutter, while the blue and purple shadows of the palm fronds above braided their spiky patterns over brown earth and brown natives.

So here was the raw coconut, potentially shredded coconut for cake, for which we had organized an expedition and come across the Pacific. There were great piles of it, chunks of white meat, and we proceeded to satisfy a lifetime of yearning. The first bite was like taking a chunk out of a piece of wood, tender wood to be sure, but with a definite grain to it. And the taste was much like wood, perhaps with not so much flavor as a civilized toothpick. That was all there was to it, one could not eat this raw coconut.

Then how about the delicious coconut milk we had read about? One of the boys took a whole nut, deftly whacked a little hole in it and then stood back to laugh. We drank straight from the nut and the liquid tasted like something that runs off your hair when you are washing it. Ivory soap flavor. So that was that, too.

Later on we had both shredded coconut and coconut milk (from overripe nuts) at a meal prepared for us by a Tongan. Each of us was served an entire chicken which had been stuffed with shredded coconut, then put in a pack of it, and the whole wrapped in leaves, roasted among hot stones. As a beverage we had genuine coconut milk which was the creamy juice wrung from shredded coconut. For dessert there was a baked mash of very ripe bananas in a thick jacket of shredded coconut. We ate all the chicken, its stuffing and wrapping, drank all of the milk that was offered us, devoured the ambrosia of coconut and bananas, and then spent all of the following night and day in seclusion. Coconut meat has so much oil in it that a sufficient quantity is one of the quickest and most thorough purges known to man—practically a pinwheel action for it sometimes works in both directions. This purging, however, got rid of the shredded coconut craving for all time.

The final stage of copra-making is simply a matter of drying the moisture out of the coconut meat. Ruavatu had a modern drying shed with rows of ovens, each with a bed of hot wood coals in the bottom. Above the bed were stacks of wire trays on which the coconut was spread, and the trays were raked over at certain set periods so that the copra would dry evenly. Everything—heat of the ovens and time for taking the finished copra out—had been worked out scientifically to meet the government standard of a minimum moisture content in copra, and the "savage" drying-shed boys worked with thermometers and clocks.

The precious product emerges from the ovens in little hard lumps of yellowish fat, shrunken sections of coconut, still with the thin brown inner shell adhering to them. Once in the sack, the copra awaits the six-week call of the *Mataram;* then over the high surf it goes on the backs of the beetle-legged Malaitans, onto the lighter, and out into the world via Sydney. From whence it presently arrives back in the islands, from England, Germany, or the United States, to appear on the table as margarine or to be lost through the floor of the house wash-wash as soap.

13

Nothing the Malaitan indentured boy does on the plantation is even remotely a "native industry," but the way he does it is entirely native. He seems to make a weird game of working for the white man. Every stage from coconut collecting to the final dumping of the copra sack on the lighter or steamer is accompanied by little yips that have the sound small boys make when they are together without grownups around. There doesn't seem to be any mirth in it, and yet there is some kind of enthusiasm. On the surface no manner of life could seem emptier than the one these plantation natives lead. They are signed on for work in two- or three-year periods, and during that time they have no annual holiday, nor are they ever permitted to leave the plantation unless they are so ill that they are useless and must be sent back to the village. They may not visit neighboring villages (the village men see to that) and are not allowed to have sing-sings (dances) on the tract—because when they are given permission for a sing-sing they whoop for a week working up for it and take another week afterward to settle down. These are all vigorous young men, and there are no women (village women may not be recruited). Yet the obvious result, homosexuality, is said to be rare, and when known to the natives as a vice of the white man, these "savages" have a hard time believing it.

For working nine hours a day every day except Sunday for three years the indentured boy receives about thirty dollars a year in cash. His head taxes are paid by his employer;

he receives medical treatment from the planter; his bunk, a blanket, and mosquito net, "kai-kai," a pound of boiled rice every day, and a pound of tinned fish or beef once a week. Every month he gets a new calico lap-lap.

The irony of this lavish cash wage is that the native does not even get all of it until he has completed his term of contract. Deferring two-thirds of it is required by law, for by some process of unreasoning this is supposed to give the boy something to take home to the village with him—where he can buy nothing with cash. On the other hand, he can buy a great deal, down to squandering the last ha'penny, right on the plantation whether his wages are paid in driblets or total. For every plantation has either a store or a stock of trade goods. The planter doles out the weekly shilling wage, then figuratively, or even literally, hops over his counter and takes back the shillings for everything on God's green earth from defunct peroxide (to bleach the hair) to alarm clocks, which the natives buy for the "sing." There is government price regulation, but it cannot be enforced unless there are complaints of violation. And the victim of wanton prices himself is too excited by his new possessions to suspect that he could have got more on the trade.

However, the "exploitation" of natives was our business only in so far as it affected the disposition and personality of our models. We went down to the store on Saturday, pay night, to see how the victims were taking it, and to pick out a model to pose for a companion piece to the Malaita bushman. We wanted a salt-water boy on the cut of the police bullies, and there were about sixty boys lined up at the store shed to choose from. They filed past the door taking their week's rations of tinned beef, two sticks of tobacco, and a box of safety matches. Legally, money should have changed hands, but the Mastah skipped this formality and gave each boy a chit. As soon as the line had passed, the boys formed

in a second line and this time went into the shed to take
their shilling's worth of trade goods. We could not get into
the shed, but we watched the victims coming out and no one
could have looked happier at being swindled.[1] For our model
we picked the boy with the biggest open mouth and the
best-muscled chest, and expected the Mastah to ask him to
pose the next day, Sunday, this being the boy's free day.
But by no means; to be asked to pose would be an order,
and to be ordered to work on Sunday was against the law.
The boy made to work on this "spello" (rest) can leave the
plantation to go down to the government station and report
the master; then the master will be fined—or so the book says.
(But any Sunday that the *Mataram* is in, loading goes on as
usual.) In any case, the sitting for the picture was set for
Monday morning and the boy was told to wash-wash good
fella or the Mastah would kill him. All the line listened
quietly to the instructions and then started off toward their
quarters. As soon as they had passed the first shed a chorus
of yips started up that had a faintly heckling note to them.

We were down at the labor quarters early Sunday morning
taking photographs with a camera which had no films in it.
It was our excuse for spying, and the fact that there were no
films made us moan. All these big-muscled savages, about
whom we had heard such awesome tales, were sitting about
on the ground in the shade of the shed, and they were not
throwing knives at one another for diversion on the spello;
they were primping. The scene was like nothing so much as
a dressing room at a dance—with slight differences, of course,
in the primpers and their methods. Most of the boys had
oblong shaving mirrors with such bad glass in them that it
must have made them dizzy to look at themselves; but the

[1] This is no reflection on the integrity of our host. Such "swindling" is
the accepted thing in the islands, just as the handlers of goods in this
country take a third of the ultimate retail cost, while the actual maker
gets little more than that.

mirrors were clasped between their knees and the boys were bent over them, earnestly plucking out the sparse beards, hair by hair, using little bivalve shells for tweezers. One or two used their copra machetes, not shaving but cutting off each individual whisker, and one progressive boy was using the sharp edge of a cigarette tin lid. But it was the hair on the head, the male primitive's crowning glory, that received the most loving attention. This "grass" was not merely the black wool that grows on the heads of our Negroes; its texture seemed to be more like wire wool; and the boys trimmed it as one shapes a hedge, combing it out and out to its full length with a long three-pronged comb of betel-nut wood, and then carefully cutting the surface down to the desired shape with the copra machete, hair by hair. There was no coiffure that merely followed the skull line. There were great round balls of wool, and points and peaks and knobs and pompadours, all

with the back of the head trimmed close and all the attention directed toward the front—that portion which could be seen in the mirror. Curiously, each boy did his own hair, even the back. Our model of Monday, possibly in preparation for the pic-a-ture, had achieved a monumental peak "do" which took him two hours, at the end of which time there was not so much as a single kinky hair standing out from the solid mass. Part of this time was spent carefully scratching his scalp with the eight-inch comb, and the final touch was a coat of shoe blacking applied over the surface of the slightly reddened, sunburned top and front. Before that bottle had been put back in the black cashbox (with a bell on its lock to warn the boy of safecrackers) we fully expected to see him touch up his eyelashes. He did adjust some new earrings in his ears. They were pegs of matchsticks that went through three little holes in the lobes—the matches being quite useless for their intended purpose because the damp sulphur will not ignite.

Some of the other boys, meantime, were doing something about their "walkabouts." Lime, made from powdered coral rock, is the time-honored delouser, but applied to the scalp it also bleaches the hair. Among the gang here at Ruavatu were platinum blonds, golden blonds, Titian reds, and a few heads of grass which had been bleached white and then colored with some other pigment. Washing bluing was popular, and the effect of blue hair and the matching blue lap-lap was extremely chic—and paintable—but hardly Stone Age. (There is no blue pigment in these islands.) The lime was made into a paste and applied to the hair and scalp with the hands, and after it had dried it was shaken out; there, behold, was a henna-brown native with lemon-yellow hair the size and design of a shako, with a scarlet hibiscus tucked in over each ear. Very flash.

The hair business went on most of the morning, but by

and by the boys got around to their mending and fancy work. Our model, who had moments of looking like Joe Louis with a razor, opened his precious cash "bokkis" and took out a darling little piece of work. It was a glass-bead, dog-collar necklace, half finished, with a red and white design of the British flag. And, with a lot less self-consciousness than we felt seeing him do it, he began stringing tiny little beads with a needle and fine thread, spreading out his bony fingers daintily like a "laidy" with a teacup. Except for flaring his wide-winged nostrils like a stallion from time to time, we might have thought he was clowning. There was plenty of laughter of the native yipping and gurgling kind. Our model, particularly, talked incessantly, going over and over some experience which had a lot of kai-kai (food) in it; that much we understood. In the house at Ruavatu we insisted on speaking pidgin English entirely, for practice, and we could understand the household pidgin; but that of the plantation boys sounded like something made with an egg beater. It rattled, staccato. But curiously, they could understand us. And it was not until we spoke to them that any of these primpers paid the slightest attention to us.

Had the model any decorations he had brought from the village? Out of the apparently bottomless cashbox came a yard-long string of big canine teeth. This was a genuine—the old-fashioned—standard length of island currency, worth five dollars in any white man's trade store. (Any such currency like heavy clamshell arm bands and strung coral or shell money—wampum—which has a standard value will be accepted by white traders.) It was a perfect ornament for our savvy, cosmopolitan, salt-water boy, and it was all we wanted; but we had to be rude to limit the pic-a-ture decorations to this one piece. The boy had three cheap five-and-ten store glass bracelets which he slipped on above his elbow, insisting that they were "fashion 'long village." His new white clay pipe, thrust into a woven arm band, was also "village," as was the wide imitation leather belt with its huge nickel buckle. It was our first encounter with a native authority on native costume. Before we left to go back to the house we examined the dog's teeth to be sure they weren't stamped "Made in Japan."

We saw the model again that afternoon. It was right after lunch when we should have been taking our siesta, but instead were lying out on the horizontal trunk of a tree hanging over the surf. The model was strolling along the beach in the company of five other boys, one of whom he walked with, their little fingers locked together (as one often sees walk-about natives). They were all yammering and laughing, radiant with glass jewelry and hibiscus blossoms "borrowed" from the Missus' precious bush down by the river. As they passed us, unaware that we were in the tree, we saw that their big mouths were gory with the scarlet juice of betel nut, the use of which is forbidden on the plantation. The unmasculine bead-workers of the morning were headed in the direction of the French mission station.

The sittings, which began on Monday morning and lasted until Wednesday, were uneventful except as an education in painting tame savages. None of the plantation boys was allowed even on the veranda of the residence, so, feeling rather martyred, we had to work down at the copra warehouse with the sand flies and other minute island torments.[2] Margaret was on duty with a palm frond and kept the air between the model and myself clear enough for me to see through. Occasionally she used the frond on the boy who, after the first half hour of sitting still without his friends to talk to, had gone into an upright coma. All his bulging muscles and the tough salt-water expression had melted together in a heap of formless brown lava. Margaret could usually wake up sleepy sitters by asking questions, and she asked questions of this one; but he answered in his sleep and it was always "Yas, Missus." I particularly wanted this native to look normally tough to bring out the contrast between him and the bewildered, meek-looking, bush Malaitaman; but none of the usual stimuli worked. Margaret asked him if he were a boy belong bush, hoping the intimation would irritate

[2] Lest anyone get the impression from our description of the household at Ruavatu, or elsewhere, that our hosts were in any way negligent as hosts, I hasten to correct it. For to lay at the door of these all-enduring people any inconveniences we suffered would be the basest ingratitude. For one thing we did not suffer. We were mostly amused by everything which did not actually stop the work, and no one thing but the nature of the islands themselves was responsible then. No hosts in the world could have been more patient and generous, and no guests could have repaid them more inadequately, because we had been invited for company and that was the least we offered, for we were made mute and helpless with sleepiness. Our Missus at Ruavatu always went into the ovenlike house cook to see that the meals started to the table without bugs in them, and she herself often struggled with the tinned foods making them into palatable dishes. Planters took time from their work to escort us to villages and get us started with the natives, and they contributed the time of their plantation gangs when we needed any of them for models. Always they allowed us the greatest freedom where it was reasonably safe for us to have it. We owe to our legion of island hosts a debt of gratitude that can never be repaid, if only for the roof and bed they gave us where these things cannot be bought and can only be given.

him, but it was too subtle. He thought she meant boy belong bush 'long Guadalcanar. No, him-he boy belong Malaita. "Boy 'long bush 'long Malaita?" Margaret persisted. No, boy belong salt water 'long Malaita. The fine art of heckling was lost in a tangle of pidgin.

We asked the Mastah for another native to stand by and keep the first one irritated, a bush Malaitan if he had one. There was no such recruit on the plantation, but it gave Margaret an idea. She got the drawing of our bushboy and showed it to the model. He didn't admire it; he said it was a boy belong bush 'long Malaita and from then on we got all the salt-water expression we needed. The drawing was set up so that the model could see it, and Margaret kept his attention focused by asking questions about the "hayseed" bush people. When the model's interest lagged she revived it by saying that the bushboy looked like a strong fella too much. Consciously or not, the salt-water muscles of the savvy boy puffed and the rubber-lipped mouth dragged down in a sneer.

But it was all uphill work for Margaret, injecting a tough personality into this soft, sleepy, colored gentleman. My difficulties were only technical; the sun moving up to noon to change shadows and reflections and light on both model and work; the difficulty of seeing clearly with the glare all around even though there was no sunlight either on model or behind him. And if you call copra bugs and ants and sand flies and mosquitoes and horse flies technical difficulties, then we both had them. But here at Ruavatu there was the house to which we could go periodically for a spello. This was painting de luxe, for the air of the double-roofed inner rooms was cool by contrast; there was safe drinking water, and when we returned to the model he was *there*; asleep, to be sure, but still present to remain until his portrait was finished. And that constancy, though enforced by the Mastah, was something we appreciated later when we began working in the villages.

When the study was finished the model had only one criticism. He had been asked what he thought of the portrait and at first he only stood back scratching his scalp with the long bamboo comb, muttering that the pic-a-ture was a good fella too much. "All-a same boy?" we persisted. Yes, it was all-a same boy. The boy was edging away from us. He had been bored to death with us for three mornings and now that we had said finish, he wanted to go finish. We could get nothing more out of him, not a spark of primitive interest in a portrait, nothing fresh like an exclamation over the miracle we had wrought by putting his face on flat paper. We let him go; he was much too savvy.

And we had forgotten all about him, cleaning up the gear, when suddenly, behind us, "Him-he no all-a same." The big fellow was standing there, holding out his dog-tooth necklace and pointing to the one in the drawing. "What name?" (What do you mean?) There were not enough teeth in the picture! Some of them were hidden by the neck of the model and I had drawn only those which were visible hanging down his chest—and probably not the exact number of them, for teeth, even in a necklace, are not individuals. But how we rejoiced over his criticism; how we laughed at the boy. We laughed him right out of sight. He was not paying for this portrait as was a woman who once made the same criticism. She was no Stone Age primitive; she was the "educated," adult, white heiress of steel wealth, and she could count up to sixty and knew there were that many pearls in her necklace which I was painting on her. The fact that I had not an X-ray eye and could not see through her neck to the pearls that were at the back of the necklace made no difference to her. To get our check we had to paint all sixty pearls right out in sight, so that whoever might inherit the portrait and necklace would know what he was entitled to!

So *how* we laughed when the Malaitan objected to our not having given him enough of his kind of pearls. This at last was the kind of portrait painting that artists dream of— allowing full independence.

We held an exhibition of the two Malaitan pictures that afternoon at teatime. And, incidentally, we were now pounding out the full two hours of the siesta like old-timers, and devouring the stale biscuits and hot bitter tea as if these punishments were meant for the palate of civilized man. The houseboys, sighting the pictures from the side veranda, were hysterical, but the minute they came around to our side with the tea things the portraits were good fella too much. "Eunuchs!" I couldn't think of any other word for people so lacking in spunk. The Sinarango "murdering swine" had turned out to be a pathetic little gnome; the salt-water bully had primped and embroidered, and all of them down to the last screaming copra loader timidly said "Yas, Missus" to anything one asked them. We had certainly had to change a lot of our opinions about Melanesian "savages" in this month. "Why, these men are almost effeminate," I said. "They're vain and interested in details—" "And sleep," Margaret cut in. "The race would probably have died out soon just from lack of vigor even if the Whites had not moved in."

I had a lot more such unripe opinions, but was saved from exposing them just in time. "*Sail-o-o! Sail-o-o!*" came the cry up through the plantation from one boy to the next. "*Sail-o-o!*" sang our houseboys just so that we shouldn't miss it. We were already outside the veranda waiting for the Mastah to tell us whose sail it was. Nankervis and the Berande master were expected for the week end but this was only Wednesday. "It looks like . . . No. My word, it *is* the Berande launch!" In midweek! Something must be up.

Something was up; Nankervis was dead!

The "bloody" plantation gang had killed him. It was cerebral malaria in the end, but the gang first. It was the Malaitan bullies. "Yes," said the Berande master stabbing his finger toward our picture of the salt-water boy, "just that bloody kind there." Nankervis dead? It was hard to believe; he still seemed too alive to be dead. He was too big and strong; he had such a joyous clutch on life. Yet he was already buried on the island where he had died two days before. The heat . . . The Berande master gave us some snapshots that Nankervis had made for us; one of Margaret and himself on the *Mataram* —laughing. That was only a month ago.

Behind this death was a regular systematic native program for the bedevilment of white men. It is even called by the planters the "trying-out system." And whether its purpose is seriously to get rid of Europeans by an underground method or simply to make plantation life more amusing for themselves, the results are the same. The system has got rid of many overseers in the past, and put a lot more over the jumps; its viciousness is behind all the stories one hears about Malaitans and the rumors of uprisings. Yet the tool is just plain, organized hoodlumism.

An indentured boy, for instance, is legally excused from work if he is ill. And to stop work, all he has to do is pretend he is ill. If the master attempts to take his temperature he can refuse the thermometer. He can refuse quinine or castor oil, or he can take them and spit them out—and still not go to work. The planter has paid a recruiter anywhere up to fifty dollars for each boy, so he does not discharge a disobedient boy lightly. Yet there is nothing to force a boy back to health if he is suspected of "gamin'" except the master's fists. The overseer is forbidden by law to threaten with a gun, but if he does use his fists he is certain to be jumped on by the whole gang. The natives do not know how to use their fists in single combat—they strike down like a girl—so the whole gang makes a mob rush "in self-defense." They can then take a couple of days off to stroll down to the nearest district office and report the master for striking "first." He will be called into court and fined anywhere up to fifty dollars.

The planter who has survived to become an old-timer licks the hell out of the first bullies who try the system on him; then he calmly pays his fine and lives happily forever after on his reputation as a demon. But new overseers, with still some respect for the law, often hold their tempers, with the result that disobedience of a few ringleaders grows into general mutiny. The bedeviled white man can get no work out of the labor and in the end he either voluntarily quits the islands, or is discharged as incompetent by the plantation company.

Ten days before his death Nankervis, fully warned of all these tricks, had been sent off with a gang of boys to clear out the undergrowth of a coconut holding on an island up west. He should have returned to Berande the following week end, and as he had the launch the master had no way of finding out why he had not come in. He did not find out until an old boss boy arrived Sunday night to report that Nankervis was "close up finish."

Reconstructed from the account of the boss boy the system which brought Nankervis "close up finish" was somewhat as follows. On the island to which they had gone to work there was no fresh water. Drinking water had to be brought over from a plantation on Guadalcanar. But there was a river which was closer than the plantation and the water was brought from it instead. And the cookie, who knew better, did not boil it. Natives are not immune to dysentery, by any means, but it does not make them so violently ill as it does a white man. Nankervis, according to the boss boy, was p-i-lenty sick too much. However—and it was like the Australian—he refused to lie down to it, and this just gave the pranksters a new opening. He could stay on the job but they could not; they were ill with dysentery and went behind trees, ostensibly for other reasons, but actually to loll about and chew the forbidden betel nut.

This state of affairs continued for most of the week and then Nankervis, weakened by the dysentery, had his first go of malaria. Apparently this was only ordinary malaria at first, but the dysentery was still going strong and, according to the boss boy, he was sick-sick-sick-sick. He was finally so ill that he had to take to his stretcher—and this was what the gang had been waiting for. The cook boy was supposed to keep the supplies of tinned meat and tobacco locked up, but with nice timing the lock sprang open and Nankervis had a moment of lucidity long enough to see the cookie handing out tins of meat to the gang. It was night but there was a lantern on the ground lighting up the scene. Nankervis made for the cookie. He knocked him out and the boy fell on the lantern smashing it. Instantly the Australian received a barrage of rocks out of the dark. One must have struck him on the head, or his sickness had made him faint, for suddenly he was down on the ground and the gang was on top of him—much as the Lilliputians sat on Gulliver, I suppose.

Then Nankervis lay still after a while. And as it must take more poise than a Malaitan has to sit on a still white man for very long, the gang finally got up. But the Australian did not rise. The boss boy said that he and another boy dragged him to his stretcher, but he was too heavy to lift onto the bed, so they had put a mosquito net over him, and then he, the boss boy, had come straight down to Berande.

Nankervis was still alive when the Master got to the island, but he was in a coma, and fearing blackwater (death is almost certain if blackwater patients are moved) he had sent the boss boy over to Tulagi to bring back a doctor. One doctor was over at the Malaita war, and the other was off on the *Renandi* patching up the *Ark of God's* epidemic. By the time the latter could be reached and get to the island Nankervis was dead. Death was pronounced due to cerebral malaria. "A guess," said the Berande master. "That takes them off faster than anything else, and that's all the doc had to go on. It was the bloody swine. . . ."

He was staring at our drawing of the primped-up Malaitan, and his face was white and hard. After a while he said, "That's a good picture."

14

If you have ever been lost in the Gobi Desert and looked up to find, propped against your breakfast of dinosaur eggs, a letter addressed to you, then you will know our sensation when we saw our paper talk-talk at Ruavatu. It was propped up against the dish of Vancouver salmon. But who knew we were here in the Gobi Desert? How had the letter got here? Who in the islands even knew us that he would be sending a letter?

And it was a very intriguing kind of letter, constructed like a Chinese egg puzzle where you had to take off shell after shell before you got to the core. The outside envelope was covered with greasy fingerprints and looked as if it had gone through a flood. The second envelope was also addressed to us but without the fingerprints, and the ink was still blurred. The final one was again addressed, but it was unsealed. Inside was our pass to the outside world. It was an invitation from an unknown at Tanakombo, a plantation at the west end of the island, inviting us for a visit!

But this was not only an invitation; it was the golden kind that provides a means of accepting. Tanakombo had no launch, but, if we wrote that we were accepting, a neighbor's launch would be sent for us at any time we named.

There was no time for writing an answer to such an invitation as this. The Berande launch was still at Ruavatu and by late afternoon of the same day we were halfway toward "liberty." We had with us on the launch the runner who had brought the invitation, and we expected to wait at least two days at Berande to give the boy time enough to take our acceptance to Tanakombo and then for the relay launch to get to us. But instead of the boy being put up overnight at Berande, he was given our letter just after we had landed. "He'll have to spend the night *some*where," we protested to the Master, "he won't be running all night!" Oh, but he would be. The moon was full; plenty of light to travel by. "But won't he want to *sleep?*" But it seems that natives do not sleep much anyway when the nights are light. The boy on his trip up the coast would find the villagers very much awake, and in those of his own totem he would probably stop to pick up gossip and something to eat. This sixty-mile sprint up and down the coast was just a holiday walkabout for an indentured plantation boy.

So, with a bellyful of rice, a present of two sticks of tobacco stuck in his arm band, and our thrice-enclosed acceptance tucked deep into the top of his towering coiffure, the boy jogged off up the beach. It was still raining a little from the squall we had passed through on the launch trip, but soon those clouds followed the setting sun, and before the boy was out of sight a moon was rising out of the water in the east. The thought of that polite little acceptance jogging along through the night, into sticky spider webs in the spirit-haunted bush, around measles-stricken villages, swimming over alligators in the brown bogs of rivers, trotting along mile after mile of moonlit beach with the surf booming silver in that steady pale-blue glow—all this gave that note a glamor that must never before have accompanied those hackneyed words "We are delighted to accept . . ."

The real war of these islands, the most persistent and everlasting and vicious, is not the one between the white invaders and the dark people who own the land, nor the feuds between the natives themselves, nor yet the one between all humans and the bacteria and insects and heat. It is the fight of men, both black and white, to get and keep foothold on the land. For without unceasing vigilance the vegetation would push the puny human beings right off the islands.

The picture of lying on one's back with the food dropping into one's mouth is pretty, and it may be true of other tropical islands, but not of Melanesia. Food must be cultivated here, and the land has to be cleared for cultivation. But wherever the sun shines on the rich virgin soil in the hothouse air, rank vegetation springs up overnight. The women in their gardens weed and weed and weed a soil whose very composition is nascent. There is no rest from it. A cleared plot left unattended for a short time can be identified only by the fact that the huge trees are absent and the undergrowth thicker than elsewhere. Every sprout of green that springs up under and around the plantation house is plucked at sight. This is largely because the growths harbor poisonous snakes and insects, but also because, once the weeds take over, the fight to master them is the harder. And it goes on eternally. The plantations keep herds of cattle, not for meat or milk (because the danger of dysentery is too great with natives butchering and milking) but to graze down any sprouting undergrowth. Along the borders of the tracts armies of boys whack incessantly at the green arms of the bush reaching out to reclaim the cleared area. The hot moist air fairly sucks growing things to their maximum development almost as soon as they emerge from the earth. Flowers and vegetables of a temperate climate cannot be cultivated except by constant attention; they turn to seed almost immediately, neglecting the stages of blossom and fruit. The natives depend for food chiefly on tuberous vegetables like the root of the taro and a kind of sweet potato. Even gardens for the native banana trees have to be cleared and kept clear, though the trees themselves need no attention. The very village itself is an area wrested from the bush, and murdering any green thing shooting up above the barren clearing is the constant work of the women and girl children. All along the shores you see the coconut palms leaning out toward the sea as if pressed that way by the overpowering bush behind them.

This bush, which is the unimaginative Australian name for it, has all the earmarks of being jungle to an Expotition. We had explored the outside wall of it for days, searching for a colorful Gauguinish background for our Malaita figures. There were no flowers. (The clusters of red which we finally used were the seeds of a species of palm.) We never, anywhere in the islands, saw the exotic flowers Gauguin painted, nor anything like the gigantic or massive flowers that grow even in California. Here along the bush wall the sole color note is green, and it is here one gets the sensation that the bush is a living entity, capable of reaching, trampling, and strangling.

The wall is a solid mass of growth, a real wall (for there is no opening in it anywhere) a hundred or more feet high, and above it extend the dead tops of trees that have been choked to leaflessness by the smothering parasites on the lower limbs. Thousands of flying foxes (properly bats) hang head down all over the dead branches, beautiful targets for pot shots. A shot raises the whole mass, which circles and settles again a few feet beyond, to continue the daylight sleep. Below where the green begins there are flying curls of vine creepers reaching out into the air toward the cultivated palms, if there are any near, and draped below them over the mass of tree foliage are the loops of lawyer vine rope, and tops of the taller native palms.

It was the lower part of the wall that Rousseau painted. Here is all the intricate design of a frosted windowpane combined with the massiveness and variety of Nature gone crazy. Only God could create a bush wall, and few masters have the technique to copy the combinations of patterns and textures and kinds of green—or, for that matter, the ability to describe them. There are all at once things glittery and furry, gummy, warty and glassy, shirred, saw-edged and slit, massive and minute. There are little fragments of lace, the most delicate blue-green with copper-colored veins, and so transparent that we could see their whole circulatory system. The leaves grew facing flat against the bush wall like patterns on a Chinese silk.

There are great hairy leaves as big as umbrellas; there are hundreds of kinds of palms, so diverse in leaf shape that only an expert would recognize them as belonging to the same family. Down near the ground are the elephant ears of the taro, and fern and the slashed leaves of stray banana trees with their huge purple seed hanging toward the earth—something so "artistic," and frankly biological, looking that Georgia O'Keefe should always be posed with a propagating banana tree. And near the ground are all the thousands of kinds of insects and their cocoons on the undersides of leaves; the praying mantises that look like green twigs and act like intelligent animals, and the ants that look like ants and bite like dragons, and the spiders that spread their shimmering nets over the whole and make it look like a Christmas tree in tinsel.

The Australians call it "bush," and we might have called it "jungle" if we had never got beyond the wall. Neither "bush" nor "jungle" was the word.

We were on our way to a hill village to work and the Expotition at last had the appearance of a genuine safari—but only the appearance. The village was only two hours inland and we had a picnic lunch to tide us overnight in the patrol officer's hut and one mosquito net and one blanket. Leading the column was our escort, a neighboring planter, mounted on a white charger, and wearing two wide-brimmed felt hats one on top of the other—the equivalent of a pith topee. Margaret and I had got "all gussied up" like lady explorers, but before we had reached the border of the plantation our immaculate white breeches were caked with sweat, black grease, and parts of the old saddles whose stirrups dropped off even as we mounted. They were wired on again but the moisture-rotted straps kept breaking above the wiring until we were seated more like jockeys than lady explorers. The horses were almost as bad as the leather; all of them had noisome island sores on their heads and branches of leaves to keep the flies dislodged, with the result that we rode along in a banner-like cloud of black bottle flies. And these flies have a nasty instinct for locating the cracks in one's face, the corners of the eyes and mouth. So we carried palm fronds and when the horses walked we fanned ourselves gracefully.

Then, Margaret's steed was a mother, and the colt accompanied us. Her unit should have brought up the rear but my animal refused to be followed. He was a victim of shock. From his jaw to his shoulder was a wide hairless scar where an alligator had grabbed him when he was fording a stream, and it was a compliment to my horsemanship, or nerves, that the planter had put the two of us together. But for our carrier his behavior would have ruined the whole picture of an expedition on safari.

The carrier was only one, to be sure, but he made up in quality what we lacked in quantity. He was a masterpiece of bleaching and combing and hedgecutting, and the reason he was not carrying our boy scout sandwiches and blanket on his head was that on top of his snow-white hennin was a hibiscus blossom which could not be crushed. The gear was in dilly bags hanging down his back, and he kept a safe distance in the line far in the rear of my kicking kangaroo.

We had started out from the plantation house at a walk, but that was soon corrected. Even the normal Australian horse knows only two gaits, and there is nothing between a sleepwalk and a swoop. We took the plantation on the fly, branches flapping like banners, the colt running in wide, delighted circles, and my kangaroo staggering the course like the afternoon-of-a-faun. The flies held their cloud formation even at high speed, and far behind us, Friday, the carrier, ran holding onto his flower. It was like tearing up a boulder-strewn creek, for the clover was littered with fallen coconuts; by the time we reached the edge of the plantation our hands were raw from trying to keep our horses from making the trip on their chins. We were frothing like the animals—and this was still in the shade.

Now we came out on an upward-sloping expanse of tiger grass. It was one of the few low growths we saw anywhere in the islands, only ten feet high, and revealing no trail whatsoever. The lead horse seemed to know the way, however, and plunged straight into the wilderness of grass. There was no shade here, nothing save the tassels hanging over our heads, and the tunnel was an inferno. Also, now at a walk, the flies settled down in earnest, finding our juices just as tasty as the horses' sores. Walking on my own feet is one of my phobias, but I felt so desperate that I very nearly did get off the heaving stead. I was saved from such an extremity just in time by our reaching the bush wall.

So far as we could see there was no opening of any trail into it. With the morning sun striking it, the façade was a solid mass with even the patterns swallowed up in the flat light. We followed along it for some distance, and then suddenly we saw the planter duck forward and he and his horse disappeared straight into the wall. Only an animal could have smelled out that trail. The opening was overgrown with a thin curtain of leaves, but just behind it was a dark tunnel exactly horse size. We lay over on our horses' necks and did not rise until the planter called, "All clear."

Everything was black at first, and there was the chill of a cave. "Coo-oo-oo-*ee*!" Margaret yipped—the Australian cow-hand's "Whoopee"—and sure enough back came the hollow echo from somewhere far up ahead. Gradually our eyes became adjusted to the gloom, and then we pulled up awed, enchanted. We *were* in a cave, a cave going up a hillside, complete with stalactites and stalagmites. The first astonishing thing was the missing jungle. There was no thicket, no underbrush, and not one robust green thing growing anywhere on the surface. There were just gigantic tree trunks spaced wide apart, rising absolutely straight and branchless to eighty or more feet above us. High up there they branched out into a solid ceiling of leaves through which came only a glimmer of light. It was like being under an enormous circus tent, with the roof hung with great leafless loops of vine rope. Below, knotted and twisting with the powerful roots of the trees that spread all over the surface, these vines crawled like strangling pythons up and around the trunks, growing into them, covering them in a network of thick arms. No wonder there were no low branches; only the very tops of the trees struggling toward the sun could hope to keep ahead of those writhing parasites.

Underfoot it was a labyrinth of huge aerial roots and black muck, drooling with centuries of undried rains, and the cold air was pungent with the odor of rotting leaves and wood. Some of the giants had fallen, yet there was no break in the leaf roof anywhere. How these mountain slopes reforest themselves is hard to explain. Only here and there stood a timid sapling, shooting up branchless and as straight as an arrow toward the feeble light above. At the very tip were a few transparent green leaves. But these were the only color throughout the great cave. The muck underfoot was a deep brown, almost black; the towering pillars of the trees were a cold gray with here and there patches of brown moss. Yet all through the forest was the curious green glow which is the peculiarity of all great forests, even the leafless redwoods. We should have missed our first island flower if the planter had not pointed it out. High up on the trunk of a tree was a tiny cluster of yellow and green, very pale. It looked like a

butterfly, and it was an orchid. And it was consistent with the nature of these islands that the only place a fragile bud could survive to become a blossom was hidden away from the competition in the sunlight.

This was a great cavern in every respect except sound; here was none of the hush of the palm cathedral through the night. It was a Rackham haunted forest come alive. All the sounds of a birdhouse in the zoo, and of a madhouse; all the weird piping and wailing, croaking and lowing and sawing and thumping. Something cried like a child—and there was not a visible creature to make these sounds. Even the cockatoos of the plantation could not be seen, though we could hear their raucous screams above the tree roof. It is little wonder that the bushmen, living for centuries in this eerie gloom where the very air moans and cries so mysteriously, are animists.

But the singing close to our ears was made by no spirit. The air was filled with gloom-loving anopheles. We had left most of the flies behind in the bush wall tunnel, but now our tortured horses, ourselves included, were coated with blood-swollen mosquitoes. My kangaroo had long ago exhausted his adrenal glands and was now stumbling up over the high roots with his head hanging nearly to the ground. All the horses were heaving painfully from the incline, and were white with froth as if they had been cantering. It was sheer torture sitting on them and I was shivering with cold, so I got down with the idea of walking. What I did was mush, in the truest sense of the word, for the higher we climbed the deeper the muck and the higher the roots above the ground. I was panting and boiling (and back on my horse) before I had gone ten yards.

And now up on the horse I was immediately shivering again—and still hot. A storm was coming up. We could hear the roar of it over the treetops faraway from us, and long before we felt the first gusts of wind. Like magic the clamor of spirits ceased. The distant roar swelled in volume, and then we were in the darkness of a moonless night. Wave on wave of wind passed over the roof and then finally the whirlwind hit. The sound has no parallel. It was howl, roar, and moan together but with unearthly volume. Man's instinctive fear may be that of being dropped, but certainly a good runner-up is the terror of having things dropped on him in the dark. Our roof split open in flashing gaps of light, showing briefly the vine ropes slashing about as if whipped by some mighty hand. Showers of leaves fell through the whitened air, and then dead limbs. The terrified colt dashed off into the dark and my own animal tore frantically at his bridle and then stood stiff with his flesh quivering. I expected him to bolt from under me. We were all off then trying to find something to tie our horses to. Friday was useless. He would not come near the frantic animals.

Then came the rain. It came in a deafening roar and fell, not in drops, but in streams from the high branches and vine loops, and in bucketfuls when the roof split open. The trunks of the trees were upright rivers gleaming white in the ripples, and our trail, what there had been of it, was a freshet pouring over already saturated earth. And all the while the roof was screaming and being pitched about by an icy wind which corrugated our wet hides.

And still I felt hot. Even while I was shaking with cold my nose was hot. Something had happened to the back of my neck; it felt as if it had been hit with a club. My eyeballs must be on rubber bands hitched to sore places in my brain, for every time I moved my eyes I could feel the stretch clear to the back of my skull. And my spine hurt and all my muscles and joints, and my skin felt raw and dry even while it was cold and wet. And I felt very tired and dizzy and hot and cold—and utterly miserable.

I had "it"—malaria.

The planter had malaria, Friday had malaria, and my kangaroo had it. Only the colt and Margaret, who had been taking preventive quinine, escaped. We were a miserable little safari that returned to the coast—without ever reaching the village. I thought I was dying—without the Melanesians immortalized in paint. I dwelt on cerebral malaria, the kind that had killed Nankervis, and almost cried thinking of Margaret having to bury me here, perhaps even the day after tomorrow, in this abandoned land. Then she would have to make that long journey home alone, only to be greeted by "I told you so." It seemed hundreds of miles to the plantation and I lived through it like a drowning man, thinking of all my sins, but mostly of how much I ached.

My malaria turned out to be the favorite kind: intermittent. It was intermittent in forty-eight-hour attacks for about a week and then quiescent until I caught another chill. At one time we even thought we had it synchronized with the rains. During the wet season the cloudbursts came at a regular time, a few minutes later each day. If I happened to be having a go, my fever would rise as the sun went behind the clouds; during the night while the heavens poured my temperature would soar anywhere as high as a thousand; but as the sun came up I would break into a sweat and the go was over—until the afternoon rain.

I had none of the planters' philosophy regarding a pain in the neck, and I went to bed with a bottle of scotch sarsaparilla, and a peck of quinine, while native models, thinking I had died, disappeared into limbo. One may be able to conduct a plantation while in a state of vertigo and acute anguish, but pictures aren't painted that way. However, I even began to look forward to a scorching fever after a while. Between goes I was just the normal sluggish European in the tropics where work, any kind of physical or mental effort, was difficult. But after the attacks were definitely over, there was a period of curious elation and energy during which I got more work done than in any normal time. Margaret was even envious of me, having only island sores and "ants" herself.

In any case, after this first attack on Guadalcanar, I was indisputably an old-timer, initiated, while Margaret was still a new chum. And somehow the siege restored us temporarily to the dignity of an expedition: we had got on the "inside" of the islands.

15

We knew that Tanakombo was different the minute we sighted it from the launch. For one thing the residence was not down on the beach flat. In the dark we saw its lights high up, even above the tops of the coconut palms. Behind it was the solid black of the bush, not the feathery shadow of plantation palms. It must be set in a clearing in the bush wall. The slope of the roof was faintly silhouetted and it had a magnificent long curving line from the high peak to the low edge of the veranda, one never achieved by corrugated iron. It was, in fact, a palm-thatched roof, like those of the natives' huts. And as we came closer we could see the soft fringe of the edge of it hanging into the orange light of the lamps on the veranda. The pillars supporting it had the wobbly line of unfinished logs, and were logs with only their bark removed. Then we were up the hill and on the veranda seeing, with delight, the flooring of springy betel-nut saplings —and our unknown savior, for the first time.

It was her voice that had best prepared us for our new missus. In the dark of the beach as we landed over the surf, and above the roar of this, had come a cultured English voice exclaiming with un-English enthusiasm, "Oh, I'm *so* glad you could come right away." No intimation that the speaker had been so stunned by our promptness in accepting her invitation that she could not even give us a proper bed. On the way up the hill all we could see of her were her lantern-lit ankles. They were bare and thin and the feet were in worn oxfords. Now in the light on the veranda we saw a tall woman—no, little more than a girl—a thin, pale face framed by curly fair hair. If that hair had been loosened a little the face would have been less angular, almost beautiful. "Oh, I'm so glad you could come," she repeated. Then hastily, "I get so lonely here by myself." The first appeal toward endearing one human to another: that one is needed by the other.

By the time we had turned in for the night all we knew of our new circumstances was that the house was beautiful—it was native-built, and entirely of native materials—and that our hostess was a widow with three little boys, and was running her plantation unaided. And as she had talked through the evening—like a dam suddenly freed—her pale, lined face had grown younger by the minute. She was a dear, the best luck in the world for us, for we were to live together without escape for at least six weeks.

It was a princess-and-the-pea night, that first one at Tanakombo. A bed was being borrowed for us from a neighboring plantation but it had not yet come up, and we turned in on netting-covered camp stretchers lined up along the veranda on an inside court behind what was eventually to be our room. That room was a little native hut (without the roof) the walls of saffron-yellow bamboo laced together with vine rope in a diamond pattern. The "court" was simply an omission of a center square of the veranda floor. Four feet below was the ground which proved later to be the "laundry." At the moment it was a black pit of unknown depth and containing the rustling, creaking creatures that black pits hold at night in a strange place. Here we were, three white women with three babies, alone in a house tucked into the bush and surrounded by native villages.

There was a bright moon but the clouds of the launch trip squall were still with us, and all night long the wind stroked the roof of the forest behind us. It was a different sound from the rustling ticking of palm fronds. When the moon came out from behind a black cloud we could see the tops of the plantation palms between us and the ocean. It was a great sea of glistening highlights on the shiny fronds. But up in the forest behind us I could hear Smetana's "River," singing on and on and far away, while the rain from the afternoon's squall went *dri-drip, dri-drip* all around the fringed edge of the thatching. Every now and then the range of high mountains to the east of us lit up, showing the pale-blue crests of ridges and black valleys. Out there it was silent but under our high roof there was pandemonium. Lizards *geh-eh-cko-ed* hollowly, rats in pursuit of them raced across the rafters and squeaked in their frustration. They romped up and down our mosquito nets, having some sort of trapeze act on the top that bounced and joggled the whole structure. Something back in the forest sawed wood endlessly, and only when the blue beyond the fringe of the roof lightened with dawn did the creature finish his task.

Soon after, a rooster screamed under the house and then hens popped up out of the black pit of the court, plunking onto the edge of the veranda, and shaking the whole house as they landed. Then they went about making happy little noises in their throats and beating a tattoo on the betel-nut floor, cleaning up the insects which had expired around our lanterns. Three dogs, remotely shepherd, wagged up, sniffing with embarrassed curiosity all around our mosquito nets, and presently the houseboy thundered up the steps to the house cook where he began methodically breaking dishes.

Hearing a new clucking-scuffling sound I rolled over toward the court, raised my mosquito net and looked straight into a pair of black eyes peeking at me over the edge of the veranda floor. They belonged to a pickaninny who had shinnied up the pile, and as I raised the net the top of the pickaninny's head dropped out of sight like a clock cuckoo. Instantly the air was split by screams of fright, and an explosion of native gutturals. At the far side of the court sat a native woman in only a grass petticoat; the little naked girl was clinging to her mother's back bawling, and the woman's face was almost turned inside-out with what sounded like uncontrollable rage. Yet both her hands were engaged calmly digging up grass sprouts with her fingernails—her mouth and hands apparently not sharing emotions.

The child continued screaming and the mother "soothing" for five minutes before our Missus stalked out of her room at the rear end of the veranda. We were delighted to see her in her nightgown—because we had heard that white women had to be fully clothed, even down to stockings, with natives in the house—and she was Lady Macbeth with long braids hanging over her shoulders and imperious command in her advance. The whole house shook under it as she came around the veranda, bawling pidgin English at the weed picker. Hens flew and dogs scuttled, and reaching the

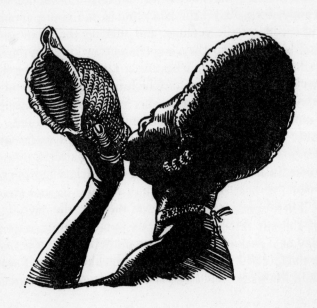

house cook she started off morning tea like the linguist and general she was. We do not like to accuse our hostess so soon of walloping houseboys on the head with pans, but from the house cook came a muffled bang, a yelp, and out of the doorway sped the boy with a pink conch shell. He went to the edge of the veranda and blew eastward, the veins standing out on his neck and temples. It was a beautiful long huntsman's horn blast that echoed back from the hills. Instantly somewhere down in the feathery palm fronds of the plantation a rumble began—the rumble of a drum. It was the signal for the day's work to begin. The sun moved up an inch, striking a thin white shaft of light down onto the dark-brown weed picker and her silenced pickaninny. Two cups of hot black tea came out of the house cook, the boy stubbing his toes on the uneven saplings, spilling tea on the mosquito net. "Teamissus!" he announced quite unnecessarily. And the Tanakombo day was on the wing.

When we had fought our way through the house wash-wash and had reached the breakfast table on the east veranda—just about the time the flies and mosquitoes were seating themselves—we saw a striking procession coming up the plantation trail. A bed mattress was moving up on the heads of two brown caryatids—in bright red lap-laps, which identified them as male. The flat springs followed on the heads of two more caryatids and after them came headboards and side rails, and finally our neighbor, the Planter himself, riding, and leading by long tethers two horses which were followed by a colt. Like a good island neighbor he came bearing gifts for guests, no matter how unattractive they might turn out to be. There was a bottle of scotch, the bed, two horses, and a boy, the last three to be our servitors for the duration of our stay at Tanakombo. And with no delay these gifts were laid at the feet of Margaret even before breakfast was finished.

While Margaret was abundantly thanking the Planter by

merely sitting listening to him, I went out with the Missus to see how a lone woman could run a plantation when even brave men had to use a hard hand on the Malaitan labor. But on the way down to the copra shed I learned that there were only two indentured boys on the whole tract. One was the houseboy and the other the boss plantation boy, both of whom the Missus felt she could not get along without. Because of heavy mortgages on the plantation's produce (on which she could barely keep up the interest payments) the Missus could not afford indentured labor at twenty-five-dollars-a-head recruiter's fee. She depended entirely on the indifferent help from the villages. The native men worked for a shilling a day and worked only long enough to get the tobacco they needed; then they just stayed away. It was therefore one of the duties of the indentured boss boy to keep rounding up village men and keep them on the job as long as possible, as well as get the work out of them while they were on the job. All this the Missus could not do herself because the village men did not take kindly to being ordered about by a woman, even a white one.

But for the moment the Missus was delighted that, by buying up additional coconuts from the villages, she had been able to swell Tanakombo's regular monthly copra shipment enough to pay, not only the interest due on the mortgages, but some of the principal, long overdue. The loans were from one of the big plantation and shipping companies (the one appropriately known as the Octopus of the Pacific) and this was only too anxious to foreclose and take the plantation now that it was in full bearing. Before the Mastah died three years ago (of blackwater fever) the Missus and he had starved and labored through seven years waiting for the tract to come into bearing before it could hope to pay off the debts. (It was the expense of Southern hospitalization, having the babies, which had necessitated the mortgages).

Anyway, the time of fulfillment was at hand when the plantation could be cleared of debts—perhaps David could be sent South to school next year; he was almost eight and his time for getting out of the islands for his health was long overdue.

We went into the copra shed so that the Missus could gloat over this precious shipment of copra which was to begin paying the way to freedom. The shed was not a fancy fireproof iron building like the one at Ruavatu. It was simply a large native hut with bamboo walls and a palm-thatched roof. And like the residence it had long been waiting a new roof (which must be supplied every seven years to be rain-proof). All the "meat" had dried out of the palm leaflets in the thatching, leaving only the spiny skeletons, dry as tinder in spite of the rains, for the other compartment of the shed was the copra dryer whose constant fire kept the whole place dried out. All around three sides of the compartment were stacked those sacks of pure gold in the form of coconut fat. While the Missus counted the sacks which had been prepared the day before I went through the door to the drying oven. And remembering the clocked ovens of Ruavatu I "lumped up," seeing what this girl had to make shift with. The Malaitan boss boy was tending the one fire by throwing coconut husks on an already blazing bed on the ground, and the flames were licking up toward the racks of coconut fat above. And the racks were smoked and oil-soaked *bamboo*. The whole room was black with the oily soot of years of fires; it looked like a stacked bonfire to me—especially with the drops of oil sputtering down into the fire from the racks above it. But I supposed the boy knew what he was doing; he had been doing it long enough. He was an old war horse. When I came into the compartment he did not even glance at me and I saw only his brutish profile with a short thick neck and a muscular chest. He was below average Melanesian height and much more powerfully built—bad-looking company for a white woman living alone, I thought.

And I was standing there watching him and thinking about it when I got the most sudden reverse of opinion of my life to date. The boy was standing with his back to the door of the entrance from the storage compartment, leaning over a little to rake the coconut meat on the bottom rack above the fire. I never even saw the Missus. All I caught was the flick of her foot as it swung past and lifted the rump of the boy. He nearly fell into the racks. The shed was sizzling with pidgin English in a cultured English voice—pitched a little high. The boy swung around and for an instant I thought he was going to use his crowbar rake on the Missus. He raised it and his big face looked like that of an infuriated gorilla. I backed involuntarily, but the Missus reached out and grabbed the rake, still scorching the air. The boy answered, but could not be heard, and then suddenly his face had "withdrawn" into the obscure black look of the normal Melanesian. When we went out of the shed he was raking the coconut husks *off* the fire.

Once out in less curdled air I could laugh as if I hadn't been scared to death. "So that's how frail woman runs a plantation!" I observed. "Can every English clergyman's daughter kick like a kangaroo?" "As a matter of fact," the Missus answered, "I've never kicked before. Your being with me must have given me the courage to do it. I've been wanting to ever since I've had that boy—he *will* use coconut husks on the fire. My talk-talk-talk doesn't do any good and he'll burn the place down one of these days. He's too lazy to cut wood —too obstinate—coconut husks flame too much. He'll burn the shed down." "Do you mean to say," I was aghast, "that you have never struck that boy before?" "No, and I think if you hadn't been with me the brute would have used that rake." "Well," I said, "don't go around, inspired by me, kicking any more natives. If I had known that that kick and gorilla face weren't routine I'd have been at Berande by this time. That man *is* a brute, black or white. I wonder . . ." But I didn't finish it.

All the same I kept on wondering, and it was not until the second night that we got the answer.

By the time we had got back to the veranda the Missus had calmed down a bit and was feeling almost pleased with herself. She thought she should have kicked the fellow before, it did *her* so much good; and, still bubbling, she called for a kettle of boiling water and began unwinding a dressing on her hand. There was about a fathom of bandage which, she explained as she unwound, covered an infection she had got from a sliver under her thumbnail. It seemed like a lot of bandage for a sliver, but when finally the thumb emerged I could only think that in any other country that finger would not have been bandaged; it would have been in a hospital garbage can. It was no recognizable thumb; it was the size and color of a nude banana, the skin had broken in little slits, and pus was oozing out of it down to the bottom of the second joint. Boiling water was poured in the basin and the Missus was preparing to plunge her hand in it when I got my stomach down far enough to offer to lance the thumb. The only possible way I could do it was to pretend that the Missus was a cadaver and that I was back in the dissecting room slicing off muscles (which I had once done in order to learn my anatomy thoroughly). We sterilized one of the safety razor blades from the cigarette tin drawing outfit, the Missus looked out over the mountains, and I sliced down the palm of the thumb. I could not look while I was squeezing. The Missus, her jaw set and face the color of a real cadaver, was pointing out a black scar on the hillside nearest us. "That was a forest fire," she croaked. "It broke out the first week after my husband died. The first time I'd ever been here alone. I can remember the sound of it yet. It was night. The natives . . ." And her voice faded away. *I* had fainted. And when I came to, Margaret, so help me, was stretched out on the floor white as a sheet, and the *Missus* was administering!

It was midafternoon the next day when another event jangled everyone's nerves. Paul, the "middle" son, not yet five years old, was missing. The houseboy was supposed to put the youngsters to bed right after lunch, while the Missus got them up and dressed them after siesta. And Paul was not in his bed. The bed had been mussed but not slept in. We were wakened by the Missus shouting "Paul—*Paul!*" as she ran around the house. The houseboy and our man Friday were just coming up the path from their post-lunch spello. No, the houseboy had put Paul to bed with the others and then returned to his dishes. Both boys were dispatched down to the river. Margaret and I had a sick feeling; being Americans our first thought was kidnaping. The boss boy to be revenged for the kick had stolen up when we were all asleep and somehow got the child out of the shaky house without being heard. And if he were a civilized savage Paul's body would have been thrown to the alligators by now. "Oh, I'm sure he's got down to the river," the Missus kept saying. The river with its alligators and tides was a constant threat to the mother of three lively little boys, and the indentured boy was less housemaid than nurse to see that the youngsters never played beyond the clearing. Such horrors as one or the other of the boys disappearing for good were almost routine, because the houseboy seemed able to count up only to two and if he produced that many children intact he acted as if he were doing his job properly. But so far a lost boy had always unlost himself by answering to the call of his name.

But Paul did not answer. The houseboys came back from

the river reporting that they had found no tracks, and then they and the Missus, armed with machetes to whack out a path, started back into the bush. Margaret and I went down through the plantation and did some inquisitioning of the boss boy. He no savvy anything 'long Paul, but he would have looked just as guilty dead; he had that kind of face.

It was four o'clock before we were all back at the house, and the British being what they are, we had tea as usual. And we were sitting there automatically gnawing on the stale biscuits when Paul unlost himself. It occurred to us afterwards that this was the first time we had all been in the house since the baby's disappearance—and we had waked him up; he had been asleep in the rafters of the roof! "Moth-ah," we heard the high-pitched little voice, above us, "might-t I have a biscuit-t when I get-t down?"

In the morning the houseboy and three youngsters had been teaching our man Friday hide-and-seek, and after being put to bed, Paul, lying there looking up into the high roof, had apparently decided that the rafters would be a grand new place to hide. We couldn't find out if he had gone to the houseboy and asked him to keep up the game, or had just climbed up into the roof to see if it could be done. Anyway, he had gone to sleep waiting and remained in the coma produced by the noonday heat through all the shouting outside the house. Probably it was only the smell of the tea that had awakened the Englishman in him. After that we began to understand why our Missus, who was only a little older than ourselves, looked haggard and harried and at times acted just a little unstrung.

That same evening after dinner we were sitting in a row along the south veranda, our legs in pajamas as mosquito protection, and those legs comfortably up on the veranda railing. Margaret and I had our "wha-whas" (ukulele and guitar) and we were all singing those fine old English madrigals which sounded magnificent under the huge roof. The sky to the south and east was changing tones like one of those color organs. There was something special about the evening; perhaps it was relief from the storm of the afternoon. The Missus suddenly pulled her legs up like a little girl, "Oh, I don't know when I've felt so jolly!" To feel "jolly" so seldom that she had to mention it!

We were silent, thinking about it, when I thought I heard a new sound. And the palms down below, a curious tint to them—slightly orange. Then there was a roar. "My God!" The Missus was off the veranda in a flash. Fire! It had the sound of a subway express roaring through the station. The trees, the palms in one spot down in the plantation were livid. Sparks were shooting up above the fronds—rockets of them. We tore down after the Missus. "The copra shed!" she screamed. "My copra . . . !"

We were racing down through the deep weeds stumbling on coconuts. I fell flat in a hidden irrigation ditch. The fire was now a solid column of flame rising from the ground, tons of coconut fat going up, a holocaust. The sound of it was terrifying, and the Missus was charging straight toward it screaming. Half-naked natives were running toward it from all directions through the tract, they screaming too. The burning geyser was sending out comets of flame which were igniting the dry fiber of the surrounding trees. I felt perverted thinking how beautiful it was; the whole cathedral was lit with an awesome glow and there was the color of burning sulphur at the base of the flame. The fronds of nearby trees flapped violently in the suction of the heat which was like hell itself. We were all, natives and Missus and ourselves, suddenly working furiously spanking out ignited patches of undergrowth with palm fronds and copra sacks— the sacks too soaked in oil to last long. The natives never left off screaming. They scrambled up the trees and tore at the flaming fiber in the crotches. Fronds as they ignited were whacked down and pulled into a pile. Someone had gone to the drum and was thumping out a steady roll which must have spelled "Fire" to the listening villages. The sound gave the scene its essence—infinitely barbaric, an ominous undertone to the excited native screams and the boom of the fire. I saw the boss boy; he was working just as furiously as the rest of us.

The wind was off the ocean and I suddenly noticed the flare of sparks swing over in the direction of the hill on which the house stood. That roof, a pile of dry hay! If one spark fell on it, it was gone. I tore up to the house, methodically falling in the same irrigation ditch, and roused the children who were still sleeping. Then we were off to the beach. I carried the baby and somehow got over the ditch without falling and even laughed hysterically because the baby kept saying: "Pretty fire. Pretty fire." I left the youngsters on the beach with instructions to David not to move from the spot and then raced back up the hill (falling in the irrigation ditch), got a pail of water from the house cook, tore down the clothesline in the "laundry," and, with one end of it tied to the pail and the other to my waist, I clawed my way up the outside of the roof. The thatching was a foot and a half deep and my knees sank into it, sometimes clear through, and great chunks of it came off in my grasping hands; but I got halfway up—to the length of the rope—and there wedged in. I was prepared to save the roof, but it was no sin to enjoy myself while waiting to do it. And I did thoroughly enjoy myself.

It was a god's-eye view of disaster. The column of fire had gone down a bit, but the breeze was whipping sparks all over the place, and all around the core of fire the fronds of other trees were flapping and flaming. The orange-colored natives hopping about looked like demons in Hell's inferno. Yet above me the great white moon shone steadily in the serene sky, and off to the south the mountains "slumbered" with that curiously eternal look which mountains in the moonlight have. Natives all over those hills must be watching this white man's spectacle, for forest fires are almost unknown to these inhabitants of forests. Did they think that we were merely having an unusually large sing-sing bonfire, or was the guv'men burning a village in reprisal? It was reprisal, I was sure of that—reprisal for a kick.

A circle of trees two lanes around had been burned to stalks before the fire was stopped. Probably not more than an hour and a half had passed since we heard the first roar and by this time that precious shipment of copra was a heap of white-hot, sputtering fat. The ignited trees with their fronds torn off were left, pillars with glowing stubs. The moonlight shone down into the cathedral through the blackened opening, more eloquent of destruction than the fire itself had been. The plantation was quiet again, the night so still—just as if the island spirits, having spoken, had resumed their eternal indifference to the petty efforts of men.

When we were all on the veranda again the Missus called for her kettle of hot water for her hand. There was nothing to be said. We sat, miserable and inadequate, while she unwound the frayed and blackened bandage. She plunged her hand in the water and then snatched it out. The water was too hot, but she thrust the hand in again and held on. Then I saw the tears drop-drop-dropping around the basin. It was the fact that she did not throw her head on the table and sob like any woman that undid me. I went for a walk down on the beach and did it for her.

Nothing was ever said about the copra shipment. It was like a death in the family. Until we left the plantation the shelled coconut was kept protected from the rains by coconut fronds, and by and by a smaller new drying shed started going up, the materials cut from the bush around us and the building in charge of the boss boy. No charge could be brought against him, for it could not be proved that the fire was not an accident in such an inadequate shed.

16

We recalled our first sight of the *Mataram* as we had seen it in Sydney Harbor; it had looked like a silly little ferry tied up alongside the ocean liners from all over the world. But now, as we chugged out to it on the Planter's launch, it looked like an ocean greyhound, something on the lines of the *Queen Mary*, only more beautiful. We should never have thought the sight of a single steamer could rouse such emotions. It was like coming home, for there on the bridge was the Voy's round, pink face, glowering in a dear familiar way. "You've brought our paints!" we rejoiced. Our mail, pounds of it, was handed over—and can anyone know what this one-sided conversation with home meant!—but *there was no freight!* "Look again," we demanded, "there's a whole shipment of paints from Sydney for us—are you sure you didn't drop it at Berande or Ruavatu?" They were sure. The wharf strike was still on in Sydney and no one was getting any freight; none had been dropped for anyone at either Ruavatu or Berande. But ours wasn't *big* freight; the art supply store could have put it on the steamer itself. "We've ordered it. It *must* be on the steamer." The *Mataram* was turned inside out, but there were no paints for us.

This time we gave our order to the Voy, as hundreds of white islanders before us had done, and he promised to shop for the supplies and bring them up himself, next trip—six weeks off! "But I don't know what you want store paints for," he bawled. "All you need is dirt diluted with island sores; smear it on a sail and touch it up with hair mattress stuffing and season with walkabouts. There you have a real modern picture of a cannibal." He thought he was being funny, cheering us up, and he *had* struck something. Sail? . . . sail canvas? What was the matter with it? And boat paint? It was not permanent, but what of it? Our studies would all have to be copied anyway. It was pigment and we could mix colors with it.

The Voy turned us loose with the ship carpenter and the first thing we got was ten pounds of white-lead paste. It was poisonous and dangerous for a painter to use, but we should have to be careful not to get it in an island sore. The red lead was also bad, but it was a fine vermilion. Then there was a quart of black paint and some spar varnish. That was all the pigment we could get. From a large bucket of brushes we chose some well-made varnish brushes which we proposed cutting down into small brushes. The only new canvas on board was some orange tarpaulin, already made nonabsorbent by the orange pigment, which would save our having to size it—so that our paints would not sink in. We could have all the turpentine and linseed oil we wanted, and we took it. And now, for a complete painting outfit, we lacked only a few colors. A madder red was handy, but we could get along without it; we could do without green, but to make green we had to have a blue and at least one yellow. Masterpieces have been painted in the past with only the primary colors. The primitive headhunt was just getting into its stride.

Luckily it rained all of the following week at Tanakombo and this gave us time to get our outfit into working order. It was not quite so simple as Robinson Crusoe would have us believe. The orange tarpaulin had to be painted white to keep me from going color-blind while painting on it, and the wide bolt was unrolled down one side of the veranda and given a coat of white lead. And inasmuch as there were three dogs, three children, two houseboys, and ten chickens living in and under the house, the wet canvas got some very individual markings on it. Whenever the sun came out we hustled it out to dry on the ground, and here it attracted such a horde of insects that after a while we became fed up picking them off. They were left on to be incarcerated for-ever under additional coats of sizing. And, if anything, they gave the too-smooth canvas a rather intriguing painting texture.

It was when we came to making little brushes out of big ones that we got into trouble. The difficulties were too numerous to describe here, but the results were simple; the bunches of hair, clipped to the right length on the "far" ends and very carefully bound with wire, then put into a bamboo handle, looked like nothing in the world but the flaring end of a child's pigtail. We used glue and had to fight the ants and cockroaches to retain the binding overnight; but in the end, with the patience of genius, we got some very decent tools made from an old shaving brush shaped and held together by a tree gum brought to us by our good man Friday. This is the kind of gum the natives use for attaching flying fox teeth to their spearheads. And at last I had brushes with handles long enough; some of the slender bamboos were old spear and arrow shafts, also provided by Friday, and we left them eighteen and twenty inches long, so that I could stand back (like Sorolla) and paint from a distance.

Picture-painting linseed oil and turpentine (binder and dryer) are refined and bleached and taught the Lord's Prayer before an artist will use them. These mediums yellow with age even when purified, and if they are used in their natural state, which is golden, they change delicate tones as they are mixed with the pigments. Our *Mataram* turps and linseed were already a rich golden hue with age, and we experimented trying to bleach them by putting them in bottles and pans out in the sun. The old masters could do it, but we couldn't. We just drowned a few more thousand insects and then gave it up; we didn't expect to do very delicate work with this outfit anyway.

While the *Mataram* was still loading the collected copra from three plantations up and down the coast, we had broadcast our need of pigments to the planters on board, and all week long tins of paint were coming in by runner. We got the most awesome collection of boat and house paint that ever came through the bush. Most of it was half used and dried to a paste—which could not have been better for our use, because we wanted paste pigment. But the colors! Everything from livid yellows to sour greens; almost everything that is known to be impermanent to the color chemist. But we poured off all the yellow oil, when there was any, and strained the paste through wire screening into cigarette tins. And in the house we found an old tin dispatch case which had once carried secret communications in the First World War (as it was fought in the islands) and which was just deep enough to take the round cigarette tins—a trim paint box.

Things were shaping up now; a kitchen knife for a palette knife and a palette made of one side of a three-ply tea case from Ceylon. When the board was given several coats of spar to make it nonporous it had the color of a Stradivarius, and was just as inspiring. Stretchers of box frames, on which to tack canvas, could have been made, but we planned to thumbtack it to the drawing board, and put the board on the ground to work (our little field easel being too light to hold a drawing board) propped up against a handy tree. But our neighbor, the Planter, had grown passionately interested in seeing that Margaret provided me with a correct painting outfit, and he did not fancy the substitute of the board on the ground for frames on an easel. It was he who had ridden the five miles up from his plantation, to take Margaret the five miles back, and return with her the same five miles with all the old shaving brushes he could find in his house— and then ride the five miles home again, all in the same day. That was twenty miles for a couple of paint brushes, but I appreciated it. And whatever the cost, we appreciated the stretcher-easel that came out of the same impulse.

I claim honors for having designed it and the Planter may have the cheers of posterity for having built it correctly with mechanical improvements upon the design. Margaret, of course, can smile quietly in her corner. With a drill, a saw and chisel, two hinges from an old toolbox, and a good part of his veranda railing, the Planter made an adjustable frame something like an old-fashioned curtain dryer—but only a sketch can describe it. We highly recommend it for

painters of primitives, especially if they have someone else
to carry it, for it is a full cord of wood when broken down.
Its virtue is that, primitive models being what they are, a
half-finished canvas can be removed simply by taking out
the thumbtacks which hold it to the frame, and a fresh
canvas for a new model be substituted in a jiffy. There are
no bales of stretchers to carry as equipment, and finished
paintings can be taken off and hung up on a handy tree to
dry. Then, when dry, they can be rolled up (paint side
out to prevent cracking) to carry, any number to a roll—
with waxed paper in between if there is any danger of their
not being thoroughly dry. We used our drawing paper, after
giving it a coat of linseed oil. The frame can be adjusted
to any size canvas simply by fitting the notches together
at different places; which makes it suitable for painting at
any height, for standing-painting, or for sitting on the ground.
And we particularly recommend it for hurricane countries
where an ordinary, light, field easel with a painting on it is
likely to rise in the air in front of one.

Now, with the completion of the wonderful easel, our
painting outfit was flawless, and I was as full of urge as an
excavating shovel. The village was four miles from us, but
the Planter had left horses for our use and lent us Friday
to hand us things. And in my solar plexus was "the" picture,
already sketched out both in drawing and in a color plan. It
even had a name—"The Garden Women." Now, all that we
needed were the women models.

We had seen the original of the picture one late afternoon going down to the Planter's for dinner. The trail from
Tanakombo led along the shore, sometimes cutting into the
bush, sometimes running out on the beach. The time was
sunset and the ocean was unusually quiet, for the tide was
going out. All of that amazing eastern sky was reflected in

oily water which made three-quarters of our view a giddy expanse of cloud color. We had been riding through the darkened bush when we came out on this glory. Opposite this point the beach was wide, and it was a deep lilac in the shade, for the sun was going down over the land behind us. A long pool of tidewater had been trapped by the beach being higher at the water edge. That sand bar formed a narrow causeway between the ocean and sky color beyond and the faultless mirror of the pool. We backed hastily into the bush path as we saw, coming down the causeway strip of sand, a procession of natives. From the distance they looked less like human beings than like some strange bird —something with thin legs, pouter pigeon middles, and Florodora hats.

They must not see us. The horses were snapping around at their flies, and I led my kangaroo back on the path and tied him. Margaret's mare was always asleep when standing, so she stayed on him, and I grabbed the colt and pushed his muzzle into the nursing area, hoping he would take advantage of a stationary feed bag and keep quiet. The figures were

now opposite us, moving along in single file both in fact and in the mirror of the tide pool. They were all, with one exception, women and girl children—dark, purplish-brown silhouettes stalking across a stage of indescribably radiant sunset colors, all the rose and violet and clear blues and strange yellows of the rainy-season sky the last ten minutes after the sun has set.

The women were returning from the gardens and each one had balanced on her head an enormous palm basket filled like a cornucopia with garden produce. Strung from the shoulders chevronwise were slings of calico containing more vegetables and sleeping babies. These heavy loads were partly supported on hips and rumps, but they pulled down the shoulders giving a cocklike length to the neck. The spines were held stiff to support the weight on top of the heads, so that the hips, clad only in brief grass petticoats, wagged extravagantly to maintain the balance. Long bony legs planked out straight ahead, for all the world like stiff-kneed birds, and though some of the legs were slightly less stiff on account of the added weight of pregnancy above, there was not one woman who had not the stylish rumpy wag. Little

girls stalking between the women tried desperately to imitate the wag and still not upset the small baskets on their heads. They were delicious miniatures with bulging "banana bellies" and brief petticoats, and their pride in taking part in an adult task was the most evident feature of the line.

There must have been twenty-five women in the procession and every one was loaded to the crown of her head; even the baskets the pickaninnies carried were not exactly toy burdens. These were native women doing what Melanesian Maries have done for centuries: bringing in the harvest from the gardens. And behind the line, about ten yards to the rear, was a Melanesian man doing what the men have been doing for centuries. Rather, he was the vestigial remains of a traditional masculine inactivity. The man was not exactly young but he was not so old and weak that he could not have been carrying something when even the children were seriously burdened. Yet all he had in his hand was a dainty cupid-sized bow and some arrows. He did not even carry a pigeon or a cuscus as an explanation of the arrows. He was simply a tradition, a male "protection" to the pack-mule females. Formerly, in those days before the guv'men when raids were sport, it was the custom for some of the village men to accompany, as protection, the women to the gardens which were often some distance from the village. It created a vicious circle because raiders attacked the gardens, not to destroy the produce nor ravage the women, but because at the gardens they could be sure of finding men with whom to fight. Today, in the government-controlled villages along the coast, there is naturally no danger of raids, but the custom of sending a male escort with the women persists. Escort is all he is officially. We often saw the men load up the women, but never saw one doing the traditional woman's work of carrying. Nor, for that matter, did we ever see a woman doing a man's work.

As the line filed past, not more than ten yards in front of us, there was not a word from any of the women. The babies in their slings seemed to be asleep, and the youngsters walking were certainly too busy just keeping their head baskets balanced without using their hands, to endanger the loads by wagging their mouths. The ambition seemed to be to carry the basket without using the hands. They were like figures moving across a stage, especially with the color in the background softening to a finale as the sun sank lower over the mountains behind us. We held our breath, ecstatic and fearful lest something disturb this stunning picture. Then something did; my kangaroo back in the bush sneezed.

The effect was instantaneous and so suddenly comic that Margaret and I could not control our snorts. The women who had passed could not look back because of their head loads. They grabbed them with both hands, swung a little and stared out of the corner of their eyes in our direction. Then the entire line bent its knees and started running—rigid of spine and long-necked, the necks thrust out like ostriches to keep the load on top of the head in balance. If you have ever watched the tail of a racing horse, which keeps an even level with all the flying hooves below, you will know somewhat the effect of those huge baskets moving steadily along without a jerk and the spindly legs below going like mad. Moreover, there was a double line of this, another centipede in the mirror of the tidewater. The head woman in the procession splashed through this and sprinted off into the bush, followed by the rest. Meantime the man had not quickened his pace. He even walked past our spot without glancing in our direction and would not have seemed to know we were there if we had not called hello. He paused then and after a minute said "Thankyouverymuchpleasefineday," only a little less clearly. "Boy 'long village?" we asked and pointed up the coast. "Yasmissus." 'Long tomorrow, we told him, we

were coming to the village to make a picture of the "Maries"
—the old missionary name for women—and here was a present
of a stick of tobacco. The man stuck the tobacco in his arm
band without a word and remained standing while we went
about our business. That business lay in the same direction
the Maries had taken, and we passed them at a swoop going
down the beach. They were all huddled under the low growth
like quail, still loaded, even with their baskets still on their
heads. And like quail there was not a sound out of even the
children, for the papa quail was theoretically on guard watching us.

Our picture was not the scuttling birds but the smartly
wagging, expertly poised food producers of the Melanesians.

17

In the village at long last! But to get to it and start painting, we had to make as many mistakes as it is humanly possible. The reader may feel that I have taken a long time to
get on with our headhunting, but the ramifications in trying
to paint a free Melanesian are not those of painting a model
in the studio. In the latter task one simply paints, and his
difficulties, if any, are merely technical. To paint primitives
the technical difficulties are left in the hands of God; the
whole job is to get out of the wilderness of civilization and
into that of the primitive, and even then one still has to
deal with the individual primitive.

Our first mistake was in letting our man Friday survive
even his introduction to us. He should have been murdered
on sight. The village was only four miles from Tanakombo,
but we had to take the horses to carry the painting gear,
and the horses, which did their grazing at night, had to be
caught and saddled by Friday. He was as terrified of horses
as any Melanesian and so succeeded in catching only the colt
because he was bigger than it. That, however, brought in the
mare, but my alligator-bitten kangaroo was chased to the far
end of the plantation by Friday swatting at it with a palm
frond, and in the end I had to sweat down after it with a
bucket of precious oats. It was, consequently, eight o'clock
before we even got started for the village. We should have
murdered the horses too.

Next in line for slaughter were the Tanakombo dogs. Just
after we had left the plantation we discovered that they were

coming with us. We chased them back into the tract and gave them a barrage of coconuts, but they merely smiled and said they were going off on their own hunt. They were; they were out for the village dogs, between whom and the plantation dog there is a to-the-death feud. We did not know this—of course, Friday did, though he wouldn't have mentioned it—and after losing another half hour in futile chasing we gave it up. The dogs accompanied us, chasing the colt and darting up behind my crazy horse or grabbing onto the long tail of Margaret's mare. They were having a field day under our "protection."

It was eleven o'clock before we came to the edge of the village clearing, and we entered an expedition in a state of riot. The colt tore out of the bush path ahead of the three dogs, all swooping past my brittle animal like a herd of yearlings. At the risk of having my hair eaten I had been walking ahead of this animal, and at the shock he bolted past me, raked Margaret's leg as he crushed by her, and snorted into the clearing in high. Two leaps in and he stepped on his bridle, staggered into a banana tree, and then backed into a hut, squashing its bamboo wall. Then he and the colt charged around the village clearing, sped by Friday with a palm frond. Our dogs tore into the village dogs, and then Margaret's mare, the old cow-herding blood up, took the bit in her teeth and went after what she apparently took for cows, but were in reality our models! They disappeared into their huts and that was the last we saw of them.

The next hour or so we spent gathering up the Expotition. Margaret's mare had followed her child into the wilderness and it was a half hour before she returned as Casualty One. She came back leading her charger and showed a long abrasion on her forearm, a fat island sore in the making. Her horse had gone down to the beach and stopped suddenly before a piece of driftwood, whereat Margaret, who had been riding on the horse's neck anyway, shot off into the coral sand on her elbow.

Casualty Two seemed to be our enormous easel stretcher. We couldn't even find it. Friday had been carrying it and of course could not remember where he had dropped it and taken up the palm frond. It was eventually found, dropped over at an angle in a grove of bamboo where it was camouflaged by its like color. There were precious paint brushes, cigarettes, lunch, and parts of our clothing scattered all over the tribal ground, and my kangaroo had gone back to Tanakombo with the paint box. At least he was gone and we hoped the paints were still with him. The Tanakombo dogs had also disappeared when the fight carried back into the bush, and the nicest thing we could hope for them was that the village dogs would soon return with parts of them on their chops.

Amid this scene of devastation, however would we now establish a harmless reputation with the villagers? The surface of the clearing, which had been faultlessly smooth and clean, now looked as if a rodeo had just left; banana trees were lying over on their sides, the wall of a hut was crushed in, and the hidden natives were probably thinking that our dogs had killed their dogs—a thought that was not far from my own mind, for the Tanakombo dogs were big and had the white man's sense of superiority, while the yellow dogs, for all their number and nastiness, were mongrels.

The most unpromising feature of this situation was that no native came out of a hut so that we could apologize and perhaps pay for some of the damage with tobacco. The huts, about thirty of them, extended down the clearing in two irregular rows, trim little blond buildings with thick, brown thatching and bamboo siding. The roofs extended almost to the ground on two sides and there were no windows, just one door on the side facing the wide avenue. And these doorways were covered with a bamboo blind—no way of looking into these houses and catching the eye of a resident. We took out several sticks of tobacco and strolled down the clearing, holding them out fanwise like "popsicle" hawkers at a baseball game. "Hello!" we called to the blank village, trying to strike a nice balance between a white overlord and an apology. Getting no response we tried the British, "I say"; then "Boy stop 'long village?" No answer. We wondered if we should get a spear through the eye if we tried to peek through the cracks—as we deserved. Then we recalled not having seen any men. All the natives who had run were women and children. "Marie stop 'long here?" we asked. Silence. Margaret was at a door running her finger down the bamboo jalousie. "I wonder if I could interest modom in a Fuller mop?" she chimed, and slid her foot under the blind. I grabbed her back. I don't admit being afraid, but—well, we weren't in the United States, that was all. Anyone we knew would not hide in his house after a stranger had battered up his property. And we could hardly count on the Melanesians' sense of humor—what we had seen of it.

"How about charming them out with music?" Margaret suggested; and that was what we tried next. We took up a place in the center of the clearing, under the shade of a palm, but not in any way hidden by its trunk, and there for the next hour or so we sang! Margaret's ukulele rang through the clearing and we sang everything from American tom-tom to Russian dirges, and through it all the invisible audience made neither sound nor sign of interest. Two or three times we heard an infant whimper and but for that we might have thought ourselves alone. It was comic, but at the same time slightly uncanny, sitting there yodeling to a blank village, knowing that all around us eyes were glued to the cracks of huts watching every move.

There was nothing we could do but retreat. We stored all

our gear inside the hut we assumed to be the government rest house. It was the only building up on piles and with a veranda. And to make sure that it was not occupied by spear throwers we looked up through the slats of the floor from a cautious distance, and then as an extra precaution made Friday take the gear up. He had been sleeping down on the beach and came into the clearing so reluctantly that we remarked about it. Could he be afraid? Perhaps this boycott was more serious than we thought, and the idea helped to hasten us out of the village. When we stopped to untether Margaret's mare at the edge of the clearing we found she had chewed the bark off what was probably a very valuable tree and deposited the roughage in a great pyramid behind her. And in this neat village that would probably be a popular touch, too.

On the return to Tanakombo we accidentally learned of another thing to do for the morrow—besides throttling the Tanakombo dogs if they still lived, and tethering the horses for their night grazing. We were heckling Friday for being afraid to come into the village, thinking we should get an explanation. He would admit nothing of the sort. Well then, we asked, why had the villagers stayed in their huts: were they afraid of *us*? "Nomissus," Friday was sure, "Marie no fright 'long you fella. Him-he fright too much 'long horse." It was the mare, tethered at the edge of the clearing, and her colt that had kept the village hiding all afternoon!

Anyway, that was what we assumed—that it was the horse.

The next morning we arrived at the village late again. Margaret woke up with a swollen elbow which might have been a fracture—we never found out—and the delay was caused by my having to outargue her about staying home and treating the joint with hot compresses. No one had the slightest idea what else to do even with a broken arm. I won in the end and Friday and I finally got down to the village, but only after the men had left on the day's hunting and fish-ing, and long after the women had gone to the gardens. The kangaroo was tethered far down the beach, and all should have gone well, for the women of the day before were still in the village. But the minute I entered the clear-ing with Friday the women scuttled. "What name?" I de-manded savagely of Friday, as if he were responsible. But the boy no savvied, and he acted as injured and innocent as if he really didn't know what was the matter.

I spent the day on a consolation picture of the village, resigned to a program of waiting and stalking. With our animals of destruction absent from the clearing I could not guess what made me so revolting to the community. The natives inside those huts, however, were not only human beings, they were women. I thought along the lines of "What would I do was I a horse?" and decided I would stay in-side my hut until the stranger went away; and if she didn't I would have to come out by and by to carry on the day's work; but I would snub her unmercifully so that she wouldn't come again. And being a woman myself, I planned to snub first. In the end, if I didn't explode first, I expected these native women to make the advances—only I hoped it would be some time before we wore out our welcome at Tanakombo.

It may seem diverging to go into the fine points of snubbing here, but as fresh young Americans living in a British culture we had learned a great deal about the snub. It is not deliberate with the British as it is with Americans; it seems to be in-stinctive, the aloofness of a cat which mistrusts too frank and effusive an approach from strangers. We had even put our interpretation into practice and found that by being equally reticent, "getting in the snub first," the "cat" did not back off, but presently made the advances. So, if snubbing was an instinct, these natives would possess it like any other human beings, and the ones in the huts, being women, could be expected to express it in superlatives and understand its mechanism. Anyway, there was nothing else at this stage to try on them.

In the meantime, my consolation was enchanting. The village clearing was a circular bower with three-quarters of the background the hundred-foot-high bush wall with its glittering bizarre leaf patterns and creepers reaching out toward the palms of the opening. These were "native" coconuts which had been left for shade, and the exaggerated angles of their trunks were posed just right to streak long trunk shadows and sunburst frond shadows in the most spirited way across the yellow and brown huts and earth. The area of the huts had not one green thing growing on the ground, but all around the edge of the clearing were banana trees with their great swaths of leaves, split and ruffled and shining, with here and there an accent of yellow in a big stalk of bananas. In sharp contrast was a feathery, pale-green clump of bamboo, and through the dark silhouettes of the palms to the right I could see gleaming surf and ocean. It tempted one to paint a panorama with no regard for composition, for it did not seem that one thing could be omitted or rearranged in this picture without spoiling it. One could not paint the hot moist odor of earth and surf, and the scene lacked human beings; but if I ever saw a human being again he would be "pasted" right on top his habitat.

If I had been a Marie peeking through the slats of my hut the behavior of that white woman out there would have been suspicious enough to keep me hidden until she was safely out of sight. She kept walking backward around the clearing and glaring at something at the other end in a threatening way. Every now and then she put her hands up in front of her head and made an ugly face through the opening between her fingers and thumbs. Then she turned around, stooped over, and stood looking back between her legs with her head upside down. She was certainly daffy because in the end she sat down in the *sun*, screamed for her boy, and then sat there jerking her head back and forth and squinting in a mean way.

Conscious suddenly of being watched I was aware of the utter idiocy in the motions of an artist finding his picture view. The only thing we apparently don't do is foam at the mouth; at least, not all of us foam. And for some three minutes after Friday arrived from the rest house with the gear I tried desperately to pretend I was sane. But it was in setting up this gear that we achieved our recognition from the hidden audience. Quite close behind me was a hut which I had thought to be empty, because by running back and forth past it very fast I could see straight through it between the cracks—the way one can see through a baseball fence when driving past it. There were no human-shaped forms to be seen inside. But when Friday started digging a hole in the earth for the pole of the painting umbrella we heard a very audible chuckle from the hut. Following this we heard muttering when the big black beach umbrella was opened and the pole stuck in the hole in the ground. I did not know it then but that umbrella, though a little large, probably helped to establish our respectability in the community. Only missionaries ever carry umbrellas. But the muttering only meant to me that there was more than one person in the hut.

The wood bars of the easel were unstrapped and slowly became a big frame set up with a canvas tacked on it, but it was not until the paint box was opened that we heard a quite brazen sound behind us. I had dug into a tin with the knife and brought out a gob of beautiful yellow paint which I smeared on the palette, and I purposely put a swab of brilliant blue beside it—not that this is the order in which paints are laid on a palette, but because of the exciting vibrations of this combination. I got my reward, for the bamboo wall behind me bulged and creaked, showing that the heads were being pressed against it for a better look. Instead of turning around I thoughtfully held the palette up so that my audience could see the colors going on it. Native pigments are limited to white, yellows, and browns, and there are a few earth reds, but animal blood is used mostly for red coloring. There is also a black made from soot, but purples, blues, and greens are unknown except in nature, and my palette of house paint must have looked stunning. It did to me.

I think what followed the laying out of the gear was less interesting. This was the blocking in of the composition, with numerous corrections, in charcoal. The picture, as such, develops slowly in this stage, and until one begins making a tree look like a tree, the business does not hold the attention even of persons who know the intention. There was complete silence near-by. It was nearing noon, when the whole island world seems to close up like a clamshell; no wind and not a leaf or frond stirring. The quiet was intensified by the muffled booming of the surf and drone of insects. As I began to paint I felt haunted—as if I had mice—for the instant I plastered a streak of brilliant purple shadow on the canvas the ticking and creaking began again. Once I backed too far to see what I had done and cracked into the thatched roof, and the sounds of scuttling over the earth were like those of an animal. And then for the briefest moment I felt a curious sensation. As nearly as I can trace it, first, I saw Friday walking away down the beach. I thought, "I'm alone," and the next instant a wave went over me and I literally spurted perspiration. For a few minutes afterwards I thought I must be actually ill; must have got a wog somewhere. Then the whole thing passed. I forgot about it, working.

Painting at last! And this was the fun end of the picture; the first unafraid hour when one slaps on the big color patterns. You feel like a god, making things grow on a blank canvas. Then follows the shaping up when objects are given bulk, and lines greater meaning. But as the detail grew on my canvas I began to forget my admiration for my own godliness in wonder at the artistry of the primitives who had built those huts. I had been painting huts, shelters patched together by Stone Age primitives out of anything they could make shift with from the surrounding bush. But these were no shacks. The hut nearest me was architecturally as well proportioned

as the Parthenon; the deep thatching of the roof was just the right "weight" to balance the area of the front wall; the width of the whole was right for the height, and the construction throughout was beautiful. There was not a slipshod piece of workmanship anywhere. There were no gaping holes where siding had rotted and fallen off, no places patched with tin cans, no ragged edges to the roofs, nor structural timber too long or too short because someone was too tired or uncaring to saw it to the right length; nor doors falling off their hinges, nor old scraps of building material lying about—

none of those things which one sees on an afternoon's ramble up our garage alleys, or in our hobo jungles. These little primitive bungalows, made with only an axe and knife (modern), were as trim and sturdy and altogether all right as the houses one would see in any civilized self-respecting community. The layers of pandanus palm leaf had been "sewed" on their bamboo poles and placed on the roof frame so evenly that, with the lawyer vine binding, their ends formed a beading design down the front edge of the roof. The bamboo uprights of the walls were exactly matched in thickness and bound to the framework by vine which formed an all-over diamond pattern. Everywhere that bamboo was bound to the betel-nut wood framework, the vine was employed in such a way that the juncture became a decoration. But the true artistry of these structures, which was almost marked enough to have been sophistication, lay in the total absence of any unnecessary material. And no material had been tortured into an unnatural form to make it look like something else. Nothing had been plastered on as ornament, but everything that had been done as a necessity had been done so painstakingly that it had become ornamental. This was functionalism of a high order, and it did the heart good.

It was some time before we saw the interiors of these huts, and we found them just as satisfactory as the exteriors. The immediate impression inside was total blackness, then coolness, and finally the odor. The blackness was only contrast to the blatant glare outside, for plenty of light was reflected up from the ground outside through the cracks of the bamboo walls. The sense of coolness was also partly contrast, for no heat came through that eighteen inches of thatching which covered all but two walls of the single room. What warmth there was came from the heat beating on the ground outside, but if there was a breeze blowing it came straight through the two end walls. The odor was the acrid one of old fires and not at all unpleasant. In the center of the single room was the fireplace—a few blackened rocks and charred coals— but the rest of the earthen floor was immaculate. The huts were brushed out with a palm leaf every morning, and if they were not occupied through the day there was not so much as a footprint or an ant to be seen. The only furnishings were the bamboo and sapling bunks built into the walls on the low sides of the roof, the overhanging thatching preventing the rain from coming in on the beds. The bamboo slats of the beds were resilient and well aired, for what air there was could breeze up from underneath as well as from other directions. This construction of the bed with bamboo slats also had another virtue which we learned about later. Heat is one of the time-honored remedies for bad spirits that lodge in the body and hurt a fellow. So, if a man aches, a mound of hot rocks is put under the bed, and the heat comes up between the slats of the bunk and bakes out the spirit. (After we heard about this we began treating our island sores with dry heat—from a flame—and got much more rapid healings.)

The central fireplace was used for cooking only during the rainy season, but it was also kept going every night with damp wood to smoke out the mosquitoes. And as there was no chimney nor any hole for the escape of the smoke, the thatching and cross saplings were dark with soot. The interiors of these huts were not handsome, but they were adequate. They reduced housekeeping to a minor chore. All the personal belongings were kept in the framework of the roof: spears, bows and arrows, paddles, banana leaf bundles (packages of sago "pudding" which can be kept indefinitely), perhaps a wicker fishtrap, and any number of plaited dilly bags and sections of bamboo for drinking water or gnali nuts (looking like yellow rice and tasting like nothing else in the world so delicious), dozens of gourds, all with stoppers, and sometimes a carved wooden food bowl. And every one of these objects was ornamented in the same way as the huts; only incidental to the making. There was, in fact, nothing in the hut that was not strictly utilitarian, and everything useful was beautiful because, as John Dewey says, it bore the imprint of man's hand working lovingly on an object which is needed. Who, then, were the professional artist-craftsmen of this community? In fact, who—confound them, wherever they were hiding!—were the highly civilized residents who had so solved the problem of existence that they were unencumbered by anything not necessary to a comfortable living?

I was lying stretched out flat on a palm frond for a spello and I must have dozed off, for the heat and glare made me weary and headachy. And when I opened my eyes the whole village was out! The women were not scattered all through the clearing; about twenty of them were sitting on the ground all down at one end of it, and that end was behind my work. How they had all got down there without waking me was certainly very puzzling, but if they stayed, here was my opening to begin snubbing.

I got up and without looking in their direction began to show off in front of the painting. But I couldn't stand it. I finally stuck my pocket mirror onto my painting with a wad of lead white, and then tipped the easel until I could see in the mirror the entire group of women. They were sitting in the shade about six huts down and their brown naked bodies against the brown shaded earth were pretty well camouflaged except as silhouettes against the sunlit spaces behind them. But I saw that there were a surprising number of infants with them. How had they been muffled through the two or three hours I had been working? Some of the women appeared to be working on something—and it was maddening not to go down frankly and see what. But I stuck it out bravely and started to work, or pretended to, and very soon got results. Two of the women rose to a crouching position and scuttled to the next nearest hut. There they sat down close to the wall so that the shade made them almost invisible, and after about ten minutes three more women joined them. As nearly as I could tell in the mirror they were all faced in my direction, and until it got too painful and unproductive, I obligingly painted standing at an acute angle to one side so that they could see the miracle I was performing. There was no applause, but when I resumed a normal position again, which blocked out their view, one of the women with a baby in a sling walked up quite brazenly to the second hut behind me. Then, not being able to see well enough there, she made a detour behind the hut, and the next I saw of her was two dark eyes and a woolly, closely cropped head peeking out from behind the thatching of the nearest roof. The top of that head looked like the skull of the famous "pin-headed sisters" of circus days. I had to pretend to keep on painting, but I did such a poor job of entertaining while watching her in the mirror that in five minutes the woman had gone.

And that was the nearest I got to the women that day. The sun was moving down the western sky and my subject of the village was lit from exactly the opposite side to that when I had started the picture. I bawled for Friday and began to clean up the palette—still with my back toward the women. Friday must have been asleep because it was fully five minutes before he approached languidly from the beach. At the same time I happened to glance in the mirror on my canvas; there was not a native to be seen. I turned around. The clearing was deserted!

18

It made us weary to have to do it, but there did not seem to be any other way out. The Expotition, an independent female expedition, had to let a man help. We had spent two days carefully snubbing and another day trying unsuccessfully to unsnub at the village when the Planter came to dinner. He listened and laughed and said he knew all the answers. He could get us a model in five minutes, God bless him, if we would meet him at the village not a minute later than six-thirty in the morning. We were to wear skirts instead of slacks so that there would be no doubt about our gender and we were to tether Friday with the horses some distance from the village, for the villagers were afraid of horses. But why tether Friday? And when the Planter explained, I didn't see why we couldn't go on from there alone after all.

So it was Friday! Friday the wicked Malaitaman, flash boy with the ladies, and boogieman to the village husbands! And Friday trying to blame everything on the horses. No wonder he had always entered the clearing dragging his toes in the sand; he knew I should be no protection to him in the event of a barrage of rocks or arrows—though possibly the Maries were less afraid of him than of their husbands. Adultery is a pretty serious offense through most of Melanesia and a careless glance can be misconstrued by the best of us.

However, the time was set: six-thirty in the morning.

Six-thirty is just a half-hour after sunrise this ninth degree south of the Equator, but we were already tethering the horses at a little after six. We found what we thought was an excellent place for them, well off the path to the gardens, as instructed. It was a clearing in the bush perhaps ten yards square which looked as if it might be a garden in the making. The soil was loosened all over it, but it was a very uneven surface and showed no indication of anything having been planted. The horses could roll in it to get rid of the flies, and off to the south side under the bush wall there would be shade all day long. But Friday was very glum about the place. We heckled him a bit about wanting to see the Maries in the village, instead of staying with the horses, but he said the clearing was a no good fella. What was no good about it: was it taboo? We looked around for garden charms—peculiar-looking rocks or branches stuck in the ground to ward off evil spirits. Friday just watched us with a sad eye and to all our questions answered, "Boy him-he no savvy." That could mean he didn't know whether the spot was taboo, or didn't understand what we meant by taboo, or even that he hadn't understood the question clearly. It was one of those common horrors where one can spend the rest of the morning repeating the same pidgin English words in different juxtapositions and emerge sweating at high noon knowing nothing.

We rolled our slacks up above our knees, rolled our skirts down to the same point, and telling Friday that we would break his neck if he did not unsaddle the horses, we set off for the village. It was precisely six-thirty when we got to the widening of the path entering the village, but the Planter was not there. Everyone else was. The clearing was alive with natives, perhaps sixty or seventy of them. It was amazing after having seen the settlement so deserted during the day. We stayed back in the path to wait and watch until the Planter appeared, for he would be coming in from the other side. It was so quiet, for so many people—almost like a funeral. The natives spoke to one another, but it was not in the shrill piping voices of the plantation Malaitans. There were any number of youngsters and infants, but there was not a morning bawl out of them. A few women sat in patches of sunlight nursing their babies, a few more were brushing the earth with palm fronds, but most of the women were moving about, picking things up and putting them down, baskets and slings of calico—I wondered what we should look like going about the house in the morning straightening it up; perhaps just as aimless. The men and boys, on the other hand, were frankly doing nothing as we know it: rather, they were waking up, sitting in patches of sunlight yawning and scratching under their arms. Some of them had got as far as applying the long comb to the scalp and were digging away with that blank look of an eased itch. There was no breakfast on the fire and no fire. Those who were eating had large chunks of violet-colored sago which they were gnawing on, sitting off each by himself with his back to the central activity. (This happened to be one of those communities where it is considered immodest to be seen chewing.) The emaciated little dogs darted forward after the crumbs of the sago and were kicked back, again and again, as if they were on elastics.

The wind must have changed, or perhaps we let out our held breaths, for suddenly, at no conscious signal from ourselves, all these dogs scattered through the clearing began to howl. And they rushed together in a pack. They still did not know in which direction the danger lay, so they stood pointing out from the center of the pack, precisely the way sheep do when they are attacked. The cry of the dogs had as curious an effect on the villagers. There was a brief pause in what they were doing, as if the motion picture film had got stuck, and then as we marched boldly into the clearing all completed their arrested motions—as if the film had started going again. We strode up the center of the plaza smiling sweetly to right and left; and we might just as well have been invisible. Not one full-sized human being paid the slightest attention to us. I looked back suddenly and not even the villagers we had passed were staring. The dogs continued to scream until someone scattered them with a handful of pebbles; almost all the toddling pickaninnies scuttled behind their mothers' legs, where they stood looking out at us as through a fence; infants-in-arms bellowed or followed us with huge black eyes, but no man we passed spoke and no shy Marie fled.

We arrived at the guv'men hut feeling like Admiral Byrd without a public. What price South Pole?

When the planter finally entered the clearing we were set, like cats, to watch every little move he made. If he could procure us a female model in five minutes, then his method was one we had to learn to use ourselves. And to our surprise, instead of leaving his horse outside the settlement as we had been instructed to do, he rode straight up to the guv'men rest house where the horse was tied to a pile—a privilege that was explained to us later, but not by the Planter; we had to learn the reason the hard way. Then promptly the village luluai voluntarily identified himself by detaching himself from a group of scratchers, and approached the Planter. The bait there was easy to see. Against the protests of the Planter we had given him about a dollar's worth of stick tobacco with which to pay the natives for the havoc of our first visit, and this, being held up conspicuously, the luluai had come to as a grain-hungry island horse comes to oats. The headman was only too pleased to overlook our offense—if he felt any. (He seemed to be even overlooking ourselves, for his attention was focused entirely on the Planter.) About three quarters of the tobacco was for the village in general to cover the ruined banana trees which were communally owned, and the rest of it was for the owner of

the battered hut. These two presents were handed over separately and explained, but an additional handful of sticks was
given to and accepted by the luluai without explanation or
thanks. This was the usual present given when some favor is
expected of the recipient. So now the luluai waited, our
obedient servant.

We looked around in back of us expecting to point out the
model we wanted in the listening crowd. There was no
crowd! Unnatural humans. We remembered in another life
the scene of a flat tire on our car one day on Fifth Avenue;
a taxi had pushed the car to the curb where we induced the
driver to put on the spare tire, and in ten minutes there was
such a jam of sophisticated New Yorkers watching this operation that the corner traffic officer had to break it up. Then
there was the time I had stopped to ask simple directions of
an officer in Havana and before I had translated his answer
all Havana seemed to have collected to see if anything might
happen. Yet here in this "savage" village where one might
suppose the inhabitants more inquisitive and easily amused,
not one native, not even a little boy, had come nearer to hear
what was going on. Yet, that everyone was about normally
interested and determined to know what we wanted of the
luluai was evident because the village had not emptied. The
men were still sitting in the sun scratching and the women
were still picking up and putting down, but now with that
preoccupied expression so familiar to other women. It's the
listening look. Some of the women, however, seemed to be
making a half-hearted attempt to get organized for the gardens. One was stacking several empty palm-leaf baskets;
another, her long deflated breasts wagging enchantingly, was
leaning over from the waist (knees stiff) whipping up a
palm leaf into a new basket on the ground. I got panicky
lest these women should start off to the gardens before the
Planter "produced." "I'll take that woman for a model," I

said, entirely at random, pointing to a group of five or six Maries. One of them, though she hadn't appeared to notice us, promptly cinched the ends of the calico sling which contained her pickaninny and got to her feet. "Hurry—hurry!" said the American. "Don't let them get off."

But we were just someone who was along on this trip. The Planter was talking Sanskrit to the luluai and the luluai was standing there looking profound, nodding and saying, "Yasmastah." No one *did* anything. "Why don't you ask the women themselves?" we burst out. "They must have *something* to say about posing." We were ignored. This was one of those familiar men's transactions and they had to go through just so much conversation and brow-knitting before they could reach a decision; and they had to reach a decision before they could take any action—and apparently before then I would have exploded and the Maries would be digging up yams a mile away.

However, it was impossible to do anything without these men because the women could not understand much pidgin English. And evidently the women could be reached, both lingually and ethically, only through their husbands.

The Expotition got as far as a husband.

The Planter oiled his palm with two sticks of tobacco; both he and the luluai then explained what we wanted; the three men stood knitting their brows, the last-comer looking profound in an apelike way, nodding his head and saying "Yasmastah" in a very Melanesian way.

And no one *did* anything.

"Are you making it clear," the American demanded testily, "that we expect to *pay* for posing?" The Planter actually hadn't thought of that, but he did not admit it. He went right on yammering, but we saw the new light in the native husband's eye. The savage! Anything we gave a woman for posing, her husband would naturally take, because he owned her; she was only a pack mule. Still, we were delighted when the avarice of the brute moved him to speak to his wife.

This wife was a young woman; she looked thirty and she might have been under twenty, and she was certainly—now that we were looking at an individual—the nakedest woman we had ever seen outside an art class. Her grass petticoat, from belt to the longest fringe, was exactly thirteen inches long—a measurement confirmed by a ruler later on—and she did not even wear earrings to give a civilized illusion of garments. Her head looked somewhat like a large eggplant with a mouth on one end and a black woolly fungus on the other, and her two legs, spaced wide apart, might have been designed after Harry Lauder's famous stick. Her whole structure—neck, shoulders, arms and legs—was so angular and unpadded with fat that we might have thought that she was ill if all the other Maries had not looked the same. The only plump thing about her was her façade: she was bulging ripely with child and child nourishment. This was a little irregular for a modern picture. The old masters were always painting pregnant virgins, but this race we were painting was supposed to be vanishing and it was certainly contradictory to show a generation in the offing . . . However, a model in the hand might produce two of the bush later. And besides, the woman looked so utterly beaten that we should be Samaritans keeping her home from the garden work on any pretext. Posing would be a rest for her, and we would give her enough extra tobacco to keep for herself so that her husband would think he had got all of it.

The woman had been twiddling some dried banana leaf when her husband called to her, and at the first rap of the vocal machine gun we expected her to start cringing as we did from the very sound of it. Instead the wife kept right on twiddling. She neither looked up, nor slowed her aimless movements, nor changed her expression of martyred womankind. She fired, in transit, a fusillade of whining screams that fairly fogged the air. The husband retorted with a sawed-off shotgun from the upper window across the street. "*Ptptptptpt*," said the wife. "*Prt!*" said the husband. "*Prtprt-prtprtprtprtprt!*" said the wife. No one blanched except ourselves. And it was the more surprising because so far we had heard not a word out of any of these women; they had all looked so defeated it did not seem possible they were capable of making such a sound. And presently, but only for lack of wind, the solo scream dwindled to a mere high-pitched whine—like a fingernail going round and round on glass. The brute of a husband occupied himself stuffing our tobacco in his clay pipe. He did not look in the least embarrassed and, in fact, seemed to have forgotten about the whole matter. Only the Planter had a slight flush. We waited, trying not to look delirious, and saw more sticks of tobacco passing along the line to another husband.

No less than five individual husbands were tried, with the same results, before the Planter, very red in the face, at last admitted that getting a Marie to work for one was a little "different." The fact is that he had never tried to hire a woman, but like most Europeans he presumed them to be under complete control of their husbands. And he knew how to handle the men. Melanesian men are usually so polite that they seem incapable of saying no to any request of a white man, even when they have no intention of complying; but when they say yes and mean no, tobacco is usually sufficient to change their mind. Patently not so, Melanesian women. At least these women were not too polite to say no through their husbands.

This was the feature that had surprised us most: the open rebellion against the "slave-driving" spouses. But we were to be further surprised out of a lot of our ideas regarding the position of the sexes in Melanesia. No one in this Stone Age society even pretends that the husband holds the whip hand over his bartered bride. It is true that pigs and shell money are paid to the guardians of a bride, so that in a way she is "purchased" and the husband may be said to own his wife; but actually the business is nowhere near so simple as a purchase. For one thing, the gifts that pay for the bride are produced by the bridegroom's guardians, but at the wedding feast it is the girl's family that provides pigs and other food for guests numbering sometimes two and three villages, an expense which probably far exceeds the bride price received. However, this exchange is not just a gracious social gesture; if the husband should treat his wife badly she may go home to mother, and instead of the man getting back his bride price so that he can purchase another wife, he not only forfeits it, but has to return the wedding pigs (which have already been eaten) to his wife's family. (Particulars vary in different districts.) Then, to obtain another wife, the man must produce the dowry gifts himself, for his guardians will have fulfilled their obligations in providing for the first wife. The whole system has a nice restraining influence on the savage fist.

As for the beast-of-burden slavery: Stone Age Maries do not work half so hard and long as the average American farm-wife, partly, of course, because all of living is so simple and there are no artificial standards of what is decent. There being no unneeded rooms in the house, no purely ornamental dust-catchers, housekeeping is simple; especially there are no dozens of sheets and towels and tablecloths and diapers and playsuits, men's shirts and underwear, and women's whatnots to wash and iron weekly. Eventually we followed the women through the day, from village to gardens and back, and the only work we saw them do which could compare even remotely with the colossal never-ending task of that American family laundry was carrying the vegetables back from the garden nightly. The planting and weeding and harvesting in the plots was conducted in a leisurely fashion and enlivened by gossip, for all the women work together, each in her family plot of a common clearing. And though the loads that were carried home at night were mountainous, the cooking of the produce afterwards was a simple matter. All the women helped to prepare the meals baked in a common rock oven, and afterward there were no alps of dishes and pans to wash and dry and put away. Even the garbage was disposed of by the dogs as soon as food became garbage. Woman's work *is* sometimes done in the simple life.

We wasted a lot of unnecessary sympathy, too, on the "pregnant virgin," for she was not bound for the gardens. She was one of those cussed women who remained in the village through the day hiding from us. For these "female animals" do not work up to the last minute when they are pregnant, drop their young in the field, and then go on working as do, for instance, the Slav potato harvesters in our own Colorado. There is usually a conventional rigidly adhered-to spello period on both sides of childbirth, and in some districts even the husband has a lying-in spello too, when he receives special food and attention because of his delicate condition being a father. Native women are just as liable to septic poisoning at childbirth as are white women, and sometimes they even recover, but when they die it is not because of neglect. It is because they are treated for bad spirits instead of bacteria. The average birth receives as much delicate attention as and a lot more privacy than it does in our society. A special lying-in hut is built in the bush wall away from the village—a new one for each birth— and there are a half-dozen old midwives attending who aid matters with massage. Any man who stumbles close enough to hear a scream calls down on his head the fury of the birth spirits; and when everything is neat and quiet again the mother returns to the village with her new infant which everyone will adore, including Expotitions.

However, if an obligation to work is slavery, then the Maries are slaves. But not to their husbands. Every adult Melanesian has the same obligation, for the work necessary to hold a village together is just enough to keep every adult engaged at a comfortable pace. The tasks of the sexes are allotted to each by tradition—and incidentally with a nice regard for the weaker one. With the exception of the garden stevedoring the men do all the muscle work; the felling of trees for house timber and the building of the houses, clearing for the gardens, as well as enough lighter work like hunting and fishing to keep them equally busy with the women. The care of the children is shared, for after the nursing and toddling period little boys accompany their fathers through the day and little girls their mothers, each learning as play the jobs they will have as adults. Thus by the time the villager is adolescent he is bearing his share of the community work, as unconscious of its being work as he is of breathing.

This was all very idyllic as a solution to Melanesian living, but for a painting expedition it was just plain torture. The thing that made it torture was that though we knew the traditional allotment of work existed (having read about it at length) it took us a long time to find out a way to get around it, and the same way never worked in two different villages. In any society where tradition is the god of behavior, all members are automatically opposed to anything irregular. And women being what they are, these Melanesian Maries exhibited extreme opposition to an untraditional task like posing. It was the custom for all able-bodied women to go to the gardens, and so all able-bodied women went—though hell froze over and expeditions exploded. All the left-overs, the women nearing labor or with very young babies, the aged or sick, remained in the village through the day, but they had their village tasks, and none of them was posing.

The normal voice pitch of a Marie is not especially high but when any men are present it becomes a whine, and the marital attitude seems to be something on the order of Jiggs and his wife where a word from "him" sets off a vocal diarrhea in "her." Yet there is a difference. It is all in fun. The woman screams, the husband remains serene, and all the listening village ignores a blaze which is certainly routine. We never saw any native husband and wife actually angry with each other, or trying to get anything by argument, even the obedience of a child. But that stymied us too, for what an American finds he cannot buy he hopes to get by persuasion.

In the present instance even the luluai lost interest in trying to persuade a husband to persuade a wife. He stuffed his pipe with our tobacco and then went and sat on his heels in the shade of a palm tree to smoke and brood. The husbands, armed with bows and spears and paddles, and accompanied by boys and dogs, went off happily also smoking. With nothing left to whine at, the able-bodied women went off out of the opposite side of the clearing, baskets on heads and tongues in cheeks. The Planter looked at us with a red face, raised his arms helplessly, and then rode away to see about his planting. We were sorry he had not been able to get a female model in five minutes, but at the same time it gave us a comfortable feeling to know that as a female headhunting Expotition we were no more handicapped than a party of men would have been.

We even had a certain advantage. The only thing we could rely on now to get women models was that superior female knowledge of females, which the Expotition happily possessed.

On our return to Tanakombo we came on a picture to

make a perfect companion piece to the garden women—if that masterpiece ever got painted. It was an egg garden in the process of being harvested.

When we got to the clearing where we had left Friday and the horses they were not to be seen, and the place was a spectacle. It looked as if it had been bombed. All over the surface were holes and mounds of earth, and, to increase the impression of havoc, out of the holes were sticking bare brown legs and rumps, twisting and squirming in what might easily have been the throes of death agony. They were masculine rumps, and the arms and shoulders and heads of the sufferers were deep in the holes, while sand and pebbles flew out in every direction. While we watched, fascinated, a pair of legs backed out and the remainder of the native came in view. He held a single white egg in his hand which he very carefully put into his dilly bag off to one side. At sight of us he gave a gurgle, and all over the plot men righted themselves. And who should be among them but our old friend "Thankyouverymuchpleasefineday" with sand in his hair and no welcome on his face!

It is always hard to describe a native encounter, because while it is happening there is neither sense nor sequence to developments, and afterwards all one can rationalize is the conclusion. In this encounter the conclusion was that we had violated the holy of holies, not only in leaving our horses in the clearing, but in entering it ourselves. It was exclusively a men's garden and that made it taboo to even white women.

Somehow, whatever there is about a female is simply poison to a man's industry. Fishing canoes sink, papaya trees wither and die, and pigs fail to reproduce if we pollute them by touch or even by being present at the wrong time. (The one food-producing tree which escapes contamination when we touch it is the sago palm. The men cut the trees down, but they have evidently found beating up the pulp of the core of the trunk into sago pudding too boresome, so the women can handle this part of the job with impunity.) We thought the natives were more annoyed by ourselves than by the horses which had done the damage, if any.

The plot actually was an egg garden, even a cultivated one.

There is a brush turkey called a megapode, or mound builder, which buries its eggs for hatching by scratching up the surrounding earth into a mound. The natives have found that if they soften the earth, the megapodes will bury their eggs all in one plot, especially if the earth is warmed by the sun. Hence, egg garden. Such plots are so enticing to the megapodes that the men can dig for eggs twice a day and always get a harvest—always, except when Expotitions defile the holy place.

Our horses had been in the clearing until almost noon before they were discovered, and then Friday had the choice of being murdered by either the kangaroo or the village men, if he did not remove the animals. He saved his life by untying the kangaroo and throwing a rock at him, at which the horse went home to Tanakombo. Then he took the colt down to the beach and the mare followed. When I called, there was no answer from him, and still no answer when Margaret used her phenomenal taxi-calling whistle. But that shrill blast, which is made in some way by gifted persons with a prehensile tongue and the right-shaped teeth, had a surprising effect on the natives. They had seemed to be ready to bury us in the holes which had produced so few eggs, but they were so startled by the sound that they forgot. They just stood foolishly looking at Margaret and then at one another, and then back at Margaret. She obligingly emitted another blast and then opened her mouth to show there were no whistles in it. This was one of the rare times when we caught natives too surprised to conceal it—for it is frightfully bad taste for them to show astonishment. Thankyouverymuchpleasefineday came up and stood in front of Margaret looking straight at her mouth; so she arranged her tongue on her teeth with her lips open so that he could watch. Then she blew. Presently all the outraged men were standing in front of her trying to blow out their front teeth. One of them actually succeeded in making a very wet shrill and everyone burst into yips of delight. We were a great success. The ordinary whistle, made between the lips, seems to be unknown among Melanesian natives, though Papuans we met were enthusiastic whistlers—but not of tunes; they used the whistle to express admiration. Probably the reason for the absence of the whistle is that it demands a tune and Melanesian music is too abstract, too noteless, to be interpreted on any one instrument.

In any case, we got out of an objectionable situation here by a whistle and in the end we had given each man a stick of tobacco for the eggs the megapodes had not laid, and they in turn gave us an egg. It was about the size of a duck's egg and we can now report that a fried megapode egg has the delicious flavor of rancid cod-liver oil. We never knowingly saw a megapode, but we suspect that he is a beach scavenger, and he is certainly one of the most treasured food producers in the islands.

It was Thankyouverymuchpleasefineday who retrieved Friday for us. He took his ackis—otherwise ax—by the head and, after glancing around the bush wall, went to one particular tree and with the handle of the ackis beat out a tattoo on the trunk. It sounded hollow, and in a minute we heard Friday's soprano coming from the bush in the direction of the beach, "Missus?" We ordered him to show himself but he would not come into the clearing. On the way home we tried to find out why a Malaitaman would know the drum talk-talk of Guadalcanar, but Friday just said, "Oh him-he talk along me." In other words he just understood—and that was as far as we could get with most questions.

But we were very happy about the whole encounter; if we could not get the garden women to pose immediately we could begin a canvas on the scene of men food-gatherers, the miraculous whistle having given us the privilege of entry to the plot by exalting us above mere gender.

19

We three women held a council of war that night at Tanakombo and the result of it was the "bitich bokkis," instituted just for Melanesian Maries. Actually it was a new copra sack and it contained almost everything one would find in a trash barrel around Flappers' Acres. Unfortunately none of us was the rococo feminine type, or we might have got together a more exciting bokkis; but by going through all the cases in the house, our own included, we managed to collect a good many enchanting objects from a Melanesian point of view. There were some defunct rubber girdles, one with rosebuds on the garters, and an entire garter belt with six exciting metal fasteners which would look well over a grass petticoat. Then there was the last of our silk lingerie, now in a rash of tiny slits from the heat and moisture. The jewelry department had three unmatched earrings, some stubs of bright-colored crayon pencils, also for the ears, and half a broken string of pearl beads, which were to be paid out about three at a time because they were large. Margaret threw in the evening slippers the Empire Builders had shredded and I added some tarnished gold slippers which the Missus thought, because of their gleam, might be presented one at a time as neck pendants. One never knew what was going to be popular nor how it would be used, but taffeta evening frocks were "out" this year. The one we wanted to put in the bokkis because it would have rotted before we could ever wear it again, the Missus took instead, trading us some fathoms of new bright-red calico which was always "good." The men used it for lap-laps and the women for slings in which to carry babies or garden produce. (These Melanesians were not the savages of fiction; they never wore the cast-off outer garments of Europeans.) The rustiest (but still cutting) of the safety razor blades, used-up lipstick tubes, pocket combs and purse mirrors, and every kind of metal container from cigarette tins to empty spinach cans—all were thrown into the bokkis.

We reflected on the power and wealth in a rubbish heap at home and felt sad like many an exploiter before us at having supply on one side of the world and demand on the other. At least, we hoped for demand. These treasures in the bokkis could not be bought from the plantation stock, nor from the Japanese traders who hawked their wares from launches along the coast—taking coconuts in exchange and soundings everywhere. If the Maries were normally feminine the very exclusiveness of our stock would sweep them off their feet.

But there was a daffiness about these transactions-to-be. The unique wages for posing were to be given to the Maries in *advance* of the work, as presents. For this is the system of trade among the natives themselves, the exact reverse of ours. One pays in advance for work or material as much as one is able, while the seller tries to outdo the buyer in generosity, giving more than the value received. For the only profit a man can make in a deal in this absurd society is a reputation for generosity.[1] And he does not get his prestige

[1] There is no profit in either labor or goods. When men work for one another it is an even exchange: "You helped me build my house; now I help you." Or, in goods: "We salt-water men catch more fish than we need, so we give them to the inland villages which have no fish. They will make us a present of taro which grows better inland. They will try to give us much more than we give them, so that next time we give them fish we will 'lay it on.'" The only transactions in the entire culture which show a clear profit for individuals are for wood working (the artists) and the sale of magic (the "doctors"). For such services as

for generosity the way some of our public "benefactors" do: by getting the best of so many bargains at the expense of his fellows that in the end he can endow a hospital for the ones he has crippled, or give an art collection to people who have neither leisure nor energy left to study and understand it. But the whole native system had nice weak spots in it which we capitalistic Americans saw immediately could be exploited. By making presents to our victims first, we could get them in our power; we would simply overwhelm the Maries with tin cans, shredded brassières and slit panties, and to maintain prestige in the village the women would have to give us something. And we would take posing, and our choice of models.

Everything seemed to be under control when we left Tanakombo that morning. It was a handsome tropical dawn, the sort of beginning that makes you know the day is going to be all right. And it was; it was so lacking in major explosions that I hesitate to report it lest the reader take a breath of relief and strangle on it a few pages along. We sailed straight into the clearing to the rest house, and even the dogs gave only one brief piercing scream before they scuttled. The villagers had not yet gone about the day's work, but they did not hasten unduly. The luluai came up for his present just as Friday was bringing from the rest house the easel with its painting of the village on it; and though the scene looked exactly like creamed spinach with strips of purple bacon in it, the headman thrilled us by saying that it was a good fella too much. We were prepared to work on this canvas awhile, or start on another village angle until the citizenry settled

having rain sent to the gardens, making the taro and yams grow big, producing an abortion, fattening pigs, or making someone fall in love with you, or die (this costs about twelve dollars), the sorcerer is paid shell money of a definite value, so much for each job, and this he keeps for himself. The only magical service which is not paid for in advance— and physicians please take note—is that of healing sickness. The patient pays only if he recovers good health.

down for the day so that we could see what victims there were for attack. But no such delay was necessary.

A Marie approached *us!*

I heard behind me, perfectly clearly, "Cheeriomissus!" and turning saw a little sandy-brown wren of a Marie. She was even grinning and had her hand held out, palm up, the fingers slightly clutching as if to grasp a stick of tobacco. There was no mistaking it; and this was the one morning we had been so clever that we had brought no trade tobacco. "Margaret," I croaked, "cigarette!" But Margaret had been watching the woman and had everything from rubber girdles to the cigarette lighter ready. While we stood gaping, the little woman poked the cigarette in the exact center of her leathery mouth, lit up from Margaret's lighter—not blanching at its sudden flame as most natives did—and, blowing out smoke like an old war horse, jerked her arm toward the picture and said, "Missus savvy pilenty too much." It was not divided into words but we understood it.

Would paradoxes never cease? Where had this unnatural Melanesian woman come from? And that she was not the average citizen was certain because when she took the cigarette there was a sudden surprising yip of laughter from the near-by women, and another when she lit up. And she seemed to be deliberately clowning, for the way she tapped the ashes off her cigarette with her first finger was just a little too much like Margaret's gesture for innocence. Perhaps this was some kind of female Malaitan bad boy putting us through the local "system." But whatever the woman or her purpose, if she would pose it did not matter. We asked if she savvied along pic-a-ture, and she answered, my word, she savvied pilenty. And to prove it she stood off and struck a pose with her arms akimbo, hands on thighs, the fingers rigidly spread, and her face raised to the sun. It was the pose of a Daumier martyr waiting for the firing squad, and the in-

evitable one of a savvy native at sight of a camera or mention of a pic-a-ture. This old Marie had been around.

The pose brought another shriek from the villagers, and now we noticed, happily, that more of them were busying themselves at our end of the clearing. Margaret seemed to think we had accidentally got the village idiot because the woman did not resent being laughed at; but she had a good head for a picture, no matter what was lacking inside. She was not particularly old, perhaps not more than forty-five, but she seemed to have lost most of her teeth, and the sunken cheeks brought out the bone construction of her head, which was useful for study in our stage of painting Melanesians. Also, like the other women we had seen in this village, her hair was closely cropped, a fact that brought out the pin-headedness of the skull and also identified her as a married woman. She was not any more strikingly feminine-looking than the rest. If you shut off the view through the chest and abdomen you got something about as genderless as the Malaita bushman. There were the same flat boy's hips and thighs, the knotty knees and pancake feet; and above, the big features and sinewy arms. The Melanesian Marie hasn't even a woman's waistline to tie a grass skirt onto; she ties the belts of her numerous grass skirts just below the swell of the abdomen, and the well-developed rump behind keeps them from falling. This rump and the breasts are two features by which one can definitely tell a Melanesian woman from a man, but the older the subject the harder it is. Our model, for instance, had breasts which were merely two strange flat sacks, so unlike any human anatomy we had ever seen before that they appeared to have been added as an afterthought. They were not even attached to the usual place, but hung from the lower ribs down over the abdomen. And they were not the color of the rest of the woman's skin, but a grayish violet. The abdomen below was equally interesting. It looked as if the woman had been drawing pictures on it. The distention of former pregnancies, probably numerous, had split that thin layer of pigment which makes the black man, with the result that the scars were all white. This was not true of the other women present, and we wondered enough about it and the peculiar gray breasts to ask about them when we brought the woman's finished portrait home. And in the answer we found the explanation to everything.

The first thing we discovered was that we had been flirting with a case of "buckwa." The gray scaly skin is a ringworm disease, one of the hardest to cure and most contagious of island gifts, one however which we miraculously escaped until the final chapter of the Melanesian adventure. The only comment I can make on it in passing is that it is disgusting and itches abominably, and about a tenth of the natives have it.

And the reason the model had scars on her abdomen and the other village women did not was that she had been bearing a European's "outsize" children.

The woman (whose name was Dogaru) was a joke in the community, but it was not because she was a halfwit. It was simply because she was too much of an individual in a community where the ideal is to be exactly like everyone else. Years ago she had been the "housekeeper" of a planter, and it was from him she had picked up her pidgin English and familiarity with Whites. And hers was the usual end of such alliances—which are not as common, however, as the journalists would lead us to believe. After bearing three half-caste children, one of whom had lived, the planter had left her to go home. The surviving child was placed in one of the mission schools with a trust fund to see him to maturity, and there was nothing left for Dogaru but to return to the village and re-establish herself as a native as best she could.

To the outsider this would seem to be a simple matter:

but community life in the village is not the individual career it is in our towns. It is all bound up with and made complex by endless clan taboos and observances, relationships and conventions, and our prodigal daughter on her return was greeted with cackles from the start. This was not because she had been off on the primrose path for a number of years but because she was an odd figure, a mature woman with no husband. Her natural guardian, who was her mother's brother, had died during her absence, and had she been young it would have been the duty of the next-in-line of her mother's totem to provide pigs for a wedding feast, which would have made a husband possible. But she was not young and somehow that made a hitch which we never cleared up. (It was Dogaru herself who told us much of this story and it was clear only in generalities.)

In any case, Dogaru must have a husband to keep from being laughed at, and being a spunky little woman, she proceeded to earn the wherewithal for one herself. And she did it in the oldest way known to woman; she became the village prostitute. This was, unfortunately for Dogaru's reputation, in a community where prostitution was unknown; but what now made all the women cackle was not that Dogaru was immorally "cleaning up," but that she was again doing something irregular. (When in doubt, laugh, should be a maxim for the whole world.) She had probably got her original idea from her white mastah, but it was successful. Our poor heroine, scorched on all sides by cackles, worked and worked and finally had enough shell money to buy some pigs; and now that she had the pigs, all was ready for the wedding feast, for a husband automatically materialized with the wealth.

So now Dogaru, being of the same status as every other woman, was "respectable." But she was still a nonconformer, inviting derisions, perhaps helplessly in most cases. We think she was a lonely little wren. Something made her attach herself to us; perhaps she was showing off her familiarity with Europeans to the other women, or possibly we were just a source of cigarettes which Dogaru preferred to the rank trade tobacco the other natives, both men and women, liked. It may be that she was even sensitive enough to ally herself on our side because she knew we were going to be the butt of cackles as she had been. But even with time and a common language and some experiences in common, we never felt we knew Dogaru. One minute she was a sprightly, old, colored mammy, purposely clowning, and the next she was off and away in the Stone Age; but even when we were wanting to kill her we dared not because she was too useful as a savvy interpreter.

Our first experience with Dogaru as a model was all Stone Age. She was perfectly willing to pose for us, indeed as pleased as a child, and the very next minute when Margaret tried to show her where we wanted her to sit, she balked. And she would not explain. I wanted to work sitting on the veranda of the rest house so that I could have a background of the black and white matting of its wall behind the model, but Dogaru had to be almost pushed up the rungs of the ladder. And when she had seated herself (having been pushed down on the sapling floor) she lapsed into a sulky silence that not even cigarettes could break—though she accepted the tobac' willingly enough. The women who had remained in the village probably did not help. They had formed themselves into a "sewing circle" two huts down, and though they did not let themselves be caught watching us they kept up a continuous yapping and cackling that had all the marks of being intended for our ears. And every now and then Dogaru would pipe out a shrill squawk to the village in general, then at the first rest we gave her she stalked out of the village and never came back!

That study was not finished until we found out that the

guv'men rest house was taboo to the villagers between the visits of the patrol officer. It was the one piece of property belonging exclusively to the government; which was why the Planter could tie his horse to its pile without any criticism and why we, not knowing this, got in trouble every time we brought our horses into the clearing. In any case, the white men's taboos were ones Dogaru thoroughly respected. She posed again quite willingly when she found she would not have to sit on the little veranda of the rest house.

That first portrait established our reputation in the village. Of course, no one except Dogaru herself (who repeated like a parrot that the Missussavvypilentytoomuch) admired it, but it must have interested the populace. When we left the village the night it was finished, we put it outside the guv'men hut, on the veranda, so that it could "work while we slept." We suspected the natives were curious though they would not come up to look at the portrait while we were present. And this roundabout advertisement, or something, worked to show that our intentions were harmless. We got models . . .

20

For the next few weeks the Expotition progressed somewhat like a "borderline case," with moments of complete
sanity and even loftiness, alternating with pure madness. It
was a period of becoming adjusted to what was to become
merely routine. I painted—there were models galore, for after
a few days of despair we became just as popular as we had
been obnoxious before. But there was not one unblemished
model and not one pose which did not develop in the middle
of it some unexpected and unexplained horror. Margaret
stood by like one of those assistants to a vaudeville artist,
switching one unfinished canvas for another as models appeared and disappeared, and then as unreasonably reappeared
again. We no longer tried to rationalize or understand anything. I was a sausage machine grinding out on canvas whatever Margaret and Dogaru put before me.

The women who daily remained in the village (they were
not always the same ones) did not make a bargain-counter
rush for our pretties in the bokkis. They made us think of cats;
sniffing and spying around corners, pretending indifference,
retreating if we advanced but never going very far away. But
Dogaru, who was posing for us spasmodically—for parts of
anatomy left unfinished in pictures by the disappearance of
the original model—was showing the profits therein and she
could not help exciting interest if not envy. She wore unblushingly what she earned and the front of her looked
like an arsenal. A satin and lace brassière with the part-
elastic shoulder straps stretched to strings was worn not as

a control but as a catchall for her
loot. Her long breasts hung down
below it and in the storage space
were sticks of trade tobacco, a
brown medicine bottle, a cigarette
tin with beads and safety razor
blades in it and a pink satin petticoat in slits and rolled in a ball. This
last she had taken for the feel of it.
It felt like the inside of her lower
lip, she showed us. Sometimes the
gold slipper fastened by its strap
hung ornamentally over the arsenal.
Dogaru wore the slipper on her toes
when she was sitting down but she
could not walk in it because of
the high heel—and the howls of
derision from her sisters.

All of these objects Dogaru had chosen herself, and when
the other women became less suspicious of us this was our
method of capturing them. We let one woman at a time
choose one thing from the whole supply, and it was at this
moment the eternal feminine asserted itself. While the other
women sat back pretending not to be even interested the
chosen one went over the stock picking up each article and
turning it over and over, laying it down for something else,
then going back to it, until after an hour or so she had
decided—or almost. For whatever she took, she cast a glance
back at the rest as if she had made a mistake. She never
thanked us, because no formal expression of gratitude is
known to Melanesians; the return gift is the form.

In this village there was no superstition about the portrait being the captured spirit of the sitter which we would
use as an effigy to do harm; there was consequently no objec-

tion to posing on that score. In fact there was no objection to posing itself, though the models always looked a little embarrassed by the cackles of the other women that launched each new pose. Still they got onto posing very quickly considering that they hadn't any idea why they had to sit still, and they were intelligent about holding the head faced in one direction or an arm this way or that until I got it blocked in. Almost all of them had pickaninnies who pushed them around, nursing and just plain mauling. The reason the babies never cried, we discovered, was that they were never denied anything they asked for. If a whimper did start up it was plugged by the breast being shoved into the baby's mouth. Our long experience painting and drawing American babies was invaluable here because it kept me from having fits trying to see the fussing, scratching models.

But one thing we could never make clear was the matter of resting temporarily between poses. Even Dogaru, savvy as she was, always thought we were finished with her when we told her to take a spello or walkabout. Unless we wanted to keep the model in a pose until she began to ache (which would make posing unpopular), Margaret had to follow her during a rest to see that she returned. But there was not much chance of the woman posing beyond her endurance. A subject, when she thought she had enough, simply got up without explanation and walked away. Sometimes she even came back; but because of certain conventions it was never safe to follow a woman who went on a walkabout without being told to. She might be going to relieve herself and, as the spot for this duty was one of greatest secrecy and the performance itself highly private, it was dangerous to intrude. The cause for this extreme secrecy was the age-old superstition that the residue of one's body—nail parings, hair, excrement, spittle, and so on—taken by an enemy to a sorcerer might result in sickness or death to oneself.

As a rule a model stopped posing simply because she was bored and sometimes because she had work to do. Knowing the importance of each performing his allotted task we dared not interfere when a model left for this reason. The women who did not go to the gardens had numerous light tasks; they kept the gourd and bamboo water-containers filled from the river and gathered shellfish off the reefs when the tide was out, and from the edge of the bush they cut big leaves in which to wrap food for roasting. Also they kept the fire going in the central oven so that the rocks would be hot for the evening meal. (Wood for this was brought in nightly by the young boys.) They shredded coconut meat into big clam shells, using the sharp edge of another shell for shredding—this was for meat packs—and they sometimes made coconut milk by wringing out the shredded coconut through a tough fibrous leaf. They buried bananas (a week underground) to soften them for puddings, and in between times they made garden baskets out of palm fronds, and grass petticoats for themselves out of banana leaves.[1]

We disgraced our patroness, Dogaru, by playing with some of these skirts one day. Seeing some new layers of them lying on the ground I tied them around my waist and went into a hula-hula. Margaret got out her ukulele and played for me. The women watching shrieked with what we thought was appreciation, but Dogaru was disgusted. She said the

[1] "Grass" is a pidgin term for any stuff that resembles grass in collectivity; thus grass on the head and a grass petticoat, though the latter be banana leaves. To make a skirt a wide leaf is separated down the midrib and the meaty part of each side shredded so that it makes a fringe; then the pieces are laid out in the sun to dry. In drying they turn a soft yellowish brown. A single petticoat is made from several sections bound in layers along the midrib, which form the belt. Anywhere from a half-dozen petticoats on up make a proper skirt, and brief as they are, never more than a foot long, and for all their lack of solidarity, we never saw a woman expose herself even in the process of rising from the ground or sitting down. The shreds seem to fall naturally where they are most needed.

women were laughing *along* us and she meant *at*, not *with*. Well, what was the difference? we asked. A laugh to us meant one step nearer friendship. But it did make a difference. For the same reason that we must not be seen in breeches or slacks because they were a man's garment, white women could not wear a native woman's skirt. It was not because the Maries considered themselves inferior; it was just *not done*. Which suggests that conventional behavior is not the exclusive invention of "civilization."

We need not have worried about prestige, for even the miracles we performed in paint did not produce any local esteem. Dogaru's first portrait exhibited on the rest-house veranda *had* worked but only to show what we wanted and could do, and that we were harmless. There was the most surprising indifference toward Art here; not even the models appeared to be interested in their own likenesses. They had to be *asked* to look at them, and if the other women were asked for an opinion they just cackled. And posing had to be paid for at both ends; out of the bokkis at the beginning, and with trade tobacco at the end, whether or not the model sat until her portrait was finished. No one demanded such wages, but Dogaru thought that since we were white we should pay like the white man on the plantation—at the end of the work. The prepayments therefore proved to be only bait, not pay.

About the fourth week of work we had a little accident which interrupted the even horror of our days.

We were still getting individual studies for the garden picture and had to paint an infant sitting in the sling of calico tied chevronwise to its mother's shoulder. It was a bad choice of models because the baby seemed to be teething. It drooled and fretted constantly, and the mother was forever shifting it from one hip to the other so that we had long waits for the original view of the child. And it was in one of these waits we got into trouble.

In picking her prepayment gift from the bokkis the mother had had a painful struggle in her choice between a comb with most of its teeth missing and a package of gum which we had brought along for the bright tinfoil wrapper. Finally, to save time, we had allowed her to take both. I do not know how old the gum was, probably two years anyway; we had found it under the bottom paper of one of the trunks, and it was soft from the heat and moisture and smashed flat. And some malevolent spirit suggested that we find out what a primitive thought of gum. Dogaru was absent so the only way we could explain its use to the woman was by a demonstration. The gum still had a flavor, but it was so melted that it did not wad up; it strung. The woman was shy of taking her portion in her mouth at first, but the minute she had tasted it she looked as pleased as a Wrigley advertisement. She kept her big mouth open while chewing and clicked her eyes around with evident surprise and enjoyment. There are few sweet things to eat in these islands (though sugar cane grows in Papua) and probably the flavor was an experience. Anyway, the infant suddenly got the scent, or perhaps he saw his mother chewing something he was not, and he set up a howl. Instantly, before we could stop it, the gum was popped into his mouth. Rather, the mother had taken it out of her mouth—with dry fingers—and was trying to scrape it off on the child's gums. In less than two minutes the picture was webbed in gum. Strings of gum were stretched over the infant's face and into his woolly top, gum was spread up and down the breast of the mother and all over her calico sling. She tried to rub it off her fingers onto the ground and only collected sand. There was nothing we could do about it without getting entangled ourselves, and when we tossed over a paint rag soaked in turpentine with which to wash it off, the woman got to her feet and stalked off with her howling pickaninny. And for the next few days careful mothers made wide circles around us.

In the doldrums we asked Dogaru to find us a "beautiful girl" for model, one whom the men admired. There seemed to be a shortage of young girls in the settlement, only three between the wholly undeveloped stage and the too well developed, and it was the eldest of these Dogaru said was the beauty. The girl could not have reached thirteen, and if you like the reed type of figure her young body was beautiful. There was not a bump on her from the shillelagh legs until you reached the breasts, which were elongated outward and had nipples of such extraordinary size and prominence that they looked like dots on the ends of question marks. There was nothing in the least sensual about the arrangement; it just looked a little unusual. However, we could understand the "uplift" ideal, that being our own, but when Dogaru said the girl's eyes were beautiful we were lost again. Average normal Melanesian eyes are small and are set deeply up under prominent brows and thick black eyebrows, so that they appear even smaller than they actually are. And this is partly because the whites are deeply tinged a pinkish yellow and do not show much contrast to the dark iris. Even the most normal Melanesian eyes have a black obscure look, and this beautiful girl's eyes were just two dark smudges through the center of her face with sharp highlights blinking around in the middle of them. Her eyes were beautiful *because* they were so unusually small. As for complexion (the one thing we should have thought would not be distinguishable where everyone who did not have a disease was a solid brown), the girl was very fortunate in being "fair." We looked again and the only difference we could see between her skin and that of the other women was that her back was not sunburned quite so black. The older women were colored like a hand with a light palm and their backs were dark from the years they had spent on their knees in the sunny gardens. The smoothness and shininess of the girl's skin we had to admit—it was like a baby's—but this left the Melanesians cold; it was only the lightness of color that mattered. And the girl's big features were relieved a little by having the longer hair of the virgin; but what was that monstrous white bulge on her upper lip with the flies around it? Leprosy at least. Oh no, said Dogaru, nothing but a yaw! A girl had to have them by the time she menstruated otherwise the bad spirits would stay in her and when she married they would come out in her children (that is, the children would be sickly). This beauty had failed to develop normally, having escaped yaws in childhood, so as a last resort her lip had been scratched raw with a shell and pus from another's sore rubbed on the abrasion. It had taken and now the girl was purified for marriage.

Yaws, which even the doctors have a hard time distinguishing from the syphilitic lesion and which, curiously, responds to the same treatment (but is still not a venereal disease), was a prominent feature of this village and one of the reasons why we practically drank disinfectants while we worked there. Not many adults had it, but that they had gone through their preadolescence immunizing was evidenced by the white scars, mostly on their legs (though some were from island sores). The prevalence of sores on the legs has given the name of "sore leg" to disaffections anywhere on or in the body. Thus, Margaret had a sore leg along arm, and we both had a sore leg along neck from seeing bottle flies sup on the yaws around us and then speed straight for the cracks in our faces. We were not unduly cautious, but just the sight of an infant being carried toward us was enough to bring out the bottle of alcohol or peroxide. Hardly a baby in the settlement was without its crop of pustulate "blisters" or equally distressing scabs, which were always bleeding because no effort was made to keep the children from picking them.[2]

It was a toddling youngster with a mess of yaws on his chin who struck the opening note of our swan song in this village. I was painting his mother (the Expotition having been restored to respectability for no apparent reason) and she was having a hard time trying to keep her balance with a basket of yams on her head and her youngster thumping around on her crossed legs. (The control of parents in this country where one *can* murder and not necessarily be hanged for it always bewildered us.) The baby must have been at least two years old, a fat, husky, naked little fellow with a full supply of biting teeth and an appetite like a sponge. He was still nursing though the mother's breasts looked dry, and while he mauled around on her poor legs, every now and then he would take a piece of his mother in his mouth and gnaw on it, finally biting her and beating her chest with his vicious little fists because she failed to produce. The woman made no protest, and in fact did not seem to notice, unless she got tipped off balance when her darling periodically cannonaded her stomach with his head. This behavior was not in the least unusual, but it still made our skin hurt.

What we objected to most was having our model all messed up by the deposit smeared around on her skin from the yaws on the baby's chin. Margaret kept fanning with a palm frond but the flies were thick between me and my subject; and it was painful enough anyway just having to look at a woman with ten pounds of potatoes on her head. She had been sitting there for about an hour on and off, and I have done enough

---

[2] One of the steady jobs of the lik-lik doctors is treating yaws, and in localities where natives have no theories of immunization dressed up in spirit fatalism the government is having some success in controlling the disease. But we could never get an authority to admit that having the disease produced an immunity as the natives would seem to believe.

posing myself to know how painful it is to hold even an arm out for five minutes. Not the least of my agony was fear lest the woman's endurance give out and she would discontinue her suffering by walking out on us.

I needed air and something to drink, so I laid my brushes on the palette which was on the ground, and Margaret and I walked up to the end of the clearing. The natives kept a supply of coconuts there, husked and half buried in the sand for coolness, and we regularly tapped these for milk just as the natives themselves did. The water was a cool and nourishing drink, though it never got beyond the taste of a hairwash, and we also ran the chance of getting dysentery, left by the hands of the native who had husked the nuts, by putting our mouths to the holes we cracked in them. And, ah, that we might have expired of dysentery or anything else before we returned to the "studio."

For there was the indulgent mother sitting laughing at her little boy. And her little boy was smearing around on our palette! He was covered with paint. There was poisonous red lead on his knees and in his hair and poisonous white lead all over his hands and face and arsenic green in his ears. So far as we knew that was not white matter but white lead on his yaws, and he would be dead of lead poisoning tomorrow or, at the latest, before we could get off Guadalcanar.

We didn't figure it out until afterwards, but probably the mother's complacency was due to her not knowing there was such a thing as oil paint; she must have thought the color could be washed off with water. Whereas we knew it was not water-soluble—and that difference of opinion is what caused the panic. We had no soap with us and we were obliged to use turpentine—knowing very well that it stings even a toughened adult skin. Dogaru was absent again and we had no way of explaining, so Margaret very calmly took a viselike grip on the child's upper arms from behind—at which the child bellowed with terror. (We never dared go near an infant because they were afraid of our white faces.) Not at all calmly I went to work with a rag drenched in turpentine. The mother was exactly like a terrified bird who sees her young in the jaws of a huge enemy. She pecked ineffectually at our backs and got a hold on the fighting child's leg and tried to drag it away from us. All she succeeded in doing was knocking us all over onto the palette. It looked like a murder, and sounded like one. I cleaned the little paws first as best I could and then grabbed the youngster by the wool on top of his head and went after the face. But I dared not touch the sores because if there was lead white on them the fighting child would make me rub it in. There was paint and yaws all over us before we dared look up. And there were the rest of the villagers hopping about and yapping. We were panting and suddenly frightened. But the turpentine had to be washed off the baby's skin or he might be burned. And the way we did that might be said to have put the double bar on the swan's death rattle. We used linseed oil. We used it simply because it was the only other liquid we had, and it might actually have neutralized the sting of the turpentine; but we never waited to find out. Ignobly the Expotition ran.

We left everything and rode hell-bent for the Planter's tract. He would have to go back to the village with us at sundown and explain everything to the luluai (with plenty of tobacco) and the luluai would explain to the woman who, God helping us, would then be induced to let someone clean out the yaw properly. And I hoped it wouldn't be I; I felt myself breaking out in spots as it was. That the Planter took the affair seriously as we did was evidenced by the fact that he sent us straight on to Tanakombo when we reached the village, not letting us enter with him. He had a boy with him and assured us that all our gear would be moved into the rest house. He also carried the planter's faithful remedy for everything, castor oil. On the plantation it is regarded as a punishment, but anything coming out of a bottle is magic in the village, and he was prepared to treat our victims both internally and externally—for the sorcerers "wash" every bad spirit away by external treatment.

In a few days the Planter brought all our gear up to Tanakombo, which was a signal to us that the baby had died and the village was laying for us with an eye gouger. For the eye-for-an-eye principle is still in practice in these savage lands as it is in civilization. But the child had suffered no after effects, apparently not even from the turpentine, and the mother had been appeased with a liberal present of tobacco. Still it was not safe for us to return to the village. It was our man Friday's goings-on. Apparently while we labored in all innocence in the village, Friday, who was supposed to be keeping flies off the horses down the beach, was actually busying himself seducing the village beauty—the glamorous girl with the little eyes and the yaw on her lip. Just how she had managed to get away from the gardens and the chaperonage of thirty women and Thankyouverymuchplease-fineday long enough to get herself seduced baffled us. And why the village should have been upset and called it a seduction was even more puzzling, because this was one of the villages where the youngsters began experimenting with the urge as soon as they were old enough to feel it. The parents were so very indulgent that they just thought it amusing. And as the young girls never became pregnant until after they were married—for some reason even scientists do not understand fully—no one had a substantial reason for being prudish.

But Friday was a Malaitaman, and Friday was our boy, and probably the combination was too much for any community to stomach. Anyway, the luluai had said things to the Planter which made him think that art work, if continued in the village, should be reported to the guv'men as a violation of Section 152 of the Native Protective Ordinance, Fiji Islands (adopted)—something that covered immorality and terrorization.

21

When the New Year came around we were in the western islands on a plantation in the "largest land-locked lagoon in the world." There was a superb vista of Marovo Lagoon from the backhouse at Segi. That temple stood on a hill at some distance from the residence and connected with it by a white coral path hedged with gardenia bushes. There were only the three of us in the house, and our host, who was a bachelor, served every Saturday night a compulsory cocktail which he said was what had kept him in the pink of health these forty years in the islands. We called it the Segi Weak-end. It was an explosive concoction of gin, bitters, a lot of Epsom salts and a dash of water, and the secret of its success was that anyone taking it who could survive the following day was impervious to ordinary tropical bacteria. The first purge started off our stay at Segi with a comfortable informality, and as time went on we even got the matter delicately organized to avoid the Sunday traffic jam on the gardenia path. Anyone going up the hill to the temple plucked a white blossom from the hedge which he left in the middle of the path, and on his return he retrieved it to show the way was clear.

We loved those Sundays.

The doorway of the temple was unusually wide with an object of opening up the vista to the occupant, and so far as we know the door was never closed. All around below the entrance were planted gardenia and frangipani bushes, and as the hill fell away one looked over the tops of the plantation palms out to the lagoon. It was blue—such a blue! We were on the south shore of New Georgia and faced southeast to the island of Vangunu topped by a crater almost five thousand feet high. The view was as different from that of a coast plantation as if we were in another part of the world. It was intimate, cozy; the sort of thing one reads about as an "island paradise." All up and down the lagoon, which we could see from the throne on the hill, was a labyrinth of little coral-made islands and waterways that had a varying depth and a snow-white coral sea-bottom. That made the blues of the water every shade from deep purplish ultramarine to peacock and robin's-egg blue. And there were streaks of tender green and yellow where the coral castles reached near the surface. The blue of this water was the first distinct palette color we had seen in this blinding dark and light world.

There was a strong tide current through the lagoon but somehow the water never got rough, and in between spring tides the surface was so glassy that all the cozy little islands and sunset clouds were reflected in it like a mirror. Gone was the constant roar of the surf, the churning of it, and the sight of squalls passing out to sea. Here at Segi the silence and stillness of everything was the kind that let you hear your own heart bumping. It kept one "waiting"—like a Sunday afternoon in London hushed before the din of Monday. But Monday never came to Segi. Its days were without names and dates, the time measured only by the hysterical Weakends.

All the Mondays happened on the opposite shore, on Vanganui. In a little cup of a bay, less than a quarter of a mile across from us, was the native village of Patativa. The settlement was built up the side of the hill and we could just see the brown of the thatched roofs peeking out from under the shade palms. The white beach was always buzzing with activity; natives milling up and down and canoes of all sizes putting in and out, for the village lived principally on lagoon fish. Long before we got to work at Patativa we were excited about the war canoe on the beach which we could see distinctly with the binoculars. It was protected from the sun with palm fronds, but what we could see of it looked like an enormous gondola elaborately decorated with white patterns. We had read about those canoes; how many human heads they took as a sacrifice at a launching, sometimes a hundred or more. (But in these western islands any excuse was a good one for lopping off heads.) A couple of days before Christmas we saw a whole fleet of canoes, led by the gondola, put out westward, and when they returned late in the afternoon there was such excitement along the beach that we could hear the cries over at Segi. Margaret and I were having fits holding ourselves down until after the holidays.

Segi is a plantation famous for its beauty and hospitality. If we had not been invited to visit we should probably have been the first American party so slighted and this book the first one about the Solomon Islands which did not include mention of the Mastah. (All he gets is mention, however; he is now writing his own fascinating story of almost forty years' residence in these islands. Author: Harold T. Markham. Title and publisher yet unknown.) Holidays, especially, have always been open house, and starting with the day before Christmas the Mastah wore his binoculars on his neck and seldom left the south veranda from which we got our view of the lagoon. But no white speck of a boat appeared on those kingfisher-blue waterways. The combination of a shortage of launch gasoline (on account of the Sydney strikes) and preoccupation catching up on plantation work after the Malaita war holiday were evidently keeping the usual guests at home. Christmas came and went, as bleak and uneventful as the Sunday in London. The *Mataram* had brought no Christmas presents for us; our families, if they were still speaking to us, never would believe it took a good two months to get even love on a postcard to these islands. But the Mastah had got pounds of mail which took him a week to read—chortling and snorting with private pleasure which made us feel just that much more forsaken and isolated.

That Christmas Day with its enforced idleness was as long as a selfish life. We spent some of it up on the temple hill trying desperately to remember what snow looked like, and to recall the sound of church bells and crowds laughing. When we stopped talking all we could hear was the bump of blood in our own veins. Vainly we tried to visualize a familiar face. What a Christmas present it would be to see one suddenly, when we had been meeting only strange faces for almost two years! What did turkey taste like? with cranberry sauce? and even spinach? We drew up a menu and, like natives, discussed it in detail from every angle; but in the end we could still taste only tinned fish and tinned mutton and tinned beef; and they all tasted alike. What did it feel like to be cool? cold? even frozen stiff? Wonderful! We were getting bogged down by the steady heat. It was intensified to steam now by the intermittent rains. And there was the unadmitted weariness of our own unrelieved company, something few expeditions will confess in print but which nevertheless does enter the picture.

What would it feel like to be going to a cocktail party this afternoon (a big noisy crowded one) in a smart new outfit; a frock that fitted perfectly, an actual hat, groomed and scented from hair to heels—smelling of anything but sweat, at any rate? Sartorially we had gone native. Night and day, at the plantations and painting in villages, we lived in men's shapeless pyjamas because they were the coolest protection from insects, and the too-long jackets deceived the natives as to their "gender"; they thought they were proper missus' skirts. We had only one melted lipstick left, and that was being saved for emergencies. Nothing could be done with the hair anyway even by trying; it takes a Melanesian's wire wool to stand up in this steaming country. But our guilt was that we did not seem to *care*—not until these holidays came to remind us of another life we had once lived.

It was a very, very dismal Christmas.

Then it was the day before the New Year. And with it flamed that undying spark of femininity which comes to life in the breast of every woman when she sees boatloads of men coming into her arid field. The Mastah turned from examining a white speck down west on the lagoon. "It's the guv'men launch," he said, very pleased, "We'll be dressing for dinner." *Dress* for dinner? How delicious!

It took the Expotition just two and a half hours to dress for that New Year's Eve dinner, but through it all we never quailed. The first thing I discovered, examining myself from a non-Expotition point of view, was that the stuff on my head was not only limp but, because I had studiously forgotten the cork tank, it had bleached out to a startling kind of hay; dry hay on top and wet hay near the roots. We fought that awhile and then shaved off the luxuriant beards around the island sores on our legs. This was the only place that hair thrived with the pores working twenty-four hours a day. And now, having hurried through our baths so that the Mastah could take his turn and be dressed by the time the government launch got in, nothing could stop the flow of sweat, not even plugging those overworked pores with a paste of talcum powder.

While sitting waiting to cool off enough to get garments on, we heard squealing outside and saw a guest arriving; a man followed by three native boys. The first two boys carried a pole between them on their shoulders and swinging from the pole by the feet was a live suckling pig. It was a native pig, one of those ugly, long-legged, thin animals only a generation removed from wild pig and, hanging back down with its full weight making the cords cut into its legs, it was screaming with pain. It was a relief to regard the third boy. He looked like the "Hark to the Porter's Shoulder-knot a-creaking" lad in the Rubaiyat, for sticking out of the top of a palm-leaf basket on his shoulder were the necks of numerous liquor bottles. (The Sydney wharf strike had also affected delivery of this kind of freight.)

This charming tableau had barely passed out of sight when up the path came three native women with two youngsters and a baby. Like the natives of the district they were very dark-skinned, almost plum-colored; but unlike any Melanesians we saw anywhere else, they were fat. And they were modestly gowned in the beltless white mu-mu of missionary persuasion. Also, something we had not seen on women elsewhere, these three had long hair which stood up in a great round ball around their faces. It had the surprising effect of making them look feminine in a normal human way. One of them, the one carrying a suspiciously light-skinned pickaninny, was almost pretty, with Negro-sized eyes and dazzling teeth—though perhaps the fact that she was laughing with un-Melanesian gaiety was what made her look so likable. When this group passed by below our window on the way around to the house cook we went back to our primping.

Those garments! I shall skip the ones that went underneath and mercifully could not be seen. Two georgette frocks were put on, straight out of the trunk where they had been packed for months; and though they smelled a little moldy, before we got back to our wet hair the wrinkles had been steamed out on us. But so had the georgette itself. When Margaret stooped to fight slippers on heat-swollen feet the material, without a murmur, parted between the shoulders, down the behind and up the knees. I had better luck because I had lost more weight; only my seat came out, but in such a way that the dress looked as if it had a rear panel. So Margaret wore the remaining linen evening frock, which looked just the way an unironed linen frock does when it gets damp.

But what lipstick can do for a headhunting expedition even with its seat out! And what gardenias with ants on them will do for soggy hair! At least we did not have to back out on the veranda. At last we splashed forth, lipstick and gardenias first, at which five men rose from their supine position on the deck chairs to semistanding—for all the world like puppets worked only by shoulder strings. The legs were still lolling. (Planters' legs always looked weak because of the starched white trousers, which corrugated at the knees with one sitting and remaining in a sitting position even when the occupant was standing.) The Mastah made the sixth, but he did not have to rise because in all his forty years in the islands he had never learned to sit down—probably a sense of futility induced by the Segi Weak-ends. But even tottering, these half-dozen gentlemen were an exceptionally "representative" aggregate, we were thinking, for any part of the world. Rather, five of them were tall and well built, young, or well tailored, or amusing looking; and two young women with the nearest competition a thousand miles away should have had a very happy New Year's Eve in such company.

That was what *we* were hoping—in the first several hours of the evening.

The odd fifth guest was eliminated from the very beginning. We never saw him awake even when he was lopping on his feet to be introduced. He had an island plantation in the lagoon, and he was that rare living character of tropical fiction who traded his copra straight for cases of whisky from the *Mataram* and then spent the intervening six weeks drinking it up. Usually at sight of his launch the "bar" at Segi was put away, because the visit meant he had run out of liquor and was prowling the lagoon with his tongue hanging out. The Sydney wharf-strike shortage had reduced him to a pitiable state, and so because it was the happy New Year the Mastah had mercifully set a whole quart of whisky by his side and left him to do his will, which had been to get quietly as drunk as a corroboree goat. The snore from his deck chair added just the right macabre note to the dying year and our party spirits.

For no one could survive the handicaps we had to work against; it was the islands themselves we had to cope with. The Mastah, of course, played his part as honestly delighted host; and the guest of honor, the guv'men, was faultless in all ways. But he was peculiar to the islands anyway just by being so stubbornly civilized. He was the tailored one, straight from Bond Street, as faultless as faultless Englishmen can sometimes be; they make you think you are listening to a gramophone that is running down but yet, unmercifully, never does stop. As for the young doctor who had come with him on the government launch; he seemed to be a victim of one of his own diseases. In reality he was victim of something much more difficult—infatuation for a half-caste native girl. If she had been native he could have taken her as a "housekeeper," but she was a virtuous Christian who had been educated by her white father in the South, and some time would be heir to a very productive plantation. The young doctor was obliged to marry her or he could not have her and the problem was weighing on him. He said "pip-pip" at the first "sundowner" and "cheerio" five hours later, and in the meantime sat holding his pulse.

But the doctor was charming and witty compared with the Recruiter. The Recruiter, we think, actually was sick, not sick of a disease either, but like Cynara's lover, "sick of an old passion," from which he must have tried to escape, and in vain, by hiding in the islands. He was the beautiful one, a thin, wolf-eyed esthete, worldly, well born and as ageless as a woman past forty. It was said that he carried Nietzsche around in his pocket, yet he lived on a thirty-foot launch which was then returning two hens, three dogs, a pig, and a cockatoo and their owners (twenty natives who had finished their "time" on plantations) to Malaita. All evening he seemed to be thinking profoundly about the futility of life, but still with a vague contemplative eye on the phenomenon of Margaret.

The Planter from the west end of the lagoon, however, looked at Margaret and never took his eyes from her. He was the amusing one and he looked at Margaret not only openly but illegally, for he was the only one of us who was married. His legal wife, in fact, was the handsome, fat, full-blood black girl at that moment out in the house cook—because local natives were not allowed up on the front veranda at Segi. At least this was the rule and the Planter chose to observe it even though the native was his wife. And the three light-skinned pickaninnies were the Planter's, as well as the pig we were having for dinner which he seemed to have contributed just for Margaret's own happy New Year's Eve.

The pig came in to dinner still intact, with a California tinned peach in its mouth in lieu of apple, but looking as natural as if it were asleep. I could still taste the squeals of pain, and surreptitiously fed large portions of my helping to the four dogs under the table—two Segi and two visiting. With the exception of the salad the remainder of the meal came out of tins. The *pièce de résistance* was the island-famous "millionaire's salad" which was the heart-of-heart in the budding tip of a full-grown coconut palm. We had heard variously that millionaire's salad tasted nutty, like asparagus, like artichoke, and always that it was exotic and delicious; but its real virtue is that it is something crisp and fresh in a land where all other food is soggy and hot and old. Also, the knowledge that it had taken five to seven years to grow the portions we ate gave it a flavor that doesn't come with an onion.

Nothing happened to make it a happy New Year's Eve until the dog fight under the table. I suppose dog fights occur regularly at dinners throughout the world, but we do not remember attending a dog fight at any dinner so formal as this one at Segi. The presence of the guv'men would have made our dinner holy even if it had not been New Year's Eve. For though the district officer may be an ex-clerk from Wooloomooloo, when he graces the island board one winds on a cummerbund and observes certain formalities like not going to sleep until he has left, and especially not feeding one's dinner to the dogs under the table—even when one of those dogs is the guv'men's own and a guest too. Still the dog fight did revive the party. The battle among our legs got us up from the table, and separating the pack took us as far as the deck chairs on the front veranda. Then for five minutes afterward, until it began to rain, we were so stimulated that even the Recruiter said something. He observed in a dying voice that all the fights in the islands were caused by dogs or women.

The gaiety died finish with the rain.[1] It came with the roar of a copra shed burning, and a curious singing obbligato in the porous thatching of the roof of the house. Then for a while we eight isolated human beings sat mute in a small block of air under that roof, surrounded by what seemed to be solid water outside. The suction of the waterfall beyond made my thin dress flutter and cling to me, and on the top of the guv'men's faultless head a strand of hair loosened and waved undecidedly back and forth like a cockatoo's comb. There was no wind, but spray filled the veranda and the air chilled. I broke my fever schedule by getting a shiver eight hours too early. Whisky all around.

At midnight the rain had stopped and the sky above Vangunu was like the stormy one in El Greco's "View of Toledo," streaked black with broken clouds, the cold moonlight on top of them. Solemnly, at the tick of twelve, the Mastah went to the edge of the veranda, pointed the revolver he kept under his pillow toward the hidden moon and fired—once. "A very happy New Year to you!" said the Planter earnestly to Margaret and jumped off the veranda to join the other guests on their way down to the launches. As their heads dropped below the far side of the hill, we saw, off to the right moving through the palms in the direction of the wharf, three dimly white mu-mus without heads or legs or arms. "And a very happy New Year to *you*," said Margaret.

After that it was Sunday in London again.

[1] One can die and not be dead, but to "die finish" is fatal.

22

The celebrations that were going on at Patativa at this time of the year were coincident with the European holidays. It was the height of the turtle spawning season and to meat-hungry natives a traditional time for gorging and rejoicing. We had expected to watch the joy at the village from the outside like waifs picking up spiritual crumbs beyond the gates of a rich boy's party; but suddenly we found ourselves, not only guests at Patativa, but at the very core of the feast gathering. We were off with the men on a turtle hunt.

We had seen our first western Melanesians from on top, looking down on them from the deck of the *Mataram* when we arrived at the eastern end of the lagoon. A missionary was taking the steamer South for his holiday and his flock had come down the lagoon to see him off. There must have been three hundred natives in the bon voyage party; their canoes covered the water all around the steamer, and their laughter —good, honest, human laughter with mirth in it—kept the air chirping for three full hours until the *Mataram* had finshed loading copra and got under way.

That was the first striking difference in the westerners, their familiar "darky" exuberance. We made the remainder of the trip from the entrance of the lagoon to Segi on a little copra freighter, and towed all the dozens of native canoes behind us in a long queue, and it was a streamer of laughter we drew all the way. The little freighter set up a sizable wash and the canoes, tied one behind another, had to keep exactly in the center of it to stay top side. If one craft went out of line, though it might regain its own balance by paddling hard, it threw the following canoes out. Then there were screams of mirth as the long end cracked the whip. We finally lost the last three joints of the tail when they went over, and saw the dunked paddlers coming to the surface still laughing.

These laughs were like quarter moons in a black sky, for the westerners were shades darker than any Melanesians we had seen so far. Their skins were the rich plum brown one gets by mixing madder red and umber. And there were other features in which they resembled our full-blood Negroes. They had the "open countenance": eyes widely set with ample white showing around the iris, the eyebrows not so clouded over the gaze, which somehow eliminated that obscure "black" look of the easterners. It was interesting how likable and intelligent these familiar features made the westerners appear.

Actually these charming colored folk were the headhunting demons of the whole group. Until the government got the coast villages under control a few years ago every possible occasion was used as an excuse to lop off a few more heads. It never made any difference whose heads gave prestige to a christening; both friends and enemies unwillingly contributed their heads to the *mana* at the launching of a new war canoe; heads were so greatly in demand that there were even gangs of professional headhunters, something like our Chicago murder gangs. They supplied, at a price, freshly cut heads for any event, not making any delicate distinction between sexes, ages, nor totem alliances.

The explanation of this head cult is that here the spirit—all that is strong and immortal in man—dwells in the skull. Thus a chief, when he died, was fortified in the hereafter by the company of anywhere from fifty to a hundred strong immortal spirits. The heads both of the sacrifices and of the honorably deceased were retained after burial of the bodies and kept either in the rafters of the house or in a "cemetery." (The heads of deceased relatives are removed in a unique way: the body is buried up to the neck, leaving the head out of the ground, and in a short time the climate has made it possible to pick the head up and remove it to its permanent niche.)

We ran onto one of these skull cemeteries one day when we were rummaging around the lagoon. It was a tiny coral islet, merely a pointed clump of coral rock sticking about twelve feet up above the water at high tide, and all along the north face of it (probably for shelter from the sun) ledges had been cut out, one above another, and these were lined with skulls. There might have been two or three hundred skulls in the lot. At the risk of starting new crops of island sores on the sharp coral we clambered up and down the shelves searching for a complete skull for an Expotition piece. (The cemetery was so old that none of the natives in the district knew anything about its origin, so there was no violation in helping ourselves.) Brain pans there were a plenty, but most of the lower jaws were missing, probably having fallen into the sea. The shelves were littered with teeth that had fallen out, as well as hundreds of clamshell "ornaments" which must have been placed there with the heads. Most of the shell work consisted of thin disks with a hole in the center—probably wampum of small denomination; but there were also dozens of great rings about six inches in diameter, and these are worth about five dollars in trade among the natives even today. Yet the unguarded gold mine was left untouched by the local natives. The fact that they did not know whose spirits guarded the rock did not make them any more willing to violate it.

One of the interesting features of these old skulls was the

condition of the teeth. The skull of an old person could be easily identified by the stubs of molars that had been worn down through the years by a diet liberal in sand content. We examined dozens of teeth and found only a few with cavities, although dentists today claim that primitives have just as many caries as civilized candy-eaters. On the other hand, where teeth were missing or could be easily removed from a jaw there was evidence of pyorrhea. The bone surrounding the tooth cavity had receded obviously by absorption, for other equally thin portions of the skull had not been eroded any more than was reasonable by the action of time and exposure to the weather.

There are many theories offered by experts for the difference in the physical type and culture of the eastern and western Solomon Islanders. The one we choose is that the very dark-skinned natives living in the islands from Vangunu west to Little Buka are remnants of the indigenous Negroid inhabitants. They are descendants of the whole island chain's "original settlers" who somehow escaped the Mongoloid infiltration that altered the type in the other Melanesian islands. No one can give us any reason for their having escaped—for their islands are no more protected than the others—but our own theory is that it was because they were so tough. The fact that they were notoriously tough headhunters and cannibals protected the Papuans from the Mongoloid invasions, for these old Indonesian "mariners" gave New Guinea a wide berth when they were migrating into the Pacific. However, that theory doesn't get us very far either, for it doesn't explain why one island of "original settlers" was tougher than any other. Anyway, we all agree that the westerners are different.

As evidence that headhunting is an only recently expired cult, our host at Patativa was an ex-headhunter. He was also the village luluai, having won this distinction some years ago by lopping off the head of a white man—which he cached in the man's own shirt. The government thereupon appointed him headman on the theory that poachers make the best game wardens. Today the ex-headhunter was the living pic-

ture of the cartoonist's cannibal king. He had grown plump through the years of secure living, and the fat had concentrated in his abdomen which ballooned out above his lap-lap, tight-skinned and shining as if bulging with missionaries. On the most jovial pug-nosed brown face in the world he wore nickel-rimmed spectacles, so filthy that one could not see his eyes behind them. He had bleached his hair platinum-white and wore it pulled up into a pompon through the crownless top of a wide palm-leaf "beach hat." The brim of that hat had a line as coy as the picture hat of a Southern missy, but the ears under its sweet shade were hanging in ropes to the headhunter's shoulders. The holes in the lobes had been stretched by larger and yet larger clamshell rings until the flesh had given way and broken, and the result was four uneven strings of meat dangling about the neck. The ex-headhunter made one think of nothing so much as the reluctant dragon.

And it was this bespectacled dragon who gallantly sent his "car" for us on the morning of the turtle hunt.

The vehicle was the dazzling war canoe we had admired from afar, the enormous gondola with twelve-foot-high prow and stern, inlaid with mother-of-pearl, gay with banners of seaweed to keep off evil spirits, and manned by thirty polished plum-colored galley slaves. This was the war canoe which a few years ago a woman would have lost her head for touching, and it was still so downright sacred to the men that women were not allowed in it. The only explanation we had then for our special privilege was that no native ever seemed to be sure we had a sex. (It was only the women who were suspicious.)

The only thing our seat midships lacked was a gold-embroidered awning. We had a back and plenty of leg room, and the Mastah had insisted on giving us cushions—on a turtle hunt! Ahead of us were fourteen glistening black backs whose owners were sitting two abreast, and behind were sixteen more galley slaves with teeth of mother-of-pearl, every set showing as we pushed toward the middle of the lagoon where the fleet of smaller canoes was waiting.

It is hard to explain becomingly the peculiar pleasure one feels in being the only women on a hunt. I suspect one reason for it is the knowledge that this is a very special masculine job, and somehow by being only two women we become slightly invisible, which permits us to observe rites of the secret society which would be hidden from a crowd of women. Anyway one feels smug and completely happy, especially on a lagoon morning fresh enough to drink. But we were far from being invisible when the flotilla set off westward down the lagoon. We seemed to be the very cause of things. Our magnificent war canoe led the way like a triumphant flagship, our galleymen hissed in unison between their teeth as they dug their paddles into the crystal blue, forward on the left, then on the right, the muscular backs rippling with high lights. The water foamed white and sped beneath us, spraying the air with shattered diamonds. Luxuriously we lay back and watched the laboring canoes around us trying to keep up. There were ten and twenty men to each of these shells, all of them hissing and digging and spraying— and flashing white teeth as we cheered them on. We thought the speed was entirely for our benefit, but it never slackened until we reached the open sea. Then, as we cleared an island, we two did become invisible, nonexistent as women. The men were suddenly on their own hunt; the turtles lay before us.

It was a spectacle, that turtle field. There seemed to be acres of great brown shells floating on the water; the whole surface was covered far out ahead with waving islands of them: not the little turtles we know, but great shells two and three feet long, weighing as much as a man and some of them a hundred years old. They were all ladies, sleeping or comatose, preparatory to hatching on shore. The men hissed at the sight, but there was no other sound from the whole fleet. Without a signal the canoes slowed down simultaneously, then quietly, slowly, and with exquisite suspense, we glided forward, the fleet spreading out to encircle the nearest batch.

Nothing but a snipe hunt could have been conducted so silently as this wholesale turtle catch. When the canoes had ringed the nearest side of the herd, the men slid over the side into the water and swam the rest of the way with an unsplashing breast stroke. They worked in pairs, two men to each turtle. With a quick simultaneous movement they flipped turtle after turtle over on her back, and with the flippers waving futilely in the air the creatures were helpless. The long snaky necks stretched up to keep the heads out of water while the parrot mouths gaped open and shut in such a silly astonished way, and one could only think of the tortoise in *Alice in Wonderland*. Sometimes a pair of men missed on the flipping movement, and there would be a tussle and splashing which made the near-by turtles dive. Many of the great beasts woke as they were approached and slid under water before the men could get to them. We saw one boy dive after a disappearing turtle and come up a minute later gasping and laughing. He had missed, but if he had got a hold on the shell he could have ridden his catch to the surface by putting his weight on the rear end of the shell and pulling up on the front. (A native expression for a bungled opportunity is "The turtle has dived.") We hesitated at going into the water ourselves because of our island sores, but by putting our faces over the side under the surface we could see the great brown disks diving down and down on the diagonal until they disappeared in the blue depth. It was a radiant world down there under the surface to be explored one day.

The scene up top gradually became something like a muted three-ring circus with things happening fast all over the place, and only one pair of eyes with which to see it. Speed seemed important; and, as we moved on, the men were panting with the exertion and the surface of the water was littered with upturned yellow bellies and a forest of flippers, and long necks waving back and forth. It was all one man could do to swim and push a great turtle before him toward a canoe. The turtles were tethered by a flipper, each one with its own long line, to the canoes, and by midmorning we had all that the boats could tow. Still the ocean surface was covered with floating islands of turtles. It was one of the biggest fields the natives themselves had seen. The trapping had been going on for days and would continue until Patativa was gorged or the field had floated so far off that the catches could not be towed back to the lagoon.

It was a triumphant return to the village. The going was slow for, though the return had been planned for the incoming tide, the catches weighed hundreds of pounds and each canoe had a wide fan of turtles behind it. But even had speed been possible we should still have had to go slow lest the heads of the turtles be dragged under water, which would drown them. They had to be kept alive until they were eaten. The men paddled to exactly the tempo of the "Volga Boatmen"; so Margaret and I sang it, as loud as we could, in time to the dipping paddles, and by and by a few of the following canoes pulled up and lined out across the lagoon parallel with our flagship gondola. And so we came home singing and laughing, delighted with ourselves and one another, even though there was not one portion of the morning's picture I could have painted—at least, not with paint.

There were so many pictures that could not be painted, everlasting impressions that were composed of flashing color and sequences of movement and odors and temperatures and sounds; and just the things one feels on his skin and in his heart. There was, for example, the return of the hunt, and the feast that followed. Even as the fleet came in sight of Patativa the shouts and laughter started up, for the entire village was down on the beach to help pull the boats and turtles in. While still a few yards from shore the paddlers in our gondola suddenly rose, and with a whoop popped over both sides into the water after the manner of the old swimming hole. We remained in our seat while the great canoe was run up high and dry on the beach in the hands of half a hundred laughing men. Then the huge turtles were pulled up on the sand with a yo-ho-ho and yips of delight. Every canoe that came in sprayed paddlers from both sides as ours had done, and every turtle that was dragged up on the sand was the biggest yet, until the wide beach was a bedlam of racket and running to which innumerable children and dogs added their din. One doesn't have to know the language in such delirium.

Meanwhile the homebodies had been getting things ready for the "bacon." At the far end of the settlement there was a great heap of round boulders (about the size of coconuts) being heated on a bed of coals. The palm grove on the beach flat was filled with smoke from the fire, so that there were the white shafts of light of the palm cathedral again, coming down through the fronds, and in them ninety billion bottle flies. All through the grove the earth had been solidly carpeted with banana leaves, and here the slaughter took place— and everything else that happened. The turtles were dragged up from the beach and while they were still trying to get their flippers across their stomachs, their belly shells were unceremoniously whacked off. The flippers kept right on

waving and the parrot heads on the long necks gaping, while the men proceeded to carve out their "being." Entrails were thrown to the snapping dogs which rushed away in snarling packs with yards of purple tubing between them. Emptied top shells—tortoise shell worth hundreds of dollars in the right part of the world—were turned upside down and became receptacles for the masses of yellow eggs. The great muscles—worth hundreds of dollars in turtle soup—were cut up in big chunks and tossed over onto the banana leaves, where feet with sore legs on them and dogs and children and flies walked over them until the women had made leaf-wrapped packages of the chunks, adding sago mash, a few yams, and banana pudding to each parcel.

It all looked like the wildest confusion but actually everyone had his appointed task and was executing it with enthusiasm. Ordinarily we helped with any work going on in the village and devil take prestige (which was so unusual an attitude for a white person that it always amused the women hilariously—which we interpreted as friendliness). But here the combination of frenzied flies and island sores and goo and the odor of meat not yet actually dead kept us moving around for air. At the ovens the rocks had been raked into a circle from the bed of coals, leaving about two layers of stones on which a sheaf of banana leaves was spread. The packages of meat were heaped on top, sprinkled with water, and then covered with another layer of leaves, and over the whole the remaining hot stones were piled. Roast was in the oven.

The busyness of the entire grove was the picture of Melanesia: the smoky shafts of sunlight that wagged as the fronds above moved in the breeze; the billions of flies; the racing dogs and yipping children; the laughter and whacking and the wonderful color of great bowls of golden eggs on the green banana-leaf carpet all through the grove. It was busier than Breughel's "Wedding Dance." But there were also static compositions ready-made for Gauguin; here was the satiny plum-brown torso of a young girl—far slenderer than Gauguin painted his chunky Polynesians—silhouetted against a patch of brilliant yellow-green sunlight on the banana leaves behind; to one side was a mound of magenta-colored turtle meat, and on her madder-red lap-lap the girl held the leaves

with which she was wrapping the meat—they were in the shade and so a rich blue-green in color. And the girl herself was what is known as a honey. Not beautiful, nor even pretty, but—well, just the kind called a honey; young and plump and little, with a doll's face framed in a great round ball of frizzy black hair. She had the most guileless saucer eyes, almost no nose, and a full, puckered mouth with teeth so white and even that they looked like a bite of coconut meat.

There was nothing whatever the matter with her torso. In fact it was so well preserved for her age, which must have been all of fifteen years, that we assumed she had not yet undergone the ravages of maternity, and was probably not even married. And she had the maiden's look: a tricky little way of gazing saucer-eyed up from under her pompadour. But we painted this little treasure later—simply as a curiosity, because she was certainly not the typical Melanesian maiden— and had the posing interrupted by a summons to court.

Court was held periodically at the village by the district officer to settle all local troubles, and the girl came up for husband poaching. Obviously the ample meat of the turtle season, plus the attendant rejoicing, had stimulated other appetites which the little honey took care of. In the old days she would have had her head sliced off for adultery, for she was married herself and to a second husband; but all she got now for her waywardness was a threat of being sent to the mission school if there were more complaints about her. We sat in on the trial and doubted the improvement of white justice over that of the primitives. The evidence against the girl was overwhelming and so frank in detail that the district officer had his face in his papers half the time to hide his hysteria. All this juicy testimony was lost to us by not understanding the language. Very clear, however, was who was on what side: the sulkiness of the injured wives and the reluctance to give evidence of half a dozen husbands who had given way to the joy of the season would have been just as obvious if we had been deaf. Through it all the girl stood figuratively showing her leg to the judge. She let her round mouth hang open helplessly and gazed obliquely past her cloudy dark pompadour at both judge and victims, meantime twirling a plump baby finger round and round the circle of a big shell earring. She was a bad, bad girl in any language, but perfectly bad.

The preparations for the feast and feasting itself went on simultaneously all through the night and next day, as they had done for a week and would continue to as long as anyone had strength left to gorge and whack and laugh. (The natives have no way of preserving meat and the only thing they can do is stuff while it is on hand.) But as the days wore on, the grove rang with the screams of exhausted children, and weary-eyed adults with bulging bellies still wrapped and whacked and stoked the fires but with lessening hilarity. Then by and by the fleet of canoes no longer went up the lagoon. By this time we at Segi were so fed up with rich tough turtle steak that we longed for a tin of soggy old mutton. And the Expotition had gone in frantically for tortoise-shell art work.

We had at our disposal several thousands of dollars' worth of shell and no way of hanging onto a cent's worth except by making it up into articles which would be classified as "used" by the United States customs. (There is a duty on raw shell so high that the only possible reason for it is to create a false value for rarity—when the freight costs alone would do that, the raw shell being very heavy and bulky and much of it being lost in working it up.) Segi was equipped, as many plantations are, with a shell-working outfit. This was simply a small handwheel which had cloth buffers and emery stones of varying coarseness; and files, a hacksaw, a drill, and plenty of sandpaper. The only other things needed were elbow grease and ideas. Paper patterns—a shoehorn, for instance—were cut out of the shell with a hacksaw, filed down to the proper outline, thinned with sandpaper and elbow grease, and then put into a pan of hot water for shaping. The shell became very pliable when it was hot, and if held in the desired shape until it cooled, which was in a few minutes, it stayed that way. (Margaret made herself a ring set with a black opal in this way, but the heat of her hand was constantly unshaping it.) The final gloss was attained by buffing and buffing and buffing, on the handwheel buffer when a boy could be spared to turn it, or, when not, on the seat of our pants. The island connoisseurs of tortoise-shell work judge one's handiwork by the same standards as those by which hospital nurses rate one another on bed-making: the corners of things must be neat and the surface smooth, but the depth of the finishing gloss is the tortoise-shell worker's own test.

The work was fun and simple and the results elegant. We made combs of all sizes, cigarette holders and cases and boxes, picture frames, palette knives, pickle forks and salad spoons, bracelets and buttons, and buckles and even a watch crystal. By this time we had grown wantonly particular about the shell we used, and hacked straight into an inch-thick, hundred-year-old back for something no larger than a button of the right color. Our choicest pieces such as the watch crystal, which had to be transparent, were cut out of a portion of clear blond shell without a mark of dark brown in it. Entirely blond shells are not natural though they exist where they are produced artificially, as in Ongtong Java. Here the natives value only the transparent shell for nose and ear ornaments, and sea turtles are captured and kept in pools which are always shaded from the sun. In this way a blond shell is produced, a fact that leads one to believe that brown turtles are merely sunburned blondes.

But whatever complexion the turtles, they are a godsend to the meat-starved natives. The whole season of hunting and gorging, with a love interest of a chubby headhunter's daughter and the beautiful, virtuous Maike (of whom more anon) would make a complete movie story and a stunning picture. And woe is us that we could not paint pictures as a movie camera takes them.

23

So far as models went it was a holiday painting in Marovo Lagoon. The ex-headhunters were handsome, intelligent, unsuspicious, pleased to earn a few sticks of tobacco for posing (though they preferred shillings), and one and all thought the pictures we painted were miracles. They were the subjects which portraitists dream about but never meet in civilization.

There were just a few flaws. One of them was that every model who came across to Segi from Patativa came as a clan, and the entire totem remained throughout the sittings. The relatives were all charming but they created problems. First, for some reason—simply custom, we were told—every relative who accompanied the models had to be given a present of tobacco. And while trade tobacco was cheap by the stick, pounds of it such as we found ourselves dispensing ran into money. We had brought tobacco with us from Sydney but it had got soaked with salt water when the supply trunk was dunked, and soon began to mold. The village natives looked at it as if it smelled bad and we finally had to abandon it. (At which the plantation boys retrieved it and smoked it with their usual relish.) Since then we had been buying tobacco as we needed it from the plantation stocks. This was actually the Expotition's only cash expenditure throughout the Solomon Islands, and we might be criticized for our distaste of lavishness toward the models' relatives, especially when the model himself cost so little. Still, no expenditure however small increased the amount of money on hand, or decreased the hundreds of miles between us and earning more. And the relatives, when we tried to pass on old garters and tin cans as company gifts, just smiled indulgently and forgot them when they left. We had to get rid of the relatives.

Another flaw was the difference in our attitudes toward time; Western Union time which is measured by the half-minute, versus Melanesian time which we do not believe is measured at all, even by suns or moons or lives. The model would charmingly agree to come across to Segi in the morning when the sun was "there" (pointing to about eight o'clock in the sky), and it was true, the clan did appear in the forenoon; but it was anywhere from just after sunrise when our mouths were still full of toothpaste to an hour or two after the artist had gnawed her fingers down to stubs. The American idea of punctuality, even if it be as little as the artist's, dies a hard death, if ever; and creative ecstasy, in the meantime, ran a temperature.

So was the Mastah—running a temperature. He said nothing, but the sight of village natives up on his veranda must have been very hard to bear after forty years of prohibiting it for any reason. (He had once lived in a group of islands where he was the only white man in three hundred miles, and that education still made him sleep with his revolver under his pillow.) But he had given us permission to use the north veranda for a studio, probably not counting on tribes of models, and while we should have preferred to paint at Patativa there was no way of getting across the lagoon. The shortage of gasoline eliminated the launch for daily trips and our first attempt to use a canoe started up a whole new set of problems. The canoe venture itself was inspired by sheer desperation.

The little saucer-eyed siren was still posing for us and creating a minor hell at Segi, as well as at Patativa. The houseboys were two young Malaitans, bursting at the seams with about sixteen years apiece, and the daily presence of this little treasure had them in a panic. For example, their usual method of dusting the veranda when the Mastah was off on the plantation was to wrap a dust cloth on each foot and skate; when the girl was posing they skated and whooped and huffed and puffed for hours round and round "the longest veranda in the Solomon Islands," all the time pretending not to see the girl at all. But they knew and so did she, and she was constantly dropping her pose to clutch her calico sling coyly to her breasts. Not only were the boys neglecting their kitchen work, to the Mastah's justified annoyance, but their galloping about kept the whole house jiggling on its piles so that my canvas and painting arm were in a state of palsy. Whenever Margaret shooed the young hoodlums away, they fled laughing under the house where they whooped it up directly beneath the girl. Whether or not this was a Melanesian courtship, it was very comic, even though it was not promoting art.

We stood it until the climax, which finally came with an actual explosion.

The "house" on the Segi veranda consisted of two connected rooms, one the office and the other what would have been the Mastah's room if he had not slept on the veranda. (Our room was a separate little house on the south veranda.) The spare room which was nearest where we were working had doorways on both sides and was used as a shorter passageway from the rear to the front veranda. Near the doorway was sitting our supply trunk, when both houseboys suddenly tore through from the rear to the front veranda. The entire house rocked with the bump of their feet, and just as they emerged through the doorway the supply trunk went *boom!* The model fell over on all fours and scrambled; her relatives popped off the edge of the veranda like puffed wheat shot from guns, while the houseboys stood transfixed, white-eyed. As we were ourselves. There were no explosives in that trunk; not that we knew of. But we found out in a jiffy. The explosion was a big bottle of concentrated peroxide in what had once been a tin container!

The explosion was a big bottle of concentrated peroxide!

Diluted, the peroxide is an antiseptic, and undiluted it is a strong caustic, burning fingers and rotting anything it touches. The heat and joggling had liberated the free oxygen which, at the right intensity, simply blew up the bottle. We could only pour water on our poor belongings, sweep up the rotted shreds, and then go in search of the vanished model.

By the time we got down to the beach the entire clan was halfway to Patativa and we were frantic lest the girl should fail to return and let us finish her picture and, with her talk-talk of the explosion, frighten away other models. This was an emergency when we might have taken the launch to go across and patch things up, but there was a canoe on the beach and we decided to use that rather than take the launch without permission. We must finally take to canoes anyway in order to avoid all the problems of painting at Segi, and now was the time to begin using our own muscles.

We had not been in a native canoe before but they looked like fun; they slipped over the water so speedily and seemed so easy to handle. I had spent a good number of my school vacations in canoes and especially liked handling one in rough water.

The native canoe is simply a keelless barked log with a slightly flattened bottom and pointed ends with a slot down the middle for the paddlers, a "two holer" (big enough for two paddlers with their legs stretched out in front of them). This one was pulled up in the shade of the trees behind the beach and covered with palm fronds, but it evidently had not been used for some time because it was pretty well dried out. And it weighed a ton pulling it down to the water. When

Margaret stepped into it from the beach it grounded and was so heavy I could not push her off. The way to get into it, we decided, was to pull it down to the end of the little wharf and step into it like ladies. We were in the water before you could say "Pooh." The round-bottomed craft simply skidded out from under our stepping foot and went giggling off by itself while we were still coming to the surface.

It was a battle now, and no loss even if we lost because we were enjoying our first swim in the lagoon. We would try the canoe one at a time. So we pushed it back to shallow water and while Margaret held it firmly I wedged my American hips into the rounded slot, got a perfect balance, and, holding the double-end paddle like a tight-rope walker, told Margaret to shove me off. She shoved and the next instant I was hanging head down in the water, hips still wedged in the canoe. Laughing in such a position is quite a novel experience. You are not only so helpless with mirth that you have no muscles to help your hips out of the canoe, but you run out of breath quicker than is usual under water. It nearly drowned Margaret.

We finally decided to master the canoe the way one learns to ride a bicycle. I got in and practiced keeping topside by feathering with the double-end paddle, Margaret wading behind with a mothering hand on the craft. That was all right so long as I feathered, but the minute my body got off-center an inch when I started really using the paddle with my arms, I was in the ditch again. The canoe had a very definite personality: kittenish and still with a devilish kind of humor like some horses, which quietly let you get on them and then promptly rake you off on a passing tree. Yet over at Patativa little boys just beginning to walk properly skeetered their own canoes all over the water front.

The solution, we finally had to admit (returning the canoe

to its shade), to paddling a Melanesian canoe was to be born a salt-water Melanesian.

Or not be born at all. For hell hath no fury like a Malaita-man who finds his canoe split by American hips. Nor is there, apparently, any pollution so vile as a woman, even a missus, touching or getting into the canoe of a Malaitan. Even without the split (which did not extend to the bottom of the shell) the craft would never be any good again. Its spirit was violated. If the boy—he was Kesuo of the labor line—should ever try to go on the water in that canoe the spirit would drown him.

A merrily laughing Malaitan is awesome enough, but an angry one looks like an infuriated gorilla: all open mouth with big teeth in it, black eyebrows pulled down over glinting high lights and every contorted muscle outlined with deep creases. Even the Mastah was silent before Kesuo's blast, which we all realized was justified. We hid behind the Mastah and paid up five dollars' worth of tobacco to soothe the savage. Ordinarily five dollars' worth of tobacco would buy two such canoes, and as the lavish amount was our own suggestion—not the demand of the boy nor even approved of by the Mastah—forgiveness should have been ours. But we had committed some horror beyond monetary salvage: when Kesuo went to the warehouse for his tobacco he was still snorting flames.

But the damned canoe, we discovered, was now ours. And the Mastah promptly set a gang of boys to work making it into a craft that would stay topside and could ferry us to and from work at Patativa. In less than two hours it was a seaworthy little outrigger. The split in the bottom was calked, and then the boys took themselves off to the bush and in a short time came back with coils of lawyer vine, a number of saplings of matched thickness, and a young tree of about four inches diameter. The Mastah's drill was used to make holes along the gunwales of the canoe through which to thread the vines for binding the saplings to the shell—the holes would ordinarily have been burned through—and an ax was used for pointing the ends of the young tree which was to be the floater on the outside edge of the outrigger. These were the only modern tools used: the remainder of the work consisted entirely in binding the sapling to the canoe and one another with the vine.

The result was a jolly little water bug: and it was *ours*, which was more to the point; the Expotition had a yacht at last. And we even discovered we had a totem insignia figurehead. It was a flattened knob on the point of one end of the canoe which we thought at first was merely a knob. Then one of the boys constructing the outrigger pointed out the saw line which represented teeth, and the circles, vaguely eyes and nostrils. A dog! I was delighted because I was raised as one of a long line of dogs. The boys grinned. "No, Missus, totem belong you-two-fella missus," one of them joked, "*alligator*." So, our departed uncle (or any other relative deceased) was in some alligator and from now on we must not eat alligator, kill, nor injure one, nor speak harshly to any we met lest that alligator be our relative. And no matter how gentle the deceased may have been in the flesh, as a spirit he was a terror, lying in wait for us for the least offense—even offenses we committed unwittingly. It was a little confusing: was our totem figurehead an appeal for leniency from real alligators in the water? or did the figurehead itself have the relative's spirit in it to ward off alien alligators? The boys smiled understandingly and said: "Yas, Missus."

The first trip in the canoe brought its own conclusion. This was surely no relative of ours; the spirit must still be of Kesuo's gorilla clan. Or it might have been Larry, the only deceased relative I could think of with a spirit so ornery as the one in possession of this canoe. The living Larry was a second cousin we had once who became an angel by falling out of a hayloft where he had gone to collect rotten eggs. He was pelting these globules of undiluted stench at us cousins when he slipped—and quite feasibly became an alligator. The canoe could no longer tip over and it could not split because we sat up on the extensions of the outrigger which went over the gunwales; but to make any headway both of us had to paddle like side-wheelers. And the headway was in circles. For, because of the outrigger, we could paddle on only one side. And backwatering, as one does with the paddle to keep the course in an ordinary canoe, didn't work in this one. Outriggers were not used by the lagoon natives, but the salt-water Malaitamen of the plantation had grown up in them, and our outrigger builders stood on the beach watching our helpless circles, all but exploding. If I have intimated that Melanesians have no sense of humor I take it back; it was just that we had never before seen a Malaitaman seeing anything really funny.

But we finally figured it out for ourselves; one of us paddled madly like a side-wheeler while the other sat aft like an Indian going through rapids, using his paddle as a rudder. I was the dashingly posed figure aft because, while logically the exercise should have been good for us, instead, the sweating up as a side-wheeler and cooling off afterward gave me a go of malaria. So with only one of us paddling we did not go as in the rapids; we moved with the speed of a canal barge and the course of a snake; for the spirit, whoever he was, was dead set on toying with us—if not with eggs, then heavy tide currents.

But we *felt* free; we felt free to go to the village when we wished because we could go under our own steam, and so were free of whooping houseboys and the danger of pressing our generous host too far with the cluttering clans.

It was a magnificent feeling, having an Expotition yacht.

24

Now, for a week or so, there were no problems. Daily we rose with the sun and with admirable American punctuality, at seven-thirty, Margaret was side-wheeling us across the lagoon while I gracefully attended the bound-on rudder with my knees and hauled in the troll lines. We carried an emergency tinned luncheon, but preferred fresh fish, which we fried on the communal "oven" at the village when the natives approved the species in our catch. Some of the fish were poisonous or taboo, but those that were passed by the censors were delicious. And to diverge: we never could understand for a long time why Europeans ate expensive tinned fish when there were oceans of fresh ones all around them; and we continued eating fresh fish whenever we were on our own until one day we broke out with what we called "fish mouth." But I can go into that with much more feeling later when we were suffering from it. It was a good enough reason for tinned fish.

One morning on the way to work we met in the flesh our totem relative, the lagoon alligator, who had hitherto been only a rumor. He was pushing along to work, too, going east with his eyebrows and nostrils, and a few dragon points of his back out of water, long ribbons of wash behind them. We bowed respectfully and gave him the right of way which he took without a glance in our direction.

At the beach at Patativa the luluai met us, as usual, to help pull the ferry up in the shade. Then we were escorted to his hut (the shade of its north side being the studio) like the Pied Piper, collecting our day's audience as we went.

We had started a canvas of Maike, a lad who looked like Cellini's "Perseus" in weathered copper. Physically he was typical of the lagoon youths, seeming tall and elegant because he was so slender, but as steel-muscled and sleek as a racing black. In personality, however, he was a universal type, a regular young "christer" convert to a new religion. There was a house lotu at Patativa and the beautiful Maike led the Sunday singing—hymns faintly familiar in tune but with a jolly new syncopation that was entirely Patativa, or quite possibly the suppressed half of Maike's dual personality. After all, he was the son of a headhunter, and his father must have been a nippier one than his neighbors or he would not have survived to be the father of Maike. The words of the hymns had been translated into the native language, and the entire congregation, composed of men on one side of the house lotu and of women with sleeping or nursing children on the other, dozed peacefully between jazzed numbers.

This was where we had first seen Maike. He was a little self-conscious at having white company at the service and struck the opening note of the first hymn too high, with the result that all were straining and screaming as they sang, their eyes squeezed shut, and the veins standing out on their necks. When they reached the highest note of the hymn they tried, failed, and the entire congregation burst into a guffaw. Only Maike refused to laugh. He carried on horribly and alone to the end. But perhaps it was this very purism which made him approachable for our purposes.

The attitude toward Art in this village was refreshingly merry. Toward the completion of a portrait every stroke I put on the canvas which brought the likeness nearer the model was greeted by a whoop from the audience. We thought the cheers were innocent, but the models seemed to take them personally and as derision. In any case, the self-conscious young men of the community took it just the way young men do elsewhere in the world and would not risk being laughed at to pose for us. But Maike was consistent. He was so very self-conscious that he wanted to see his face on canvas more than he feared being conspicuous as a model. But on top of this he was an artist himself, and a rattling good one, though there was then no association in his mind between our kind of creation and his own. We had this very clearly illustrated when he was asked to make a portrait of the Expotition. Maike was a canoe carver, a craft he had inherited from his father who had got it from his father and so on back to the dim beginning.[1] His tools, therefore were an adz and shells of different widths with sharpened edges, which he preferred to modern tools; a pencil was an unfamiliar medium. So, with a pencil, Maike made "carvings" of us, conventionalized figures with exactly the proportions of the wooden spirit-statues one sometimes encounters along the bush paths in this district. All the time he was drawing

[1] The attitude toward professional artists in Melanesia was naturally very interesting to us. The professional artists are the canoe carvers and mask makers and they are hired to make things just as are our commercial artists. Their products are respected, but neither the villagers nor the artists themselves regard artists as personages deserving special privilege, as we do. They are still obliged to carry on their traditional work in the village, helping others to build their houses, clearing the bush for gardens, and hunting and fishing, exactly as are the other men who lack talent. This is primarily due (possibly) to the fact that an art sense is not confined to a few in Melanesia. All villagers, both men and women, make all their own decorations for everyday use, as well as all objects for family use, such as carved food bowls and lime containers. Objects for ceremonial or communal use, however, are made entirely by professionals; and as all such property is endowed with metaphysical significance there are taboos attending the making of it. Thus, in a way, in so far as the artist is presumed to have the association of spirits while working on a secret society dance mask or a totem carving, he does receive special attention while actually on the job. The knowledge of how to make a carving with proper ritualistic observances is secret and is handed down with the craft from one generation to the next in a family. Professional artists are therefore not necessarily specially gifted, and may be merely expert woodchoppers who follow conventional patterns which have been used for centuries. In fact, in some objects it is taboo to improvise or introduce new patterns.

he never once referred to us for data. He drew the representative human figure as it has been carved for generations in this lagoon and as a concession to his subjects made lines around our toes for shoes, added lacings, belts, a watch and topees entirely from an impression he had got previously. Our sex and tools, Margaret's ukulele and my brush and our ciga-

rettes, were "written" in as postscripts later. In fact, we did not get a sex at all until we asked if these were portraits of mastahs. Maike looked at us with boy-scout surprise and then, when we insisted we were missus, he simply added the symbolic patterns meaning female. There was no humor intended.

As an introduction to posing, in order to show Maike and incidentally the village the profits of association with artists, we painted his long fingernails a brilliant scarlet with some of our imported enamel. Our own red fingernails, chipped remains of New Year's Eve glamor, excited a great deal of admiration in Patativa. The children were frankly dazzled and, whenever they thought they were not being seen, the grownups would stoop and peer at our hands. There was no doubt that until we painted Maike's nails with the blood-red out of the little bottle the natives thought our nails became red from painting pictures. We obtained reports of our goings-on and explanations of things, not from the natives, but at the dinner table at Segi in the evening. So when we heard from the Mastah who heard it from the houseboys who heard it from the air that people who painted pictures acquired red fingernails we decided to award Maike the badge of our guild. It was an inspiration. From then on Maike was the sober envy of the entire village and conducted himself with appropriate hauteur. No one laughed at him when he began to pose—and he was a sample to invite laughter ordinarily. For we had induced him to wear all the heirlooms there were in the village. He wore on his head a chief's tortoise-and-clam-shell "dollah"—though he was not a chief, nor descended from one (and to step out of one's class gives everyone a fit in this society); his shell and plaited pandanus collar were "royal," and the ackis was a deadlock. Maike had introduced it himself as a head lopper-offer. To us it looked like an ordinary wood-chopping ax *circa* 1940; origin Sears, Roebuck; with a rather long, hardwood, black handle, probably native-made. But it was one of the treasures of the village, and we painted it in to keep the esteem of our friends—intending, however, to substitute a genuine headhunter's implement if we found one later.

But the Sears, Roebuck ax stayed (it seems that all the authentic weapons of civilized headhunters are in the American Museum of Natural History), and so did the "war shield"

Maike posed with. It turned out to be not a war shield, but a sing-sing shield, used in dances, and was not even local. It was Malaitan. We were lucky that it was even Melanesian, for everything the native offers is "something belong village long time before," which means something long esteemed though not necessarily owned as yet by anyone in the village, such as, for instance, the shining new safety-pin earrings seen on some Malaitan plantation boy. Thus, should a safety pin ever happen into this village it would be offered to an artist as "something belong village long time before." And if all that sounds confused it just reflects our bewilderment on having to depend on natives for authentic material.

Referring to Maike's portrait of the Expotition again, it will be noticed he has given me a highwayman's mask. This was not a native symbol of my glowering at things as I painted; it *was* a "mask," a "something-nothing" which I began wearing for painting about the fourth week at Patativa. In reality it was a symbol—but only to the Expotition—of the lowest ebb in our spirits of the entire painting venture so far. And the presence of that "mask" also accounts for Maike's entire family being included in his portrait with him.

All this not-too-clear sequence began with the second week of painting at Patativa when I found myself going blind. Not actually sightless, but having such severe headaches from the glare that I was obliged to sit down frequently because of nausea and dizziness. And I had started out on this venture with faultless eyes and a heritage of exceptionally strong ones —an ancestor, for instance, who was famed in our family for being able to read without glasses when she was nearly a century old. And I had frequently used my eyes for ordinary work ten and sixteen hours a day for days at a time and not felt the strain—except in my feet. The eyes still had first-rate lenses but the pupils were now being overworked trying to see my painting, which was always kept in shadow (but could never be arranged so that it did not catch a glare on the shiny paint reflected from some blaze behind me), and still see the object I was painting which, if not in the sunlight itself, was surrounded by glare. I could not, of course, wear dark glasses to paint in. Rest—another painful delay—seemed to be the only solution.

It was genuinely maddening. A physical handicap was something we had not imagined—not eyes. Indeed, without our painting-eyes we were no longer even an Expotition. And we were still not halfway through trying to do the job.

We retreated to Segi where I spent despairing hours "palm-ing," the Bates treatment of cupping the palms over the eyes and rotating them to stimulate something or other. That worked—until I strained my eyes again, which was the minute I started painting. Then, for a few days I painted anyway, not to be a martyr, but to experiment with timing. I worked for a half-hour, "palmed" the next, and worked the next. One can't paint a picture that way—cooling off every thirty minutes. Also the models (we had another canvas going in the afternoon) got bored with the whole idea and went back to their village work while I was lying on the ground "sleeping." We tried working half-days only, then working one day and suffering the next, and finally resigned ourselves to a prolonged mope.

"You never saw a blind native, did you," demanded the Mastah, "—not one that wasn't born blind with a venereal disease? And natives can see for miles, things a white man can't see—in the same glare that's cracking your eyes up." That was true—some of it. Most white men who have lived near natives think natives have special eyesight, but some of the far- and quick-sightedness is training: sighting objects unfamiliar to a white man. But the Mastah had started us wondering. Structurally the native's eye is supposed to be no different from that of the white man; nevertheless, in painting them I had noticed a very marked prevailing difference. The high lights on the eyeballs of our models were always much wider than they were, for instance, on Margaret's eyes when she was standing in the same light next the model. And actually Margaret's eyes were much bigger than any native's. Still a more acute curve to the conjunctiva (which would account for a greater reflection of the surrounding light) would not explain being able to see better in the glare. Nor was the dark pigment any special protection. Natives did squint in the sun, but they never lidded their eyes down to slits the way we and other Whites did even when they had eyes as dark brown as the natives'. Then what was the answer for my strong eyes failing? Or was there no difference? Did natives suffer from glare too, get headaches, and gradually grow dim-sighted in time?

But there was a difference and the answer came from the most unexpected source—out of the lagoon!—by the silliest accident, and the cure was as simple and revolutionary as a safety pin.

As our island sores had not spread any more than usual after their dunking at the canoe launching, we began swimming daily in the lagoon during the eye doldrums. The water was blood temperature and the texture of velvet, besides being crystal-clear, the kind of brilliant cleanness that makes one want to plunge in face first and gulp. But therein lay the inevitable flaw. Scientists tell us that the reason for the special luminosity of tropical water is that the water is actually a mass of microscopic marine life. It is the sun shining on these millions of living facets in liquid that gives the effect of light coming from the water itself. In any case, you don't gulp (because of the brine) and after you have had a case of "tropical ear" (an infection which is supposed to be produced by some sea wog) you don't go into this beautiful water at all.

Until then, however, playing in the lagoon is a special kind of ecstasy.

Margaret and I swam one at a time because of the alligator, now no longer a myth. He had been haunting Segi because at Christmastime the Mastah had killed a steer for the labor line, the reptile had got a whiff of it roasting on the beach, and later had devoured the leavings right outside the labor-quarters' door. He came back nightly now to see if there was anything left, meantime cruising up and down the water front with his nostrils sticking up above the surface. So long as he kept his nose out we knew where he was; it was when he was sniffing around out of sight that one of us sat on the end of the wharf smacking the water with a paddle while the other swam.

The water was too warm to do much swimming anyway—one panted and broke into a sweat after a few strokes. Our efforts chiefly consisted in diving to the bottom of the lagoon with a lungful of air and trying to stay there. For if what happens above the lagoon is too exotic to describe adequately, then under water it is even more so. How describe the sun striking the surface above to send prismlike shafts of light down through the liquid crystal, which make writhing patterns all over the pale-yellow floor? or the greenness of the distance out toward the middle of the lagoon with its ghostly shapes of big fish passing to and fro? Everything waves, the green piles of the pier, Margaret's magnified feet, and a white coral castle, and the tempo is the luxurious one of the man on the flying trapeze. All is clean and glistening as in a jeweler's showcase, the traffic perfectly organized. No one gives signals, but a round ball of a little brilliant fish with Isadora Duncan draperies swings toward my face, does a right turn, and without colliding or breaking the formation, passes a school of little yellow bullets just coming up behind my shoulder. The yard-long, pencil-thin, black and yellow snakes stayed near the piles of the wharf, weaving between them. And though their heads might be distant they knew what was happening at their tails, for those tails would always slide away before I could close my hand—luckily, because we learned later that these pretty, harmless-looking reptiles were among the most venomous of island snakes.

Neither they, nor anyone else, ever paid the slightest attention to us, but there were a few residents to whom we gave a wide berth. There were the gutty bêches-de-mer, hideous black patent-leather slugs that went places along the lagoon floor with no visible effort of locomotion. Some of them were over a foot long and inches thick through the middle, and they had nasty thin-pointed ends that they wormed around like an anteater's nose. The Oriental traders collect them for export to China where they are used in soup, and probably knowing this is what made us take a personal dislike to them. Not that we minded the Chinese using them as flavoring; it was the association of eating what gave the flavoring. On a trip we made through some shallow reef water the native crew speared the bêches-de-mer and brought them on deck, at which the slugs turned inside out through the spear wounds, exuding worms of white gut and slime.

There were no poisonous sea urchins nor men-of-war in our part of the lagoon, but the few starfish were Paul Bunyans of such brilliance and variety of color that I'm sorry I mentioned them because I cannot describe them in black and white. Also there was an octopus, big-big-big-big, which lived in an undersea coral cave at the west end of the lagoon. No one had seen it for a thousand years or more but it grabbed and pulled under water the canoes that had been polluted by women. The octopuses the natives caught and ate never had a wing spread of more than a foot and were preferred smaller, for they were eaten boiled (in a gasoline tin) and were as tough as rubber even so young. We never got beyond biting down on the stretched-out arm of one, but the high shellfish flavor lasted through many a civilized meal. Chopped up and smothered in curry as some Whites serve them occasionally (mostly as bravado to impress a new chum) octopus might slide down, but without any lift to the soul.

There was one mild but very real danger in the lagoon. This was not so much the sharp poisonous coral reefs (a scratch was a certain infection) as the giant clams which were everywhere and disguised themselves as coral. The shells of the old ones—and some clams live to be as much as five hundred years old—were anywhere up to eighteen inches across, encrusted with coral and even cemented to the rocks they had lain on for years. They lay with their jaws gaping wide for chance food swimming in, and anything thrust into the shells, like a stick or a nice digestible rock, was clamped down on with a death grip. The clams are known to be the malevolent spirits of departed villagers, and when a Marie gathering shellfish from the rocks plants her toes between the jaws of a clam she gets just what she deserves for ignoring some taboo. The seriousness of this punishment was illustrated by our toying with a big clam. We thrust our walking stick into his mouth at which he promptly clamped down. Then by and by we wanted to go home, but the clam was busy digesting the stick and refused to give it up. We rapped on his head with rocks, blew smoke into the crevice held open by the stick, and finally put our lighted cigarettes into his mouth. He still held on. Finally we picked up the clam by the stick and banged him on the rocks; but he was unbreakable too, and in the end we took him home and hung him up in a tree by the handle of the stick. In the morning the ants had got us back our stick. The clamshells were lying on the ground clean as a whistle.

All this undersea life of ours was endlessly interesting, and I was thoroughly enjoying having an excuse for loafing, but the brine of the lagoon was not helping the cure. It supplanted eye sting for eye ache and gave me Margaret's company in "pink eye." "What you need if you two *must* pretend to be fish," said the Mastah, "is a pair of diving glasses." Yes, we said pleasantly, or mermaids' eyes, or a diving bell like William Beebe's. But diving goggles were not as remote as that. The Mastah's storage cases in his office had no bottoms; he could pull rabbits out of them, and after a little rummaging around he produced diving glasses. The natives in some districts use them for collecting troca shell (which is exported and becomes pearl buttons at our notion counters).

The instant I put my goggles on I had the solution to painting in the tropics without going blind. They made my eyes like a native's. Where the natives' eyes are deeply set with a projecting awning of prominent brow ridges and bushy eyebrows, small eye openings and high cheekbones to shut off some of the glare from the ground, the diving goggles (with the glass knocked out) sheltered my eyes all around in the same way. Only they were an improvement over native eyes; it was like looking out through two dark tunnels. I could see color now and detail in the shadows of things, and did not have to squint at all. And not the least of their virtues was that the rims made a dark boundary so that everything I saw through them was a framed composition. The only improvement possible was that they might have had square or oblong eye openings the shape of a real picture frame: and a little air-conditioning plant would have been nice. But even so they were a wonderful discovery.[2]

Our return to Patativa masked was a sensation. Ordinary

[2] The goggles proved to be a godsend, for I never afterward had trouble with my eyes when I wore them. However, there were many times when I had to leave them off to work because the natives seemed to be suspicious of them—not actually afraid, but too cautious to let us approach near when I was masked. Children screamed at sight of me, and the women scuttled.

spectacles were known, of course, for the luluai wore them; but he wore his for decoration, and everyone knew he could see nothing through the dirt. But my decoration had no glass in it and instead of being merely nickel frames the black tunnels covered the whole top of my face. No one stared openly, but the company that followed us up from the beach seemed fascinated. They were silent, and, as with the nail enamel, examined me slyly from the side so that if I stepped back suddenly I was liable to step on a few admirers. So far, however, the goggles were evidently thought to be rather extreme models of the luluai's decoration.

Then I began to paint. (It was ecstasy at last to paint in physical comfort.) We returned to Maike's portrait and the first thing we noticed was that Maike was looking at us queerly. Natives posing for me always looked a little horrified because of the faces I unconsciously made. (And this was another blessing I was looking forward to from the goggle mask; that it would cover up my murdering expression.) Yet here was the serene erstwhile-haughty Maike gazing at me with that hypnotized expression. And the usual audience, instead of sitting in back of me to watch the work, now sat in front and looked at my face. Then Maike's father, with a long dance stick he had brought to show us, was standing beside Maike as he posed, peering intently at me. I blocked in the outline of his figure before he moved, and we got him to pose for us just that way. Finally Maike's mother ducked behind the two, pretending to be on her way to somewhere else. Her mouth with its betel-nut-stained black teeth was hanging open in complete forgetfulness and her eyes stared at me frankly as if she thought I was unable to see her looking.

There were more peering relatives before we were finished, and only the fact that there was a limit to the length of the canvas kept it from becoming a frieze. We have no idea what these villagers had concluded about the goggles but there was a finale from which the reader can draw his own conclusions. On the final morning when the Marovo Lagoon family was carried as far as I could work on it in the village the luluai of the plump, brown, shining face, all his headhunter charm turned on, tried to make us a "present" of the tortoise-and-troca-shell "dollah" that Maike had posed in and that we had tried in vain to buy. Very few of these "dollahs" are in existence in the lagoon district today because they are no longer made, and so soon as one comes to the surface a missionary or planter grabs it up. (Now that the government is replacing chiefs with luluais the number of practicing chiefs and their symbols of chieftainship, like the "dollahs," are decreasing together.) The "dollah" was worth anywhere from five to ten U. S. dollars in trade, and we were charmed by this parting gift (for which, however, we expected to pay in full), thinking that we had been such delightful guests that the village had decided to part with it as a token of their esteem. But not at all. The precocious luluai had seen that there were possibilities in owning a pair of goggles. He was admiring them; they were good fella too much and the Missus certainly lookem true fella 'long Maike, 'long Davi, 'long Marie belong Davi, 'long pickaninny belong Marie belong Davi. And as for the bananas we had painted in the basket, they were so good that one had to laugh. I handed over the goggles for the luluai to try on and see what a foolish bargain he was proposing. He removed his own decoration which kept him partially blinded and, naturally, the minute he looked through the goggles, which had no interfering dirt, the world became the shining colorful vision it had become to me. They were good fella too much, good fella too much; and for once it sounded as if a native really meant it. Meantime the villagers were pressing up, gazing at the luluai's face with the same puzzled interest as they had

looked at me; but when the luluai swung his head around the circle, they stepped back a little, smiling faintly, seeming self-conscious and questioning.

That was all there was to it. The luluai kept the goggles (because the Mastah had a half-dozen pairs) and we, feeling guilty, kept the precious "dollah"—as far as Segi. "Take it back. Take it back," said the Mastah, "the luluai had no right to give that away. It doesn't belong to him—and he must have wanted those diving glasses pretty badly to take the chance of giving it away."

The "dollah" got back to the village but in a rather round-about way.

A few days later Maike turned up at Segi on an apparently meaningless visit. He and two other lads came up to the edge of the veranda and after an exchange of greetings just stood. Maike had in his hands the elaborate collar in which he had posed (and which was another chief's decoration) but he did not offer it to us for trade; and after waiting awhile for the boys to say what they had come for I went back to work in one of the rooms, leaving Margaret to solve it if the boys had any purpose in coming. About half an hour later I heard her shout with laughter. Maike was after a "something-nothing belong eye 'long picature" (diving glasses) and he was offering the chief's collar in trade. The luluai apparently had been boasting about the visions he was seeing in the mask; and the equally precocious Maike, with much better claim as being an artist, wanted a similar pair of magic eyes, for he proposed going in for the European style of portraiture. He got the goggles, for the Mastah had given us the lot, and was sent back to Patativa with both the collar and "dollah," neither of which belonged to him.

There was a complicated system of inheritance in this district in which, if we understood it rightly, a chieftainship descended through the male line, but ordinary property was kept on the female side of the house. For example, all children are of their mother's totem and their legal guardian is not their father but their mother's brother, and all property descends in the mother's totem line. Thus a man does not pass on his property, which he has inherited from his mother and her brother, to his own children, but to his sister's children—all but the decorations symbolic of chieftainship, which are owned individually and go with the title (the title being, in the beginning, an appropriation by a shrewd sorcerer).

Or the whole thing may be the other way around. However it may be, it is just as complicated, and what is true of one village is likely to be the exact opposite in another a few miles away. In any case, in Patativa the chief line had run out of male descendants and the power of a chief was now in the hands of the luluai. But still the chief decorations did not belong to him. They belonged vaguely to the whole village, both to the clan of the last chief, whose claim was on the ground of general property inheritance, and to the clan of the widow, whose children, had she produced sons, would have inherited the chief decorations. Ordinarily, when a chief line dies out, some other prominent man, usually a clever sorcerer, announces himself chief, the spirits in his control taking care of any objectors; and it was on these grounds, probably, that the luluai considered himself heir to the decorations.

If all this explains anything it is how disorganized the whole orderly system of a native culture (which the natives themselves, at least, understand) becomes when governments and missions introduce new authorities. As a by-product, objects that were once sacred and that are still considered to possess mystical properties float about the village belonging to no one person, and yet are claimed by half-a-dozen factions. Meanwhile, enterprising young men like Maike and old rascals like the luluai dare to appropriate them for personal profit. It is the beginning of dishonesty in a culture hitherto innocent of it, at least in the form of thievery.

Yet all the qualities peculiar to Patativa that had made working there such a pleasure and relief, were due to this kind of "interference." The intelligence (which we recognized as intelligence because the natives were co-operative and unsuspicious), the normal interest in picture making, Maike's progressive wish to make our kind of three-dimensional portraits, everyone's happiness (which was quite genuine), as well as the divorces and adultery, the "thievery" and pronounced commercial sense (their preference of silver to tobacco and tobacco to "presents" for posing, and as much as could be got for the work)—all these qualities familiar to white men were the result of white men's education. Patativa was not only a Christianized village; it was a mission station, the one from which the missionary we met on the *Mataram* was taking his holiday. And it was because of this that the beautiful war gondola had been taken on the turtle hunt and we contaminating women had been allowed in it.

25

"Mastah! Mastah! Alligator-him-he stop!" It was gasped out in a whisper though we were two hundred yards from the beach. The boy's eyes were gleaming wildly in the light from the lamp on the veranda and his big mouth was hanging open, panting from having run all the way up from the shore. But the Mastah was howling with laughter. The labor line was instructed to report when the alligator-him-he stop, so that the beast could be shot, because he was haunting the labor quarters. But every time a boy had come up with the information he had made such a racket getting started that by the time we got down to the beach the visitor had fled; so the boys were ordered to be quieter next time. Hence the whisper!

Margaret and I sprang up like old hounds at the sound of the horn, but the Mastah was writing letters and disinclined to shoot an alligator at the moment. "Take the gun and shoot him yourself," he said, at which we were off like young hounds.

We saw the alligator, all of him, and we must have knicked him because he pivoted on his belly, either from a hit or from hurt feelings, and slid like a log into the water. But if we missed, it was not poor marksmanship, you may be sure; we had something like the side of a barn to aim at, and were not ten yards off. He should have exploded—so there must be something in the legend that one has to drill an alligator through the eye-socket to get him.

But we were down on the beach and that was a feat in

itself. The Mastah did not openly disapprove, but he did not encourage our wandering from the house at night—not beyond the temple, which we could hardly visit as a complete Expotition—and we forever had to remember that we were guests owing more than usual consideration to our hosts, who would get in a whopper of an international situation if anything did happen to us. So now being legitimately on an alligator shoot we fired another shot for the Mastah's ears, then another for the plantation boys who had assembled for the kill (but were just as happy with an explosion, as they proclaimed with a yelp), after which we retreated to the wharf path to give them the impression that we were returning to the house.

It was a blessed night, filled with the howl of mosquitoes, but with a half-moon making a mother-of-pearl path on glassy water. We continued the hunt in our outrigger going eastward down the shore, and like Venus we floated through the night in our own radiance. Every dip of the paddle made a whorl of phosphorescent light in the water, which trailed away in spiraling radiance as we moved forward. A glow ran along the hull of the canoe trailing its ribbon of light; the floater of the outrigger was a long beaming shaft, and every drop that dripped from the paddles hit the water as a small sunburst. All around us were the reflections of real stars, and fish jumped in pools of luminosity or flashed near the surface, streaks of silver in midnight blue. And in all this world there was no sound but the drip from the paddles and the occasional splash of fish.

Lights of the labor quarters had to be out at nine o'clock, but there was no law against a coconut husk bonfire on the beach, and one was going when we got back to the wharf. The fire was not for heat nor cheer, but for the smoke (a little water sprinkled on the flaming husks) which keeps a few of the mosquitoes back. We could see in the circle of firelight the orange glint on naked skins of a dozen or more natives. We circled back through the palms to spy, and got within easy spearing distance of these reputedly magna-eared natives without being heard. The reason was that there was a musical recital in progress.

Off to one side by himself, the fire lighting the near side of his figure and the path of moonlight on the water sil-

houetting it, was a native. A native sitting in an almost indescribable anatomical tangle; just like those last three words, in fact. I'm not even sure I can make a sketch of it. It was the shape one gets into trying to reach his ears with his arms run under his knees. This was the musician. He had his arms under his knees but with both hands between his feet, and held between fingers and toes was a perfect thicket of bamboo tubes. And the man was actually making music in that posi-

tion, tapping the bamboos on rocks. Even as a feat of co-
ordination it was something Dalcroze would have applauded,
but beyond this, with the most delicate touch and the speed
of a Bach toccata, the bamboo pipes were tapping out the
most enchanting sounds in the world. Not music in the sense
of melody, but wind chimes in a Chinese garden, fairy bells
in the enchanted forest of "A Midsummer Night's Dream."

We stood enraptured—and scratching, of course—by our first
Melanesian music. Sounds there were a plenty in the islands, of
all kinds, from the hand drums for dances on which the native
could get the next thing to music by beating on the snakeskin
head, to big "bellos" that were whole logs, message drums,
pounded on the top slot with one or two clubs. And there
were pipes-of-Pan of four to ten bamboo tubes, one set of
which we owned and on which Margaret had nearly blown

out her front teeth trying to produce music. But even in the hands of a native the pipes did no more than whistle huskily in melancholy discontent. Six members of a Malaitan boat crew once performed an apathetic sing-sing dance for us (stirred into action by tobacco), the singing of which was a droning nasal repetition of four notes in two-part time. It might have hypnotized us in more than an hour but that was all we could stand, for even the dance steps were uninspired, being merely a bent-knee hop up the beach and down the beach and up the beach again. And when dancing and singing and drum beating stopped, the performance simply ended in the middle, when the dancers ran out of breath.

Until now we had heard no music; only sounds. And certainly no other such delightful music in the world could have been made on rocks with tree stems, and with the musician braided into such a position. It was a Stone Age masterpiece, and we hoped we could copy it in paint.

In case the reader has not already discovered it for himself, I am willing to admit that I am one of those picture painters who are forever swimming out beyond their depth on the tide of creative ecstasy and either drowning regularly in the soup of their own paint or just managing to come gasping and gagging to shore with some kind of picture but perfectly infuriated by the entire ocean. So with the "Tapu Player" (the fairy bell pipes being "tapu"). The musician could have been painted in daylight, but this was not the "picture." We must have platinum moonlight and footlights of a coconut husk bonfire, as well as everything in the model right up to the slightly moronic expression that even primitive musicians have when they are making their favorite racket. But a picture cannot be painted in the dark, nor even by lamplight, because in the orange glow colors appear different from what they are in daylight. So we had to invent the atmosphere of the enchanted forest in the storage room of the residence. To create night we tacked blankets over the windows, leaving only the doorway open for the daylight to fall on the canvas and palette. We got a very feeble moon by hanging a lantern, further dimmed by blue tissue paper, up in one corner near the ceiling. But this had to be abandoned when the blue tissue paper began to smoke. (I should have to get the moonlight on the model later by letting cold daylight fall on his back from the window.) The coconut husk bonfire was the simplest of all; simply three hurricane lanterns in a clump on the floor. Then the model, who was to sit in the corner, had to be shielded from the daylight coming through the doorway, so we tacked a mat from the edge of the easel across to the doorway, poking back a lower corner through which I was to see my masterpiece to paint it, after which we substituted the air in the room with "Buzzoff."

And now we were ready for the musician.

The Mastah had been obliged to go out on the plantation early because he could not stand watching his house burn down, and he promised to locate our musician and send him up. We still think he was playing a joke on us by sending a tapu player other than the original one. For, to our mutual shock, the musician turned out to be none other than Kesuo, the infuriated gorilla, whose canoe we had polluted. Our shock was that anyone so utterly savage-looking—and he was still looking savage—could make fairy bell music in the enchanted night. And the boy's horror was that he had been sent to the house with his instruments to pose for *us*.

He looked at first as if he would not do it. He sat himself down on the gravel below the veranda with his rocks and pipes and stared down the plantation, while the houseboys amused themselves by hooting at him, and we tried in every known arrangement of pidgin English words to get him up on the veranda. We tried luring him with tobacco, threatening him with profanity, and finally out-sitting him, hoping meantime that the Mastah would return unexpectedly and knock his block off.

I retired to the "studio" to sulk over the ocean of adversity while finishing the tacking of my canvas to the easel. And by and by, what should come to my ears but the fairy bell tinkling of wind chimes. Looking out I saw Margaret sitting chummily on the gravel with Kesuo; she had her shoes and socks off, the Malaitan's bamboo pipes between her toes, and was trying to reach, with her arms under her knees, the rock between her feet. She was tied up correctly enough, but the knot made her incapable of moving either hands or feet. Kesuo had eight bamboo tubes between his fingers and was tipping his hands from side to side, slowly tapping the tubes on a rock to show Margaret the motions necessary to produce the sounds.

I retired to the studio again to wait, to hold my head, and to reflect on the universal consanguinity of the musical temperament which knows no barriers either racial, social, or intellectual—against fraternizing with a fellow musician. Whenever Margaret was absent she could be soon found sucking the dysentery wogs off a native's bamboo flute or showing the yaw-infected owner how to play her ukulele. And both musicians, though they could not understand each other's language, would be wreathed in smiles of mutual appreciation. It's a secret society. And it's a little late to tell it, but Margaret's and my friendship was a result of something like that. It started with my guitar's need for some instrument to carry the melody, and the need of Margaret's ukulele for something to beat out the time in good round bass notes. So the fact that Margaret lured the reluctant gorilla into our den to continue the tapu lessons was no special musical achievement for her.

The Malaitaman still did not like the idea of association with both of us, and he liked even less the black coop with its mysterious arrangements of blankets and lanterns, but before he knew it he had been eased into the corner and was posing as a tapu player. And he was actually playing; he played on and on, inspired by Margaret's admiration at first, and then by his real enjoyment of the situation. And gradually his tough face relaxed and took on that expression of pleased idiocy which identifies the amateur musician the world over. That was the face I was waiting for.

By and by I found myself painting as if there were a hole in the canvas and I had to fill it in. I couldn't *see*. When I looked from my canvas, lighted by the glare from outside, through the hole to the night-lighted model, he was almost invisible, and when I looked back at my work it was invisible. My pupils could not keep up with the abrupt changes that were necessary if I was to see in both day and night light. The temperature in our twelve-foot-square studio, aided by the lanterns, had risen, I should guess, to somewhere around five hundred Fahrenheit. Both Margaret and I were lathered, not only from the heat but from the exercise of fighting off the anopheles mosquitoes which had come out thinking it was night. The air was dense with cigarette smoke and the carbon dioxide exhalations of three human beings. It was like the Black Hole of Calcutta, but the model, holding his unanatomical position, was as fresh as a rose. He was perspiring a little but in a genteel way, and beyond his quota of CO_2 he was giving off no poisonous fumes. For here was that freak which many Americans will have a hard time believing, a Negroid with no body odor. In fact, the gorilla may have been finding Americans pretty pungent. We are the carnivores of the human species, dreadfully scented according to the Orientals, while the Melanesians, like the Chinese, are almost vegetarians and so only mildly fragrant. Among these primitives themselves, anyway, a rare and unfortunate villager who has "B.O." is an object of derision and repugnance, like someone who has committed incest. We have this on the authority of an anthropologist, though there was also the antifaction, comprising the missus, which tried to refute our findings. However, we never anywhere in the islands smelled anything human even remotely like the fumes in a subway during the rush hour on a rainy summer night. And surely this airless hotbox in which we were closeted with the big healthy Kesuo was a test that must be respected.

The two Segi pug dogs, however, smelled *something*—or I painted truer than I knew. Anyway, the sittings for the "Tapu Player" ended in a round of odors, all bad.

The afternoon of the model's release we removed the picture from the easel, to make room for a new canvas, and tacked the "Tapu Player" on a drawing board which was set up against the wall on the floor—between the two doors already mentioned which caused the room to be used as a passage. The painting was wet, of course, and I had been doing some further patching up on it, sitting on the floor with my messed palette below the picture. We were out on the veranda for a rest when we heard the growls of doom in the studio. There were the two Segi dogs, who regularly used the passage, backing off and snarling at the painting of the tapu player. These two animals loathed natives even more than the usual white man's dog, and would not even take their food from the houseboys. (They had to be shut up in a room when any of the plantation boys was called to the veranda.) Yet here they had found a strange native on the floor *in* one of the rooms.

We were laughing, delighted to have portrayed a native so convincingly that even a dog thought he was alive—there was probably a lingering scent of Malaitan in the room which missed our noses but got to the dogs. And then Pepper, the heavier of the pugs, suddenly lunged. He went straight through the air catching the portrait on the leg, at which the

Melanesian hair, while others have the big stature and curly hair of the Polynesians. Most are like the spotted guinea pig with some features of both strains. The women are said to be handsome. We never met any. The head we got was that of a man who came to us in the night when we were staying at a mission station two hundred miles from the atoll.

We had been delivered to the station with the shipment of copra by our last host, to wait over three days for the call of the *Mataram*. The missionary here was an old-timer who had once, years before, been stationed at Ongtong Java. He just revived our regret that two hundred miles was as good as two thousand for a yachtless Expotition. For the rambling old mission residence was a treasure house of Ongtong Java material. (Missionaries are great collectors of heathen curios.) There were numerous tortoise-shell nose pendants, looking curiously like the Maori "tiki," a conventionalized design of the embryo which the Maoris wear for fertility. And which the Ongtong Java men wear as an emblem of fatherhood. There was the simplest hand loom in the world even with a half-finished mat of palm raffia on it, and a shuttle still threaded. For the Ongtong Java men are weavers, one industry which identifies the group with Polynesia, there being no cloth weaving in Melanesia. And all the rich lore that went with these coral island objects, and the big box of faded photographs which illustrated the stories with people and personalities. Everything, in fact, was here at the mission station except the live Ongtong Javanese, the one model who could make our collection eventually complete.

That first evening—it must have been around eight-thirty because I had already wakened myself two or three times with my own snore—the natives of the settlement were entertaining us by singing hymns, as they did all white visitors to the mission. But they were sitting down on the ground in the dark below the veranda so we had not even their faces to keep us awake. Then at long last one of the dozen house boys —missionaries are also great collectors of house servants—went across to the good church bell on a post at the steps to bong out to the settlement an all-to-bed-whether-you-want-to-or-not. I was revived with relief, but Margaret had already spirited out our wha-whas. She somehow had a fixed idea that when we were guests we should be less regretted afterwards if we made music than if we sat and snored in our host's face. And, of course, hosts were polite; the minute the missionary saw the instruments he changed his mind about the curfew, deciding to let his flock stay up awhile for this treat. I was just hoping anyway that Margaret would control her sense of humor and not lead off with something like the flea who could tell a he from she. Those ditties might not shock this minister. He had a good worldly sense of humor himself and was more likely to think they were funny, at which we would have to keep on being "entertaining." And according to my schedule it was now about two o'clock in the morning. We were now keeping planters' hours, trying to get in four or five hours' work before the heat of the day set in. It meant getting up before the sun, but also going to bed right after dinner, and anything which upset our schedule, like entertaining a missionary after eight-thirty, was done in an upright coma.

Margaret behaved, but she made just as bad a choice of songs. There is a gay Cossack marching tune which has at least thirty short verses, each one of which ends in a shrill taxi-calling whistle. I have seen even a dear old lady slap her knees with joy when Margaret suddenly left off looking like Saint Cecilia-at-the-organ and split the air with her famous whistle. The listening natives—now just a long row of high-lighted eyes and wads of black hair running along the edge of the veranda floor—went into an impious and unanimous howl of delight at the first shrill whistle, and from then on they would have nothing but the sing alla same pigeon. (Any bird is a "pigeon.") But it wasn't to save me from dying of fatigue that the curfew was finally rung; it was to keep Margaret from shredding her tongue, which she would likely do for any appreciative audience.

Again I saw relief with the bong of the bell. But even before the obedient lambs had disappeared in the dark my erstwhile friend, still inspired, was striking the opening chords of "Night and Day," then one of our favorite songs. But, praise the Lord, in the middle of it the missionary suddenly leaped to his feet as the sing of *Sail-o-o* came from the rear veranda. Now was my chance. If a launch were in the offing, the new visitor could carry on and I should never be missed. I saw myself in bed, lying flat, with my lead eyeballs comfortably crossed as they had been wanting to go ever since the abundant dinner. (Missionaries are also well fed.) Probably for the first time in history an Old-Timer (myself) did not stir to look for the launch light. What woke me up in a minute and had the effect of three days' sound sleep was the missionary saying he fancied it was the District Officer's launch. Then he was sure, because the light in mid-blue was passing landmarks at so many knots.

We did not even know this district officer. It was just what we had heard about him that accomplished this miracle of resurrection. For there was a story about him like an invented movie plot. People liked to tell it, and so do I, but it appears in the last of this chapter only because it might have something to do with the capture of our Ongtong Java head. There was plenty of other talk, too, about the D.O., for one thing, that almost every white woman in the group, married or not, had been in love with him at some time or other. And yet he had never married, though he was a "sentimental jackass." Curiosity alone might have kept me awake to meet this paradox, but also, the D.O., too, had once been stationed at Ong-tong Java, and that gave him the charm of a mortal returned from a heaven we should never look upon.

But when this personage walked up out of the dark into our lives our interest was not so ethnological as otherwise. For one thing the man had a haircut, and it was neither a convict clip nor a glamor bob. It was just an ordinary man's haircut, which is a wonderful sight to see in a land where the nearest barber is about a thousand miles distant. Further, he wore a jacket and a *necktie*. Occasionally, rarely, one sees this sort of affectation in "trippers" on the steamer, but never anything like this tie, which was striped—beautiful wide collegiate yellow and brown stripes. The haircut and the tie alone would account for half the gossip, but such an ensemble did not go with that movie plot about the native woman. Nor did the D.O.'s personality which, despite twenty years in the islands, was still as English as a rubber quid. That is to say, you couldn't get your teeth into it, and didn't want to very long.

Then it soon developed that the visitor would not talk about Ongtong Java anyway, but, on the other hand, was boresomely interested in music, at least in the sounds we made. The minute he saw the wha-whas he asked if we would play, and when we obliged with "Night and Day"—having left off there—he was as enthusiastic, in his waterproof way, as the primitives had been over the Cossack whistle. He said it was a jolly good tune—would we mind very much singing it again? And *again?* Then finally would we mind very much letting his launch crew hear it? These boys had worked up quite a nice little orchestra among them with a guitar, a few ukuleles, and gramophone records to help them with tunes. (Pronounced "chyunes.") I was just dozing off again, but this revived me. A Melanesian crew playing chords on ukuleles! Singing *melodies*. We would like very much to stay awake and hear these unusual Melanesians. "Well, you see," said the D.O., as we started down to the launch, "these boys aren't exactly Melanesians. That is, they're from Ongtong Java—"

The trouble—and it seemed to be a complete deadlock from the beginning—was that the D.O. was to be anchored in at the station only overnight. At daybreak he and his precious Ongtong Java models would be off down the coast attending to scheduled courts in the villages. And one did not ask a Crown Officer to neglect government work while we painted one of his police boys. Nor could a model be left behind, for the launch was not returning west on this side of the island. Also, we, ourselves, dared not miss the *Mataram* because we had run out of hosts in this part of the Group.

There seemed to be no solution. Here was an Ongtong Javanese in the hand, so to speak, and all sorts of Ongtong Java ornaments within reach, and yet no daylight in which to paint them.

The crew orchestra was not bad at all, but neither was it as good as a full-blood Polynesian outfit would have been. Its repertoire was entirely "modern" South Seas, melodies of hymn origin with straight harmonies, like our Hawaiian music. They had the same good Negroid voices, and tom-tom rhythm, but no sense whatever of our eight full-note scale. This was not so evident when they were singing "native" things because of the expected slurs and liaisons, but when they sang their one popular American song, we knew that they did not know. Off-key was just as satisfactory as on the note, and any kind of accompanying chord would do so long as they all played the same one and were in time. We had heard our "musical" Hawaiians making the same kind of noises.

The boys laughed and chattered a lot, we thought, for being in the presence of lordly Whites—perhaps the extra assurance of the Polynesian in them—and when we sang "Night and Day" they even applauded. The "mean" harmonies in it were the same kind they made for everything, and so probably sounded fine. But on the whole there was a curious "un-island" atmosphere on board this launch. Something like actual intimacy between the Master and boys. There is always a lot of nasty gossip about womanless white men and native boys in the islands, but this was not that kind of intimacy—which is never revealed if it even exists. For instance, when the D.O. addressed his "orchestra" leader he just used a normal conversation voice—not the roar of an infuriated bull—and he spoke almost straight, not pidgin, English. Also, to our astonishment, he dropped his hand on the back of the boy, who was sitting at his feet—something we never saw another white man do. It was this boy whom he asked especially to listen when we droned out "Night and Day" for the third, fourth and fifth time. And while we labored away at the song the D.O. lay back on the deck chair, eyes closed, a highball on his stomach, dreaming some dream, and rousing himself only to flatter us on to another repetition.

But in an hour I was deep in my own dream from which no ordinary snore could wake me. Margaret did the whole thing by herself. She first closed my jaws for me and then whispered that the D.O. wanted his boys to learn "Night and Day." If we would teach them the words, music and chords, he would stay over the following day and his boss boy would pose for us!

So the next morning the D.O. and his entire crew, even those not in the orchestra but would-be future critics, came up from the beach and in the shade of a coconut palm (there being only coconut palm shade in Ongtong Java) the boss boy posed, pretending to work on the mission hand loom. Margaret played "Night and Day" on her ukulele, we both

sang for harmony, the D.O. wrote down words, and all the
boys listened brightly while I painted the Poly-Melanesian.
And all over again and again and on and on through that
long day. We had one interruption when I shifted the whole
stage over to solid shade. Painting an Ongtong Javanese in
his own spiky frond shade was, with the attending insects,
too much like trying to paint a running zebra in a rainstorm.
We had to sacrifice some realism for visibility.

"Nightandday," said the crew off key, off time, and with
no such clear diction, "*youaretheone . . . only youbeneaththe-
starsandunderthesun . . . whetherneartomeorfaritsnomatter-
darlingwhereyouareIthinkofyou . . . nightandday-ay-ay.*"
"No," the D.O. would say painfully, "they haven't quite got
it." So we would go over it. But I found finally that I could
paint and devote my whole mind to it because the singing
of "Night and Day" had become automatic and unconscious,
like digestion. However, for ten nights and days afterwards
I sang the song in my mind all too consciously. And we still
have the scar.

Our part in this business was daffy enough, but how could
a sane man have listened to one song that long, or ever
afterwards want to hear the depressing wail again? How
could any responsible person like a Crown Officer neglect his
work to possess a song, even if it were the best melody in
the world? We think it was the sentiment of the words, for
the D.O. was a "sentimental jackass." But then the Reader
can judge for himself.

More than twenty years before, with four years of World
War behind him which he had gone into straight from school,
the D.O. had come out from England, as so many of the
white men who live in the islands had done. Likely he was
worn out with the war—most of the triumphant Englishmen
we met had an air of defeat as if they had not won. But long
bitter wars are like that. Anyway, he had applied for an

isolated post, alone, thinking perhaps, as so many of them did, that in a simplified world he could untangle a sane one for himself. They gave him Ongtong Java and the eastward district where he wouldn't have to see a civilized man in months except to report in periodically to Tulagi. But it was in Ongtong that he met the "girl." And so created for himself a tangled world from which, apparently, he was never to emerge.

We had already met one planter who had been married, and legally, to an Ongtong Java girl, so they must be more normally attractive to white men than the Solomon Island Maries. The D.O.'s Girl was said to have been the Polynesian "kind," with curly hair and a light skin. But another element must have entered the picture to cause the un-English reaction. This was the "parade of the virgins." It was in the parade the young patrol officer had first seen the Girl—so it was said. In Ongtong Java it is the custom, once a year, for the young marriageable girls, stripped entirely naked, to walk in procession with their clan chaperons around the village clearing. Betrothals are arranged in infancy, but the girl appearing in the procession is a sign to her fiancé that she is ready for marriage. We saw scores of photographs of the parades, and admittedly the Ongtong Java virgin did not look much like her Melanesian cousin. The dark bodies shone with the coconut oil with which they dressed themselves for this important debut, their legs were long and straight, with neither the "beef-to-the-heel" chunkiness of the Polynesian leg, nor yet the bony stringiness of the Marie's. They were rounded about the thigh, the torsos were long and elegant with smooth shoulders and high breasts. One did not look at the faces even in the photographs. Chances are the young patrol officer didn't either even in the flesh, nor care much that the girl he saw in the procession was already "taken."

In any case, when he left the Group he persuaded the

Girl to go with him on the launch. And accompanying him, she certainly proved that she cared, "as much as a native can care." For one thing she had offended the Spirits in breaking her betrothal contract and, from the material point of view, all the exchange of betrothal gifts would have to be returned, which would make the relatives hopping mad at her. However, the D.O. was "decent"; he meant to marry the Girl when they got to Tulagi.

This is just where his friends disagreed with him; he was *too* decent. It wasn't necessary to marry a native girl. It would ruin his career in the service; there was no chance of advancement for a man with a native wife unless he abandoned her. So why marry one? So while some of the well-meaning friends kept the D.O. "otherwise engaged"—which is to say, drunk—others whisked the Girl back to Ongtong Java where they got her properly married to her intended native husband. And by a white parson, too, just in case the D.O. held native marriages as lightly as he did betrothals.

That should have ended the business, with finality. Only it didn't. The D.O. was transferred to his present patrol "up west," far as possible from carrying out any rash ideas, but while there he learned that the Girl had given birth to a half-caste baby. His son. He sent for the child immediately (which established his reputation as a "sentimental jackass") and for the next seven years kept him constantly with him, on the launch when he was on patrol, and even in his room at the station. The native wife of one of his boys, an Ongtong Javanese, took care of the boy until he was sent down to Australia to school.

Meantime the Girl's husband died. And in Ongtong Java a widow spends anywhere from five years to life at the grave of her husband. This is not just visits, but living at the grave, and dressed in "sackcloth and ashes," literally old mats and with soot smeared on any exposed skin. These natives

are the only group in Melanesia who erect gravestones or
have a proper graveyard. The stones are hewn from coral
rock and, as the largest island of the atoll is less than a
square mile in area, the graveyard is a crowded place, a tree-
less forest of tall bleached-white stones set close together.
Here down the narrow avenues the exiled widows erect little
individual awnings of mats, and in the shade of them they
sit day after day, year in and year out, "mourning"—whether
the one buried beneath the stone was loved or not. One
wonders what the widowed Girl thought, smoothing the sand
around her those years of days. Knowing she would still be
doing this decades hence while "he" lived, and not even so
very far away.

One wonders, too, why the D.O. never went back for
the Girl, if he was so faithful as to have never married anyone else. And what became of the son. To make this a
good movie ending, but a bad one for us, we could say that
our Ongtong Java model, the boy for whom the D.O. showed
such unusual affection, was his son. But we made certain that
we had painted a full-blood Ongtong Javanese. Our model
was the brother of the Girl—"night and day."

27

Nowhere else in Melanesia, nor, for that matter, even among the notorious headhunters of Papua, does the head cult reach the degree of fanaticism with which it is practiced on Bougainville in the western Solomon Islands. Most head-hunters are content simply to lop off the heads of enemies; the westerners go one better and include friends; but the black Bougainese of the far west actually tinker with the heads of their own young. They don't go so far as to cut them off, but they remodel them to look as unlike human heads as possible without killing the subject. The ideal is a skull shaped like an upended bullet or watermelon, and it is not surprising that it is only the boy children who are guided toward the ideal. Shortly after birth the soft skull of an infant is securely bound with a stout bark fiber, and the wrappings are tightened periodically to press the skull into an elongated shape. The bindings are not removed per-manently until the bone is no longer malleable; sometimes parents are not satisfied with what they have done with their child's head until he is three or four years old.

By the time the bindings are removed the boy has a head like a gourd which will remain like that so long as he lives. Immediately upon their removal, the boy begins preparing his head for entrance into the men's secret society. He lets his hair grow long, never cutting it, and when he reaches adoles-cence he is given a tall hat, shaped like a Chinese lantern, into which he tucks his long wool, the hair holding it on. The hats are worn during the whole six months' period of the

initiation ceremonies, after which according to some authorities, they are removed and burned. The finished young man
then emerges from the cocoon, as it were, with his hair shorn
and his beautiful melon-shaped head exposed to the girl he
will marry.

Reading that description is what now guided the Expotition
in the direction of Bougainville. For nothing in the world
could better illustrate the predominating idiosyncrasy of these
black westerners than a gourd-headed model. And all we had
to do now was go to Bougainville, trap some bullet-headed
models, and paint. That was all: just get to Bougainville.

The first thing that confused us was that Bougainville,
although one of the Solomon Islands—and actually within
sight of Faisi, the last port of call of the Solomon Islands
steamer run—is not a *British* Solomon Island. It lies across the
border in the Territory of New Guinea. That makes it just
about as accessible from Faisi as if it were one of the Philippines. To go to the Territory from the British Solomon Islands
one is expected to return to Sydney on the *Mataram*, take
another ship up to Rabaul, the seat of government of the
Territory, and then a headhunting Expotition might continue on the steamer as far as Kieta on the east coast of
Bougainville. Kieta is just about a hundred miles north of
Faisi! The lower tip of Bougainville is even nearer to the
last of the British Solomon Islands across from Shortland
Island. Here it is only *four miles*. That might easily have been
done in a canoe or with water wings, except that there was
no place on the southern coast of Bougainville for us to stay
if we got there. The nearest white settlement was still Kieta.

We could hire a launch at Faisi if anyone there was fortunate enough to have a reserve of gasoline for a two-hundred-
mile trip; or we could wait at Faisi until some launch had
business in the Territory, which, we were warned, happens
about once every blue moon. Or we could retreat. And that

would be homeward (without our Indonesian canvases), for we could never hope to earn enough money in Sydney to get us back up to the islands again.

When we arrived at Faisi on the *Mataram* we were not quite so anxious about our future as before we had boarded the steamer. The blessed Voy had arranged for us to stay with a resident of the settlement, so that we had another six weeks before we had to move in any direction. And anything can happen in six weeks. Anything can happen in ten minutes. And it took us just that long after the anchors were down to discover that Faisi was under quarantine—*measles!*

What we were thinking of the *Ark of God* then is unprintable.

Islanders who had waited three years for a holiday were standing below in their launches bawling up at us, not allowed to come aboard. Our intended hostess among them, alternately begged us to come ashore and then warned us to stay on board. If we went ashore we were quarantined for no one knew how long, and that launch which came in the blue of the moon might come and go and we should not be allowed to leave on her. And we had had too much of measles quarantines to think that we could pass the time working while one was in effect.

So we stayed on board, reflecting, however, on the one satisfaction there was to be had in returning to Sydney, which was to take the head of a wharf striker with an ax. If there had been enough gasoline in Faisi to get to Kieta and back—which there was not, because the first thing we did was to ask—we might have transferred straight from the *Mataram* to a launch, and thus have got around the quarantine by not landing. If only we hadn't left our outrigger behind!

All this time the copra loading was going on as usual, copra loaders apparently not being measles carriers. The loaders yipped and the cranes clanked, the engine roared, and the sun rose high. These signs marked the horrible passing of time, to the moment when the boys would scream and the anchor chains rumble up. Then the Expotition would retreat to its stateroom and—probably bawl. And all this time we could *see* the Territory of New Guinea, blue slips like flower petals dancing on the glaring water a few miles to the north.

During that last tense hour we changed our minds like the minute hand of a clock. The steamer was calling at Rendova again, our last stopping place, and we decided to return there and wait—for something; for the quarantine to be lifted at Faisi, likely. Then we remembered how this host would have drowned us if the *Mataram* had not brought him relief when it did, and we thought it better to face a measles quarantine, or even return to Tulagi and wait in the hotel. We seemed willing to face any direction but that of actual retreat.

Then we heard the blood-curdling scream of the loading boys.

At that minute we decided to stay at Faisi and went up to the Voy's stateroom to say good-bye. The Voy said nothing, just glowered as usual, and after examining us for a minute he took out the bottles and began mixing us our second Mataram Special. He took a long time at it and when he finally handed us our glasses he had one too. It was the first time we had ever seen him with a drink on board. He must have had a premonition. "To the headhunters!" he said simply and his eyes were very gentle. We gulped: and then choked, for at that minute there was a shout over the water and cries of *Sail-o* on board. A launch, flying the insignia of the Territory of New Guinea, was tearing up to the steamer!

Nothing like this had happened even in a blue moon before. A government official of Rabaul had some urgent business in the South which could not wait for the regular Rabaul steamer, and he had hired the launch to bring him down—almost four hundred miles—to catch the *Mataram*. And the boat was returning to Rabaul after it cleared at *Kieta!*

Then it *was* good-bye. It was not until we and our belongings were on the *Nakapo* that we realized it; realized what good-bye to the Voy meant. This was a turning point in the progress of the Expotition. From now on we were on our own, for our hosts—our harbors—we should have to dig up ourselves and on our face value, since there would be no advance notices of our charms which had made hosts welcome us sight unseen in the Voy's domain. And there would be no holiday every six weeks when we came home to the *Mataram* and to our own stateroom with that dear, glowering, familiar face heckling us across the dinner table.

"To the Scots," we called back to the bridge as the *Nakapo* got under way. "May we always meet them on the high seas." We threw him handfuls of blessings and the Voy took them, standing with his glass raised and the sun making a strong highlight on his pink bald head. He stood that way until the *Mataram*, anchors aweigh, slowly turned westward and started down to Sydney. Without the Expotition, praise be!

28

The usual charge for transportation anywhere in the islands is by the day; five dollars a person whether the vessel is the Sydney steamer or a put-put launch. And there is no guarantee of getting you there. No matter how long the trip takes, come fair weather or foul, whether the engine lisps or the skipper would rather go on a reef than use his anchor or sail, the passenger can only set his teeth and keep on paying a pound a day until some sweet providence sees him in his home port. This custom accounts for much of what happened to us on the *Nakapo*—and some of our grief was probably due to the fact that we were paying ten dollars a day for it.

Another element that may have created the wrong vibrations was the nationality of the Skipper. He was German. That did not bother *us;* we had matured during those years of sweetness and light following the First World War when the League of Nations was telling us that all men are equal and the Germans really just as nice as anyone else. But as the reader knows, the New Guinea islands belonged to Germany before that war. When the Australians took over, they expropriated the property of German residents, and were generally just about as tough as the Germans themselves would have been had the circumstances been reversed. All Germans who had actively resisted the invasion were sent to concentration camps in Australia and none of these were allowed to return to the islands after the war. To diverge, we met one of these exiled Germans in Java and he told us with a great deal of smug amusement how, when the Australians began moving in, he and other Germans retreated to the mountains where, according to prearranged plans, they erected radio-sending stations with which they broadcast the movements and strength of the enemy to their own ships, like the *Sea Wolf*, then cruising New Guinea waters. The Australians could intercept the messages but it took them a long time to locate the sending stations in the unfamiliar and mountainous bush.

As for the plantations of the German nationals, these were "liquidated." A board tried to decide upon their value, and when these efforts failed the tracts were offered at auction. The proceeds "were applied in payments of amounts due in respect to claims of Nationals of the Allied and Associated Powers." Any balance over this amount, should there be one, was to be divided between these Powers on Germany's reparations debts. Nothing went to the former owners, though they could buy back their own property at the auction. (This took place in 1920-21.)

Many Britishers we had met, and especially the Australians, were rather disinclined to give the United States credit for having swung the First World War the way it went. The Germans, however, had not forgotten our part in it, and this German Skipper, who had once been comfortably off as owner of a large rubber plantation, was now reduced to a single launch on which he traded and recruited, picking up whatever hauling jobs he could. As we were Americans, he probably hated our very stuffing. At least it had taken the Voy to persuade him to take us on as passengers, and in the end he did so, probably because he saw an opportunity for a little private reprisal. Anyway that was how it looked in conclusion.

But our remarkable friendship began with all sweetness on our side. We expected nothing in the *Nakapo*. It was a sixty-five-foot schooner-rigged launch with the lines of a tug and the personal odor of old herring and bilge. There were two hatches; the large one in the fore part was for cargo, while the aft one was tiny with a superstructure and was meant for a cabin. At the moment it was filled almost to deck level with sacks of copra, so our quarters were two camp stretchers set up on each side of a table that already almost filled the space on the aft deck. To pass down the length of the table you folded up a cot to get by or crawled down the cot or along the table. Then, in about a foot of space between the table and cabin structure, was the wheel. So the wheel boy sat on the table. That was all right; the wheel boy was a masterpiece.

When we turned in that first night—and to turn in all we had to do was lie down, which illustrates the advantage of wearing the same pajamas night and day—the wheel boy was sitting on the table with his feet up on it, one prehensile-toed foot guiding the wheel, while he used his hands to scratch, and then light a long-stemmed clay pipe. The orange flare lit up a brand-new Melanesian profile. This was a New Britain boy with blue totem "lozenges" on his broad jaws and a thick hunched look to his shoulders and neck. Suddenly, in the brief picture existing only by the flare of the match, all our grief at parting with the beloved Voy, and the unconfessed fear we felt at leaving the cozy Solomon Islands vanished. We recaptured that instant the excited anticipation of travelers just setting out on their voyage. The rising moon was to starboard when at last the steady sing of the engine lulled me to sleep—against my will; it was so delicious thinking about being on this launch going to Kieta.

The next minute it was dawn. The wheel boy was still sitting above my head, still scratching and steering with his foot, but something was wrong. The sun was on my left, to port! I rose—the land, Bougainville, was to starboard. We should have been going north and the sun and land on the opposite sides. "Boy!" Only then the wheel boy turned his head. "Boy, launich go 'long Kieta?" I expected him to say "Yasmissus," but he said "No." We were going along some place that sounded like Boom—wherever that was. Anyway it was *south!* Margaret was still asleep, the sun shining on her face and her pajama jacket up under her arms; but she was safe. Even the cook boy when he came aft with his stacks of agate pie pans, tin cups, and cutlery for the breakfast table, did not glance in her direction. Her shape was no novelty. I climbed over to her side when he began bowling things down the table, thinking he might want to fold up the cot so that he could reach. But he preferred to set the table his way, like a game of "croquinole."

Finally breakfast came up: some rather moldy bread, strong tinned fish, strong black tea, strong tinned milk, strong tinned butter. Not bad, but not good enough to eat either. (We wondered if the government man from Rabaul had eaten it.) The Skipper did not show up, which made us think, not knowing him, that he was a gentleman of sensibilities. Presently a boy brought us a pail of hot water and one of cold, and as there was no private place to which we could retire for the ablutions we performed them on the open deck in full sight of the wheel boy's back, though hidden from the forepart of the vessel by the cabin. The toilet proper was a round hole in the wide shelf of the taffrail, in front of which a blanket was hung from the awning roof. Next to the Segi temple it had the pleasantest vista of any such place in the South Seas—even though like a French *pissoir* it gave the occupant the illusion of privacy while declaring to the world, by the feet extending below the blanket, that it was engaged.

But *why* were we going south?

We did not find out until the launch had slowly pulled in toward shore, cut down, and dropped anchor. On shore there was not a thing to be seen except bush. Nevertheless a large dinghy put over the side, several natives got down into it, followed by the Skipper dressed up to go out with a sun helmet on. He did not even say "Good morning" when we spurted up to the rope ladder. But we asked him right out what was up.

He was going on a *recruiting* trip!

Recruits for the New Guinea gold fields were then bringing a hundred dollars a head in Rabaul, they were hard to get because the news had got around the islands that carriers to the fields died of cold and exhaustion in the high mountains. No doubt the Skipper was being only an opportunist in going recruiting when he found himself at the remote end of the Territory; but also he could profit by the venture even if he did not get recruits, because we were paying him ten dollars a day while he found out if men were available.

But that was not what was making us savage; it was the low fellow's attempt to slip off without us. Why, in this remote spot we might find the very models for which we had fought and bled to get to New Guinea. Boom sounded just like a place of tortured babies and gargoyle-headed primitives. "Wait!" we demanded. "No," said the Skipper firmly, and he made as if to shove off, "this trip is too rough going for laties." "We're not ladies. Margaret—" I pleaded and tore aft for our gear. I don't know what I expected Margaret to do with the Skipper, but she had always done something with persons who said "No."

What to take! It was like taking things out of a burning house. Colors, anyway, in case we found our models; some new sticks of pigment that could be used as watercolors or crayon, a Christmas present from the Voy (he had brought the paints, too); the camera (and films from the Voy). I also threw into the dilly bag the stack of sliced bread from the breakfast table. The dinghy had not yet pushed off, so I took time to grab the toothbrushes and box of quinine. How long was a recruiting trip? There were boaty sounds coming from the side. "Hurry!" called Margaret. I was plowing down through the duffle bag for socks—we had on only our tennis shoes—then let it go.

When I got to the foredeck Margaret was down in the dinghy holding onto the ladder. The Skipper was looking like a Prussian general in the movies. "We won't hold you up," I panted cheerfully—wiping off the moisture on my forehead to see if it were blood. "No?" said the general. "You haf done that ten minutes already." He did not exaggerate and there was an accusing silence while we were rowed in to shore. No doubt our added weight made the progress slower; and it certainly crowded the boat. Were we going far, we asked apologetically. The answer was "Yes"; and it was all uphill. But there was no white man's gear in the boat (though all the boys carried dilly bags as usual) so we couldn't be staying long. Perhaps we were going far, and back, in a single day. Not much time for drawing—and how I loathed walking!

We got our legs wet right away when we landed because no one ladled us across the surf in our usual luxury; and bare feet in wet tennis shoes were a good start for an uphill tramp. But the shoes would have been wet in half an hour anyway. The Skipper set off at a pace guaranteed to leave "laties" behind on the coast, or if they turned out not to be ladies, so to punish them they would never again tag a German recruiter. We began to think he had some other reason than distaste for our company for not wanting us along. *Squunch-squunch-squunch* in the wet tennis shoes; he was probably a blackbirder. Why otherwise so many boys with him unless it was to shanghai recruits?

Soon we were at the tail end of the line and panting like exhaust pipes just to keep the last boy in sight. And so far it was still fairly level terrain. But this was no bush path like the one that had introduced me to malaria. It went through the forest but had been cleared wide enough to let the sun in, so that it was hedged on both sides with jungle wall. The surface was dry and smooth (though I was wishing regularly every ten yards that something would crop out in it to break the Skipper's leg) and the way quite easy to follow when the last boy had shimmered out of sight. But when the party got out of hearing we ran, for it would be just like this Skipper to turn off in the bush somewhere and leave us to walk straight through Bougainville from one end to the other still thinking we were on a recruiting trip. Also, it was a lonesome bit of bush when the natives got out of sight. Neither man nor beast nor bird crossed our path, though we could hear, back in the forest, all the moans and snorts and grunts and screams of those bush spirits which ever existed solely as sounds.

Gradually the path began to climb and then life became a harrowing span. While our mouths filled with dry suds, streams of sweat poured down into our shoes. We waded through opaque yellow streams with our hearts pumping, thinking of the lurking alligators—which had missed the Skipper. And still we tore on. Such a trip at a human pace would have been no hardship. It would have been a joy and an education to study the wonders of the bush we passed. But speeding along on heat-swollen feet with growing blisters! Of course, we could have turned back, but as descendants of the Puritans we thought the more we suffered the greater would be our certainty of reward; anyone at the end of such a trip could not help having a distorted head—even if it turned out to be only our own.

One might almost insert here the entire score of "Bolero" to indicate the passing of hours and miles, repetitious but with mounting acuteness.

The climax, indeed, was not unlike that of "Bolero." It came with a crescendo of drum beating. We were well behind our party then, toddling along autokinetically, and the roll of the drum nearly gave us the vapors. It came from up ahead and was a very different sound from the bello beating heard from the comfortable security of a plantation veranda. This was a bello in the cavernous forest rolling out a dash-dot message of some sort. Drum codes are in sentence form, not word or phrase, and this bello was so vehement that it sounded as if all hell had broken loose somewhere ahead. Three days later (after we had met a victim of Bougainese hospitality), if we had heard this sound under the same circumstances, we would have skinned for the coast without waiting to find out whether it was butchery or just a weather report. And even now while our legs pushed forward our minds skinned back. The drumming had stopped as unreassuringly as it had begun and we were now surrounded by its vibrating absence. Something hidden scuttled away from the side of the path and both of us did a jitterbug figure. But the laugh freshened the air, and presently our legs had run us into a wide clearing in the path.

And here was our party, very mortal, though the huffing and puffing of the boys suggested that the Skipper had tried to kill them off in the same way he had us. But there were no other natives, no strangers. The drumming had come from a house bello which stood in the middle of the clearing, and one of our boys was still standing before a huge drum with the clubs in his hands. Even as we noticed him he began beating out his message again, thundering bush talk-talk to the village somewhere beyond, announcing the arrival of a recruiter. There was no answering sound from the forest, so we sat down with the others, waiting to be received.

We waited a long time.

Margaret and I stretched out in the shade of the house bello and gratefully pushed down chunks of dry bread to fill the vacuum in our middles, hoping meantime that the Skipper was dying of thirst too. He had brought no water even for himself. There were ten great log drums in the house bello as big around as canoes and, like them, burnt and adzed out hollow with a slot on top. The shelter above was merely a thatched roof with open sides, but all up the supports and along the rafters underneath were dozens of white pig skulls, some of them with enormous tuskers. The clearing outside was circular in shape and surrounded by high bush wall, and off to one side was a heap of blackened rocks, all of which suggested that the area was a sing-sing ground. Perhaps it was here the natives performed their mysterious initiation rites of the secret societies. One could imagine the clearing at night; a great fire lighting the surrounding bush wall; the gleaming rows of pig skulls, all ten huge drums booming out through the black forest, old sorcerers with gourd-shaped heads in grotesque masks whooping around possessed by their black-

magic spirits; and off to one side, huddled in the dark like the slaves in the ballet of Scheherazade, the terrified novitiates in their tall Chinese lantern hats.

And just at this climax of my imaginings, out of the bush path on the opposite side of the clearing, rode a colored gentleman on a *bicycle!*

It was not even an old bicycle such as a colored gentleman might own; it was streamlined and gleaming in the sun with chromium plating, and it even had a headlight, not, to be sure, lit at the moment—but why *not!* The tires were super-balloon and hypertread; and he who rode aloft matched the vehicle in splendor. We were so dazzled that we did not note until afterward that the native had a normal head, as unde-formed as any Melanesian head. For on top of this one was a towering white Florodora pompadour, on the crest of which balanced an equally monumental uniform cap. The cap pro-claimed the vision to be a village luluai, but below the cap he was a regal Bougainese chief. A six-inch, pencil-thin nose-bone streaked across his black face, great shell circles dis-tended the lobes of his ears, and over his pompous chest hung a necklace of the biggest dog teeth we had yet seen.[1] But from the neck on down the ensemble was sheer whimsy. The bicyclist wore a white sleeveless singlet (man's under-shirt), and though the badge on the cap above proclaimed British officialdom, on the nickel buckle of the wide leather belt below was stamped, plain as day, *Gott mit uns.* And the red lap-lap which the belt held up reached a new high for loin-covering in Melanesia. In the Fiji Islands the calico wrap-around skirt starts just under the armpits, like a Britisher's

[1] The size of these teeth was so unusually large that they could hardly have come from the little yellow native dogs, and must have been those of white men's breeds. During a rabies scare in Sydney a few years ago hundreds of dogs were killed and some enterprising white man exported the teeth to the islands for native trade. It is quite possible this necklace was made up of some of these Sydney teeth.

trousers, and extends below the calves: the lap-laps of the Malaitans and eastern Melanesians are cinched on below their bellies and just reach the knees. But our luluai's petticoat merely covered his buttocks—when he was standing up.

And he was now standing up, his magnificent bicycle run into the shade of the house bello as tenderly as if it were a canoe. Then, almost immediately, the luluai was sitting down, and he sat-sat-sat-sat. One of our boys was acting as interpreter for the Skipper, tobacco was passed over to the headman, and then conversation began. Conversation waxed, wavered, and lapsed into long silences while we waited with growing anxiety. During all this time and precious daylight we could have been producing masterpieces of gourd-headed natives had we been in the village. But perhaps this was all, all there was to recruiting. Perhaps we were not going to a village!

And with that harrowing thought to give me nightmares, I went to sleep.

It was three o'clock in the afternoon before Margaret shook me. The luluai and the Skipper were now on their feet, moving off toward the bush path on the opposite side of the clearing. The village! We had heard that the Germans flogged natives who did not get off the path in passing the overlords, but that was thirty years ago. Our German Skipper's boys were either too young to remember or only too happy to forget—or perhaps the custom never applied to white women at any time. When the line started up the bush trail (which was now a tunnel through the forest), the Expotition brought up the rear like a couple of squaws.

The village was about half a mile beyond the bello reception clearing, and when we saw it we understood better why there was a reception "hall." No one could enter this village without being announced. It was stockaded by a ten-foot

fence of logs with pointed tops, just like our old blockaded
forts of the Indian days. And the sight of it fully atoned for
the sin of the chromium-plated bicycle. It gave us an amateur
ethnologist's thrill, for it vindicated our whole New Zealand
chapter. In New Zealand we had painted the Maoris as a
branch of the Melanesian family, but much against the protests of intelligent Maoris who claim that the race has no
Negroid Melanesian blood. Yet even the Maoris' own legends
give a history of their Polynesian ancestors encountering
black woolly-haired inhabitants (presumably Melanesians)
when the first Rorotongans arrived in New Zealand. The
Polynesians never stockaded their villages in Polynesia, but
the Maoris, who were their descendants, did. (We painted
Maoris in a stockaded village.) And they, apparently, had
adopted the custom from the "pu-hu-ru-hu-ru," the "black
hairy" men who were the Melanesian first settlers. The adop-
tion by one race of the customs of another does not necessarily imply blood relationship, but to deny that there is any
is splitting hairs when customs are shared. We felt, seeing this
fenced-in settlement before us, that we had traced the Maoris'
Negroid skeleton to its closet. And that we, therefore, had
been justified in including the Maoris in our Melanesian picture collection.

The fence also jumped us at another conclusion, which was
that the neighbors hereabouts were not nearly so tamed as the
bicycle suggested. It further implied that the village was still
enough on its own to need a stockade as protection. Probably
the settlement had come under government control only recently, which would also explain the luluai's paradoxical
ensemble. And all these speculations revived our hopes of
what the village might reveal for headhunters.

But by the time we entered the gateway the clearing was
deserted by women and children. The warning of the bello
would have accomplished that hours ago. There were not

even any dogs, but a dozen or so men—none with gourd-shaped heads—were present and joined the Skipper, his boys, and the luluai in what seemed to be a spitting contest, sitting in the shade of a palm (the nuts of which finally provided us with a drink of liquid). The natives were sucking betel nut and spitting scarlet, whose brilliance the *Nakapo* outfit tried to excel by sheer volume (they not being allowed betel nut). The area around the recruiting confab looked exactly like the sidewalk in front of any cigar store in any little town below the Mason-Dixon line. And the conversation was just about as vivacious. We wandered off.

The one full-length sentence the Skipper had honored us with in the last eight hours was a warning not to get nosy in this village. Any violation of a taboo would ruin his business. But in the end it was our quite unintentional nosiness which indirectly promoted it—as far as his business went.

At first we wandered about, innocently trying to look up into the closed houses through the cracks in the floors—for the huts were on piles like the plantation houses. We were at the far end of the village taking a photograph of an architectural detail (which happened to be an ingenious vine-rope hinge of a door) when that door opened—ever so little; just about an inch and a half. A glittering eye looked out of the blackness at about head height. So it was an adult—but male or female? We took a chance. Calmly we lifted up our pajama shirts and exhibited proof of our right to female society.

There was a long wait; then the crack of the door slowly widened and was finally jerked back and a woman pushed out. Another woman was behind her, and another, and two more. Three of them were in various stages of pregnancy and four held young babies—not one of which was being tortured as we should have liked to see it, with a skull binding. But the women were delightful—parts of them. They were plum-colored, had big black pompadours, long bones in the septum of their noses, and were much better fed than the eastern Maries. But their torsos were scaly with buckwa. Nevertheless they were delighted with us as we were with them. At first they said nothing and just stood in a row with their mouths hanging open and their stomachs sticking out, looking like children who are seeing their first Christmas tree. Even the infants did not scream at us. Their general good nature led us to believe that we were the first white women these Maries had ever seen. But there was nothing we could paint of that. We photographed it instead, and it was at this point the luluai came sprinting up. He couldn't speak any pidgin English that we could understand, but he *loved* cameras and he did not have to say it. He must have heard the beautiful click of the shutter from the other end of the village, and when he saw that we were taking pictures of his wives— all five women with young were his—he had left the recruiting business to be in on it. He posed his wives in a stiff row with their heads up to the sun and their hands placed rigidly on the hips, and then he stood between them and waited— ecstatically.

We exposed a whole film to the luluai, with wives, with babies, with bicycle, with house, and without these things, but always with the uniform cap. Then we thought we had done the subject justice. But the Skipper was suddenly at our side smiling like Little Red Riding-hood's Wolf; asking us to keep on taking photographs of the luluai. For we had accomplished in half an hour with the camera what the Skipper had not been able to do in several hours.

The whole business of recruiting is nothing more complex than making a friend of the chief or luluai of the village, who then persuades village men to join the recruiter. In the old days the charming was done with white men's magic (entertainment, reduced to its real category), but now gifts of trade goods—knives, axes, calico, and tobacco—are the mode. The maximum value of a gift to a headman is set by law, because chiefs bribed beyond resistance could be persuaded to turn over to the recruiter men who were not willing to be recruited. Actually a headman or chief has no power to order a villager to do anything (except those things required by the guv'men); but if he is the village sorcerer as well as chief, as often happens, he can be very persuasive. But he can

be innocently persuasive, too, in the cause of the recruiter, if he likes the man. If he does not, that gentleman may as well retreat because the luluai has full power to prohibit men joining a recruiter. The law requires that a certain number of men remain in the village to carry on, and the luluai can use this excuse.

In this village it happened that the chief's weakness was having a camera pointed at him; and we had the camera. There were no longer any films in it but we continued to aim and click at the ecstatic primitive until dusk, when the

Skipper took over. This was a matter of sitting down again to continue the spitting contest, which promised to go on all night. There was no hope now of meeting a gourd-headed native in this village. We had inquired early where the natives bound their babies' heads and got a northeasterly wave of the hand which might have included the United States. Then the women came in from the gardens with normal heads, bringing babies with normal heads. Men, also average, entered the stockade carrying dead pigeons and cuscus, accompanied by the perennially starving dogs which bawled down our last desire to stay and see the finale of the signing-on. Margaret and I, unbelievably weary, started back for the coast alone so that we could go at our own pace without danger of being left behind.

If there is anything less delightful than walking up mountains on blisters, it is having a rest and then walking down on the same blisters. Before the moon rose the way seemed endless. Margaret walked ahead so that by her falling into things I should know what to avoid, and she held the walking stick up before her face to keep from being hung on a vine noose. It was a long time before the moon rose enough to light the path, and by then I was beyond caring or needing light. In the darkness I had kept my eyes glued on Margaret's dimly lit heels, walking like the hind end of a horse in her footsteps. And I was still hypnotized, so that when she stopped suddenly I rammed into her. My first thought was that she had stepped on a snake, the one I had been expecting for so long. The snakes always came out after dark and lay on the paths that had been warmed by the sun, and before the moon came up Margaret had several times leaped back from a snake of writhing tree roots growing across the path. But this time she did not move on, and when I saw what she did I stopped pushing her. It was two native men coming up the path toward us.

My first reaction was embarrassingly feminine; I was panicky. There was nothing to be afraid of (I thought afterward), but the scene was a little weird and the sudden appearance of human beings in it when we seemed hundreds of miles from any living thing was—a surprise. For the path was a tall narrow canyon in the moonlight, one side pitch-black in the shadow, and the other glistening with those fantastic forms of the bush wall. Some spirit with the dolorous voice of Poe's Raven was going "*cou-cou— cou-cou*." And the figures coming toward us with their backs to the moon were throwing grotesque long-legged shadows before them, one of them a thin little goblin with a monster head.

But these were mortal natives, who evidently thought we were mastahs, for as we neared them they stepped off to the side of the path to let us pass. We did not pass; we stood glued in our tracks staring at the goblin with the monster "head." It was a Chinese lantern hat!

The next twenty minutes or so were as interesting and exciting as any we had had so far on this long headhunt. By offering the natives cigarettes we got them turned around so that the moonlight fell on their faces, and for a better look we lit up for them with the cigarette lighter. The first surprise was that the wearer of the hat was not a youth of club initiation age, but an old, old man. He looked nearly blind.

His eyeballs were popped out of their sockets but the lids were squinted to slits as if the eyes could not stand even the dim light of the cigarette lighter. But the head was a "gourd," and of a truly remarkable height. Either the man was bald or his forehair had been shaved back, because the distance of the almost flat area from the eyebrows to the band of the hat must have been five or six inches. And this impression of extreme height was even modified by a brow band running across the middle of the forehead which had on it three enormous white cowrie shells.

To our dismay the men could speak no pidgin English; but like all unsophisticated natives they were mannerly and did not pass on about their business while we continued to stand. We had to hold them until we could think of some way of getting this head on canvas. We finally squatted down on our haunches the way natives do when they meet and decide to have a smoke and chat, and to our delight the men promptly followed suit. And there we had them if only for a few minutes.

It was a cozy little party squatting there in the moonlit bush of Lower Bougainville, a situation that is probably not often duplicated. If these natives knew we were white women and not men, there was nothing in their attitude that showed they thought anything of it. They conversed in their language and we in ours, all of us nodding, waving our hands, and laughing at ourselves for going on talking when we could not be understood. But try as we might we could not put across in sign language that we wanted them to follow us down to the coast.

It looked like a stalemate until we got to our second round of cigarettes. Village natives always prefer stick to cigarette tobacco and these men took their second cigarettes and lit up from us laughing giddily the way primitives always do when they are being merely polite. The one without the hat did not want to light up and for a minute Margaret held the cigarette lighter in front of him waiting. And it was in its glow we saw the "thing" which was to save the Expotition, we thought. The younger man's arm was in a thin sling and his hand in the flare of the lighter showed a gangrenous mess, swollen to the size of a baseball mitt. When we gasped over it the boy merely twisted his head to one side, admitting thus that it was a bad sore leg. It looked like an imminent case of lockjaw.

While we were still shuddering we got our inspiration. We had thought before of sending a note to the Skipper, asking him to bring the gourd-headed man down to the coast with him but the note we wrote now would persuade him to do as we asked because there was profit for him in it. It requested him to bring both the men down to the *Nakapo;* we would pay the boy's passage (at recruit rates, please) to Kieta where he could get medical attention for his hand. (We did not know that no white doctor will ever perform an amputation, such as this hand probably necessitated, on a native, unless the patient has some member dangling half off. Only the most sophisticated natives will permit any kind of cutting operation.) What we did not mention in our note to the Skipper was that we proposed holding the *Nakapo* at its present anchorage (and our expense) on the morrow while we made a painting of the old gentleman with the pop eyes and bullet head.

"Mastah! Mastah!" we said loudly enough for anyone to understand, and the boy, following our motions, waved the paper talk-talk in the direction of the village. We nodded violently and then watched to see that the two men kept on going, after which we continued to the coast on the wings of Pegasus.

Some time in the night we heard the woody sound of the dinghy clumping up against the *Nakapo,* and we were awake just long enough to remember that there was a tomorrow. It must be the Skipper coming on board, with the Bougainese model.

But tomorrow, the man-with-the-hat was not present!

The only explanation the Skipper would give was that the old fellow told the interpreter he did not want to walk back to the coast. The paying passenger, however, the younger man *without* the hat, had been easily persuaded to take a trip to Kieta—by the payment to him of three pounds of tobacco which had been charged to the Expotition.

Had the old man been brought down (with a similar inducement of tobacco) we should have had plenty of time to paint him at no expense to ourselves, for the *Nakapo* lay over at the anchorage until midafternoon waiting for recruits. The final decision of the spitting bee, which ended around two in the morning, was that the luluai would round up some recruits (none of the men present seemed to be able to make up his mind in ten hours) and send them down to the coast after the Skipper. But not a single volunteer appeared. The German seemed to hold us personally responsible. At least he told us very pointedly that we had sent members of the secret society of gourdheads (a rival club of the local Elks) into the village with our note. It had made the chief mad fella too much because now that he was a luluai, supposed to keep law and order, he could not run them out on the end of a spear.

29

For the rest of the day we sailed with the great island of Bougainville where it should have been in the first place—on our port side. The sun set behind its eight-thousand-foot-high horizon, the moon rose out of the sea, the *Nakapo's* engine sang—and in a minute it was daybreak. We woke to the rumble of the anchor going over.

Kieta, unbelievably, lay before us.

At the vision we felt like Balboa when he first looked on the wide Pacific Ocean—only more so. For us to have got to Kieta seemed to us much more of an achievement. We were not going merely to gaze on this wonder; when we landed we should be *in* the Territory of New Guinea with no danger then of having to look upon Sydney again before we started west on the final lap of our long pursuit.

Kieta, as a settlement, was not particularly noteworthy. It was on a promontory, which seemed to be a single high hill, jutting out to form a harbor. A wireless structure extended above the trees on its crest, and scattered over the near slope were a dozen or so white houses. Three iron-roofed buildings, which turned out to be two stores and a warehouse, were at the end of the landing stage, and straggling down the shore were several tiny houses that turned out to be a miniature Chinatown. But Kieta to us looked like a beautiful metropolis after our seeing only one house at a time for so many months.

The *Nakapo's* quarantine flag was up and we began to dress for our entry into the city with all the anxious care of a debutante at her own debut party. For on our faces depended our fate; Kieta was our first test of an Expotition to live without benefit of the Voy or hotels. There was no hotel at Kieta; we must find shelter in a place where every building was some man's private castle.

Dressing on the *Nakapo*, for a debut, however, was not the luxurious adventure it is for the debutante. To begin with, we were in full sight of the entire town, every householder of which owned a pair of binoculars which he was interestedly using if he were awake. We crunched down into the cabin on top of the sacks of copra in order to squirm into the elastic preliminaries, and finally emerged sweating and puffing and still seminude for the finale, which was dresses. The British women were almost as sticky as the Maries about the traditional female garments. But we could not wear shoes. Our feet had been crucified on the recruiting trip and were sprouting the expected island sores, started from the broken skin of the blisters; also, we noticed a new curse. (This is not a dainty feminine subject, but then neither were the feet.) The skin was peeling off, especially between the toes, and the already skinned areas were raw and sore. What we had were two exhibition cases of "Shanghai feet." I do not know why "Shanghai," because one can get the same condition anywhere that it is hot by continuously wearing rubber-soled shoes. It is the sweat that sloughs off the epidermis. But in these islands the usual infection sets in wherever the skin is peeled down below the protective layers. This sounds as ridiculous as mumps in a grownup; but it was almost as serious for us, for one of the things an expedition painter needs almost as much as his hands is his feet.

For the moment, however, socks and Chinese straw slops solved the problem of comfort, though not of chic. But we tried to make up for it at the other ends. Lipstick or no lipstick? The few island women we had met did not wear it, nor nail enamel, but we had become so anemic-looking that the slashes of scarlet seemed to cheer up the whole landscape. Ever so carefully we put on lipstick and just as carefully attended to our nails, and in half an hour—removed both jobs! It was better to be conservative entering unfamiliar territory. A half-hour later I restored the nail enamel to cover up the irremovable stains a painter gets under his nails, and when I had another look at my tea-colored face I returned the lipstick. We were done, as a roast is done, and overdone an hour and a half before a rowboat flying the customs flag put out from shore.

I removed the lipstick.

A native was rowing the boat and there was a white man in it, and when they pulled up to the *Nakapo* we were posed attractively behind the Skipper with our passports all ready, Margaret muttering, "One if by land and two if by sea . . ." The customs gentleman did not say "Good morning"; he sat in the boat and let the Skipper reach down his papers. There was a fraughted silence while the gentleman, probably a district officer, did what was necessary for the *Nakapo's* clearance. Then, "Passengers?" he asked without looking up. "Yah," said the German in disgust. "Passports," demanded the district officer, still unaware of our presence. We handed down our passport books which he opened, scribbled, and stamped, and then passed up for any hands to take. We might have been Japanese spies or have had smallpox all over our faces; our effect upon him would have been the same. We were entered into New Guinea Territory, but what of it? The district officer had ordered his rower to get on with rowing, and might have passed out of our lives two minutes earlier than he did if we had not reminded the Skipper of the boy-with-the-sore-leg. The district officer listened, studying the crotch of his pants, and then simply called back to send him, the boy, "up"; and this time he went off in dead earnest. Not a very good round for our faces.

Kieta may have had something to do with the district officer's disposition. The settlement was certainly a freak compared with those we had known in the Solomons.

We went ashore on the first dinghy trip in order to make inquiries about lodgings in the nearest store, and in five minutes we were out again feeling as if we had been pulled through a hedge backwards. The white storekeeper was a fat duplicate of the district officer, though not so well barbered, and he informed us coolly (simply because he was asked and had to answer) that there was no hotel in Kieta, no boardinghouse, no one who would take paying guests, and that last included himself with finality, though we had not intimated that he would.

In the second store we found our Skipper in conversation with the storekeeper and a citizen. The Skipper did not know us and so, of course, did not introduce us to the citizen. So to gain time for an idea we tried to buy some paint.

"What kind of paint?" demanded the storekeeper suspiciously. It hadn't occurred to us that there was anything but boat paint in this country, so we asked what kind he had.

"What kind are you looking for?" he parried.

"Windsor Newton artists' colors," we said with just a tinge. But it was lost on him.

"Haven't any."

"Well, what have you?"

"Boat paint . . . house paint. Just paint."

"We'll take some of that."

"How much do you want?"

"I don't know. Let us see in what amounts you carry it," we said, thinking of quart and gallon tins.

"If you tell me how much you want—" the man sounded as if he would spear us if we didn't—"I can give you any amount." It happened that he carried the paint in big drums, but we had to go through the same thing about colors. He would not give in and show us his stock and we had to order a pint of entirely mythical "yellow" before we found out where he kept his paint and could choose what we needed.

At the time of our history-making call on Kieta there were only sixteen white residents in the community, though there were wives then on holiday and patrol officers absent on duty. The settlement never had any more than twenty-five residents, yet there were as many rungs in the social ladder as there were residents. The government officers and their wives were, naturally, the four hundred on top, and the two storekeepers were down around the lower third section; but even those two occupied different rungs because one was an Englishman and the other an Australian. The untouchables were the Chinese, the missionaries, and Americans, whenever present.

We found out all about Kieta's peculiarities when we were having lunch with the wireless operator at his house on the hill. He was the resident to whom the Skipper had not introduced us, so he introduced himself by offering Margaret a great deal of paint he had at his house. It was an enormous house with rows of bedrooms, none of them occupied but his own, and it was in apologizing for not offering us a suite that we learned why an Expotition could not have even one room. For this was not the abandoned Solomon Islands where lady headhunters may stop over six weeks at a time with a bachelor and never hear any criticism. A little feebly we said we were willing to take any amount of criticism if we could stay in Kieta long enough to paint a gourd-headed Bougainese and the local types. But obviously nothing short of outright seduction could get this young man to make questionable women of us. For once we regretted gallantry and being a female outfit.

From the wireless station we went down and down the ladder to the far end of Chinatown where, at last, we came into our own. Along the short row of little shop-residences, Chinese merchants and their little slant-eyed wives came out to meet us with bowing backs and wide smiles. Whenever we stopped, chairs were pushed out into the shade of a palm and youngsters were sent scurrying after fans and glasses of water. No one tried to sell us anything. It made us love them very much. Yet there was no place for us to stay here. Every little shop-home had its dozens of grinning children and little mothers laden with fat doll-babies.

Between lunch-on-the-hill and Chinatown we had returned to the *Nakapo* to remove our stays and redon pajamas. (This change to negligee was a thumbing of the nose at the Kieta we had met.) So, for our return to the wharf from Chinatown (our feet being what they were) we hired bicycles. The strip of shore road that was Kieta's water-front boulevard was less than a mile long, but it seemed that half the "blacks" who traversed it rode a bicycle. For a stick of tobacco rent for each bicycle we hired two with their native owners to push us to the wharf.

Ours was a triumphant, noisy return to the "business section." The boys pushing us fell into the spirit of the thing after their first amazement and got us going with a running start and in a cloud of dust. Other natives we passed fell off their bikes or, if on foot, backed off the path, their mouths gaping with astonishment. But they laughed when they saw what fun we were having. We swept up in front of the Englishman's store with our legs straddling, our pith tanks half off and the pushers yodeling like coloraturas. For Margaret's horse had won.

When we had dismounted (and all but shaken hands with our landlords) we noticed standing before the store a young white couple looking in our direction. They were grinning and from the distance it looked like a friendly grin. But one could never tell, especially about Britishers. They were probably laughing *at* us; that was more likely in Kieta. In another minute they would either have to stop laughing or else have to speak to us, for we had to pass them to get to the wharf. But the crisis passed into sterile history when a loosened button fell off my pajama jacket and rolled away in the dust. When we had retrieved it the couple had gone into the store.

And just so simply, by the thread of a pajama button, were the affairs of the headhunting raid decided. For we learned afterward from mutual friends in Rabaul that these two young people—obviously treasures of the British race, for they could see the fun of being pushed on a bicycle even by a "black"—had dressed in their sportiest clothes and made a special trip down to the wharf in the heat of the day to ask us to be their guests. (The wireless operator had told them about Margaret.) And *we* had "snubbed" them!

When we got back to the *Nakapo* we learned that not even the Bougainese-with-the-sore-leg-along-hand had been able to see Kieta. The minute he was landed on the beach he streaked back for Lower Bougainville, not pausing even to see the doctor.

30

We had to go on to Rabaul.

But now suddenly that seemed the best idea in the world, and the sooner we got on our way the more relieved we should be. For Rabaul was that island metropolis, the one big settlement in all Melanesia where we had long expected to replenish our bleeding store of gold. An acute reminder of the emergency was that the *Nakapo* did not choose to sail. For two more days the vessel lay off that hateful little settlement of Kieta, during which time we dared not move far from the deck or beach because the Skipper said every next minute was the one in which we were leaving. He was waiting for business—of which much more anon.

On the second night we went ashore for dinner. The wireless operator sent a message that he wanted us to meet some friends, and again we sweated and puffed over our toilets, and again faced the dilemma of the lipstick. For "friends" could be of only one kind when the wireless operator knew our dire need. But these friends turned out to be too charming and altogether attractive to be among the four hundred who could save us. They were three young men, all in government service, and before the evening was over they had got together on a splendid scheme for Expotitions-in-distress. They would provide us with a complete field outfit—camp stretchers, mosquito nets, cooking gear—and lend us two indentured boys, and we could set up camp in the government rest house of the nearest village to Kieta. We took them seriously. There was nothing in the world the matter with the idea; but our hosts were "gamin." It couldn't be done. But why *not?* we demanded. Well . . . such a thing just wasn't done. Would anyone refuse us the use of the rest house? No, probably not, but—well, it would be too unusual: two white girls alone in a village. And so on and on.

Well, it *could* be done—unless the mute district officer did refuse us permission to use a rest house; all we had to do was to obtain camp gear, and we could buy that. And, by golly, use it from now on. We didn't know why we hadn't thought of it before. It would be fairly inexpensive living, we should be independent, and by living right in the village we should become quickly acquainted with our subjects and have less trouble getting models. There was just the hitch of convincing the district officer that we were not fragile ladies but tough headhunters.

When we left for the *Nakapo* we had every intention of getting to work on the idea first thing in the morning.

At the landing, however, when we were about to step aboard our dinghy taxi, we had an encounter that changed our minds—about Bougainville anyway. Standing on the wharf was a thin young man with his foot in an enormous dressing, his gear and some police boys waiting with him for the *Nakapo's* dinghy. "Well, Sammy," greeted our host, "so you're finally getting off to the hospital. How's the foot?" Sammy grinned, "Still bleeding flying-fox teeth." We were introduced as fellow passengers on the *Nakapo*—and learned that the vessel was finally sailing, in an hour or so! "But we're not sailing on the *Nakapo*," we boasted. "We're going to live in a village right here on Bougainville." There was a minute's silence and then Sammy asked, "Does the district officer know that?" We admitted he didn't, but he would in the morning. "The *Nakapo* will be gone then," worried the wireless operator, "and I'll have to marry you to give you a place to—" "Would it change your mind," interrupted Sammy, "if you knew I got this foot full of flying-fox teeth right up there in the bush? And I didn't do a thing—the natives just let me have it. The district officer wouldn't let you two stay alone in a village even within a mile of Kieta. He'd get in trouble if he did—and you probably would too. You can't trust these Bougainese."

And that was final, the word of an authority, for Sammy was a patrol officer. He had got his ankle shot full of flying-fox teeth when he was calling on a village where a native had died following the visit of another white man. The death was held to be due to the first man's visit, so when another white man came along, who happened to be the innocent Sammy, the villagers attempted to take their eye-for-an-eye. Sammy and his police fled; one was killed and Sammy received a spear in the back of his ankle before he got away.

That he had escaped with his life was a miracle that even Sammy did not understand himself; but when he was out of danger he found he still had the spear with him, imbedded in his ankle. Flying-fox teeth are gummed to a spearhead in an inverted position so that the head cannot be pulled out easily, especially if the point has penetrated between bones. When Sammy tried to extract the spear the shaft broke off leaving the head with its rows of dozens of teeth. And that little bundle stayed in his foot for a day and a half until the police boys had got the patrol officers to the coast.

That was two weeks ago, and even if the spearhead had not been poisoned a bad infection would have resulted. The Kieta doctor probed repeatedly for teeth and had got dozens out, but there were still dozens left which kept oozing to the surface. The foot was now in such a serious condition that to save it Sammy was on his way to the Rabaul hospital. Until the *Nakapo* came along no passage had been available.

If Sammy was in bad shape he was only one of many on the *Nakapo*. For even as we pulled up to the launch ladder we smelled another victim of Bougainville. The Skipper's three-day wait had profited him much, even if our Expotition had not; his vessel was as full of passengers "as Framelode is full of sea when tide is in." On board, when we at last got under way, were six Whites and *forty-one* natives bound for Rabaul three hundred miles away on a sixty-five-foot boat with no sleeping quarters that could be used. The natives were our crew and Sammy's police boys, and the rest were recruits. All but one. This one was a native who had just murdered his wife with a brand-new ackis and was being taken by a French Catholic priest to the Rabaul court for trial. It was the priest whose fragrance had been wafted to us across the water.

We saw none of these passengers (to meet) that night, but the next morning, on the high seas, the white "element" were all around the table on our cots for breakfast. It was an unusual aggregate—even including ourselves. At the right end of the cot opposite us was the Catholic priest, who could not speak English. He was a ghost anyway. His round Alpine head was shaven, but his face was not—though one wouldn't call what he had exactly a beard either. It was a black stubble, particularly gruesome on a head that looked like a skull with dark, burning eyes in it. The priest wore a faded brilliantine robe the odor of which would have made a Melanesian faint if he were not an ax murderer. It suffused the *Nakapo*, already permeated by an unnatural combination of doors.

But the priest was a sick man, as much a victim of this island as Sammy was.

The next two victims sat beside the priest like a couple of macabre song-and-dance men. They were both Americans, but Americans in essence; recruiters now, but formerly gold miners and traders and Florida real-estate operators! Gamblers incarnate. It was hard now to visualize these two in those natty sport tweeds riding around in installment Deusenbergs, loitering in the best bars with Florida bathing beauties, for they had just emerged from months of hell up in the bush of Bougainville. The recruits on board were their reward for an experience that included everything from blackwater fever and broken legs to being deserted by carriers and suffering from semistarvation, all miles from help among antagonistic natives. Yet, under the deathly white skins and the shaved skull heads with their stubble beards one could still see the clotheshorse good looks of the Florida boom beau. These two were tough and savvy, but refreshing, simply because they were our beloved countrymen talking slang through their adenoids as we had not heard it spoken in two years. They bewildered Sammy who was as English as a biscuit.

We now had a tablecloth for meals (a length of red laplap calico that looked as if it had already been used for that purpose), and we also had the Skipper's company though not his conversation. He sat on the aft taffrail next to the latrine with his elbows on the table while the wheel boy had his buttocks hooked on the other end. We were as cozy as eight men in a tub.

Between meals we still had the afterdeck to ourselves, but the Florida real-estate recruiters used the roof of the cabin for their bedchamber and they also—alone among the men on board—unblushingly used the taffrail temple, so that we did not have a great deal of privacy. The entire forepart of the vessel was the men's dormitory. As many of the natives as could get in, slept down in the hold on the sacks of copra (the hatch cover tightly closed), and the rest layered the deck with the three white men on camp stretchers. It was cozy too, the glimpses we got of it, as cozy as a slave trader's ship.

Three hundred miles is a sizable journey even on a civilized boat, and on the *Nakapo* it was an experience. We started out at a respectable rate of five knots and kept that giddy pace all of the first day. But the following morning we stopped to pick up more copra at a plantation—where no one called to the attention of the busily loading planter the Expotition's merits as guests—and the additional copra squeezed the recruits out of the hold. When we got under way again the little *Nakapo* actually did look like a Gold Coast slave ship. There was barely a foot of space on the foredeck that was not covered by a mess of black-skinned legs, and the natives were lying and sitting even on the awning roof that went over the aft part of the vessel. We were now so heavily loaded that there was not more than eighteen inches freeboard amidships and our speed was reduced by a third. But it was all profit for the Skipper, for the longer it took to get to Rabaul and the bigger his cargo, the better the trip. He evidently had plenty of fuel.

Or had he?

We were sailing well out from the coast beyond a point which, on Sammy's chart, gave an ominous reading, "Reefs reported six miles offshore," when the launch engine gave that familiar cough which is a clearing of the throat just before the gas gives out. When the island charts use the word "reported" they mean "maybe." Not "maybe the reefs are there" but "maybe they are six miles out" or "maybe they are under your hull at the moment." An additional note on the chart explains it: "*Caution*," it says. "As these islands have been only partially examined, and the larger portion of them quite unknown, great caution is necessary while navigating in this vicinity." The chart is compiled from the works of D'Entrecasteaux in the eighteenth century with, of course, additional soundings up to 1918.

So when the engine coughed we looked around for the expected humps and ruffling of water to indicate the reefs we should presently scrape on. There were no such signs, but the engine was dead now and we were floating southward on the current almost as fast as we had been chugging northward. Sammy had been with us—telling us hair-raising stories of Bougainville—and presently he went forward to see what was the matter, leaving us with the enlightening remark that the Skipper had probably *shut* the engine off. But whatever had happened it took him two hours to turn it on again, and the Skipper had probably made ten or fifteen dollars by the delay.

Another, more profitable delay happened when the wheel boy went to sleep on the table one night, fortunately with his foot wedged in the wheel, so that we made wide circles all night without reaching either Hawaii or Heaven. It was like the ghost *Derelict* of "fifteen men on a dead man's chest," with all forty-eight souls on board sound asleep while the *Nakapo* wandered around the ocean on its own. It took us hours the next morning to get back on the course and recover the ground we had lost. The recruiters were grumbling.

Between delays, however, our lives skimmed away by the hour in a kind of peaceful stupor induced mostly by the glare on the water. The two exhausted recruiters slept the clock around, rising only for meals, and the padre ate and perfumed the course, reading his little catechism and speaking no word in any language to anyone. Sitting there hour by hour in the shadow on the rail, his dark figure silhouetted against the brilliant water, he looked as foreign to this fantastic "slave ship" as he was to all earthly things, certainly to the experiences of the two Florida real estaters. Sammy we took to our hearts—and our cots, for we urged him to spend his days back in the less cluttered atmosphere of our quarters. He was in great pain with his leg and worried about our slow progress, because the longer the foot went without dressing the more serious it became. All of us were idle. But the primitives up forward were as busy as ants. They carved designs on their bamboo lime boxes, repaired their dilly bags, filed down the teeth of their betel-nut-wood combs and improved the decorations, primped their hair and pulled their whiskers. Some of them strung glass beads for necklaces and others played an endless and mysterious game with playing cards, the rules of which are so complicated that no white man has been able to get track of them. And all the time there was the companionable little mumbling gossip of a quilting party. All except the *Nakapo's* crew, who were from New Britain, were the bad, black-skinned westerners of Bougainville.

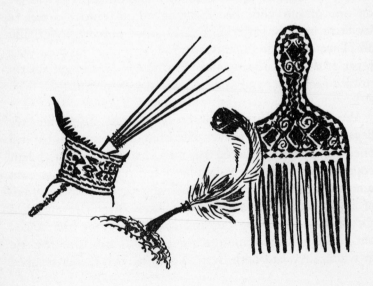

The day before we started through King Albert Straits between Big and Little Buka we ran into storm and a head-on current. For this, at least, the Skipper could not be held responsible. It was the change of seasons, leaving the wet monsoon and entering the dry, when the wind blows like a hurricane and the water comes down out of the sky with a kind of personal hatred. Natives loathe getting their hair wet, and forward on the unprotected deck the recruits huddled like hens under small sheets of tarpaulin while the water ran under them in rivers as the laden little vessel rolled and pitched in the heavy seas. We Whites had a sturdy lot of stomachs, for we never missed sitting down to the table at mealtime. Catching the food was something else. But we were all in a sensitive condition. The morning following the nastiest night of storm we had lined up at the breakfast table when the fragrant padre put in his appearance last. Whereupon the rest of us, like a group of precision dancers, wheeled around to the rail and "gave." It was disastrous to Sammy, already so ill. For the rest of that nightmarish day he lay on one of our cots, his chin hooked up onto the rail to facilitate matters, suffering mostly from embarrassment. But all of us, except the quinine-stuffed Margaret, suffered with fever from the sudden chill. The recruiters became snarly toward each other and sarcastic with the rest of us.

We had been on the *Nakapo* only a few days when we began to appreciate a packet of correspondence a planter had once let us read. The letters were half originals and half copies of an actual correspondence between two white men who had started out as partners living on an isolated group of islands miles from any other Whites. After a few months they had had a falling out and one of the men had moved out, building himself another house a few yards from the one in which they had both lived. Then the two finally stopped talking to each other, and in order to communicate, which was necessary for their combined business, they began writing letters—across a distance near enough to hear the letters being created on their typewriters.

The first letter started with a formal request for the loan of a pound of tenpenny nails which would be returned when the copra steamer called. The answer was that B would lend A the nails if A sent over security, for A was a so-and-so who couldn't be trusted. A replied in kind, with some improvements, and by the end of the correspondence both men were in such a frenzy of frustrated loathing for each other that the letters looked like battlefields, with explosions of exclamation points and shellholes of profanity and unfinished sentences. These two gentlemen had presumably been sane when they first formed their partnership; the confinement limited to each other's company day after day, month in and month out, had broken up a friendship of years.

Our climax to a mildly similar situation began bubbling to the surface in a series of little eruptions, the most consequential of which started among the natives. It might not have become important if the situation had not been one of "my boys" and "your boys" and "their boys." One of the recruiters' boys, a bush Bougainese who had probably never been on the ocean before, was pathetically seasick, and accidentally spilled over on the lap-lap of a flash boy who was one of the *Nakapo's* outfit—he was probably lying under the mouth of the Bougainese anyway. Curiously, it was the sick boy who was unmanageable. He wanted to get the dirtied lap-lap from the flash boy because it contained the contents of his stomach which it was not safe for him to leave at large. The flash boy was annoyed by the accident and refused to part with his skirt, making matters worse by intimating that he would use this stomach material for settling his score by handing it over to a sorcerer.

This was where Sammy was pulled into the thing, representing the government which punishes terrorization. The Bougainese complained to the recruiters that the flash boy was going to have him bewitched. Upon hearing this, the Americans, who were looking for a scrap, told the Skipper what they would do if he did not order his boy to let their

Bougainese scrape up his upchuckings from the lap-lap; they would knock him (the flash boy) into a week of Sundays. Sammy told them that anyone who hit anyone would land in court. While this was going on, the priest, his nose in his catechism, watched with burning eyes the scene he could not understand a word of. We lay in comfort on our bellies watching it from the roof of the cabin and were gratified when finally one of the former Florida real estaters told the

Skipper in his picturesque way what we all thought—that he was making a "bloody squeeze" of the trip. It was mutiny and made the Skipper fighting-mad, but he said nothing. And then somehow the whole matter seemed settled.

But actually it was not settled; the affair had only dragged into the open what had been fermenting ever since we lost a day by the wheel boy's dream-steering.

At lunch that morning even Sammy got mad, for the Skipper announced without a blush that we were anchoring overnight in the Pass. It was true, as Sammy explained afterward, that the Straits was filled with reefs and it would be unsafe to continue through in the dark if one did not know the channel. But even if the Skipper did not know, his wheel boy must. And the channel was clear enough for the Sydney steamer to get through, in daylight at least. The announcement of the Skipper was followed by complete silence. The recruiters just glanced at each other.

Just after sunset we came to a plantation on the port land side and the *Nakapo* pulled in and dropped anchor in order to replenish its water supply. "Now don't go," Sammy warned us mysteriously, "they'll invite you up to dinner but don't go." Why not, we wanted to know; a civilized meal on a level table would be right tasty. "If you *get* it!" said Sammy. "They'll get drunk first and it'll be a brawl." And Sammy began to figure how long it was since the steamer had passed through. It seems that the residents, a former seaman and his ex-barmaid wife, were a couple like the planter in Marovo Lagoon who stocked up with liquor from the steamer and spent the next six weeks drinking it up. The routine was occasionally broken by their trying to murder each other. It was now midway between steamers, so the situation was likely to be still very wet.

Well, it was a brawl. But we wouldn't have missed it for a

life-lease seat to the Metropolitan. This was the kind of South Sea Island brawl that happens only in the movies, although it was much more fantastic, partly because *we* started it!

When the *Nakapo* dropped anchor the ex-seaman, looking very much like the movie version, squarely built and with muscular arms akimbo, was already on the landing calling out to us. Immediately the Skipper and the two recruiters, now very chummy, went ashore. And, sure enough, in a few minutes the ex-barmaid Missus, an equally square replica of the Seaman, was seen coming down the hill path to the landing armed with an invitation to dinner. Feeling very guilty, since we knew the rule of women never passing one another in these islands, we shouted across the water our reason for not being able to go up. They were good enough as reasons; we all had sore feet, including Sammy, and Sammy and I were expecting our second rise of fever for this siege of malaria. The Missus retreated justifiably insulted.

But the Skipper had gone off leaving no order for our dinner; we faced starvation. In about an hour, after a bombardment of increasingly nonsensical notes from the Missus and recruiters, the Seaman appeared below the launch bearing the kind of invitation an Expotition could not refuse. He offered us a hot bath with dinner. Even Sammy gave in then and decided to go ashore with us; but he looked worried when, at the Seaman's request, we took our wha-whas. (The recruiters had reported that we were "hot" on them.) The least we could do for a bath was to sing for it, seeing that we had sung for many a dinner that had included nothing so exotic.

When at last we limped up that hill to the plantation residence we were prepared for anything in our hosts, and expected nothing of the rumpus house they must live in. So that was our first surprise, the residence. It was beautiful. It was a Hollywood version of the tropical splendor attributed to wealthy planters of Malaya and India, which is so far from the real thing. The house and its furnishings were made entirely of native materials and with native labor, but the Seaman and his barmaid wife had designed it—obviously after a movie, but with much more taste. The bamboo furniture the Missus had made herself with native help. It was modern but comfortable; the cushions were of brilliant plain colors; the numerous gasoline lamps had well-balanced, attractive shades; the two levels of the wide semicircular veranda (of some dark shiny wood) were spread with mats made of braided lawyer cane; bowls of flowers were everywhere—something we had not yet seen in a residence because cut flowers attract ants—and there were potted flowers and beautiful leaf plants below the veranda, and clumps of orchids hanging from the rafters. It was just the sort of home we had been thinking could be built in that part of the world with taste and time—and enough money for the native labor, for the materials would cost nothing. Obviously these residents did something besides drink and try to murder each other between steamers.

Our arrival at the veranda was greeted by cheers from the company who, we could see, had been restoring their tissues from the bottles on the beautifully carved coffee table. Highballs were pressed into our not-at-all reluctant hands and with them we were ushered through the big high-ceilinged dining room to the bath off the rear court. This room was the bath we had been dreaming of. It smelled like a perfume counter, and on a table below a big mirror—certainly the largest one in the islands that was not behind a bar—was a stock of ambrosias in mammoth cut-glass bottles. There was light, plenty of it, and privacy, for the golden bamboo slats of the walls were perfectly fitted together. There were rows of dainty hand towels and big woolly bath towels, a blue rug on the floor and, God bless barmaids, a *bathmat*. And there was space, and everything so *clean!*

The bath was still a bucket aloft with a floor of slats for the water to run away, but the bucket was blue enamel and its release worked to sprinkle us evenly with water of a temperature we mixed ourselves from a row of buckets of both hot and cold set in the room for us. By the time Margaret had finished her bath and anointed herself with two or three kinds of powder and toilet water, I had got through mine. There was still plenty of water so Margaret took another bath for tomorrow.

We hated to leave. We had been in the cloister an hour or more, but we had to let this luxury soak in enough to last for a long time. Periodically our hostess came to the door to ask how her "little Americans" were getting on. "Don't hurry," she would sing like an angel, "I'm just setting your fresh drinks here in front of the door." When we finally emerged (exhausted but cleaner than we had been for months) there were six highballs lined up across the doorway. The fact that we had taken in only two from the line had not stopped this generous hostess.

We were now ready for that dinner which would certainly be a banquet worth eating in this household. And from the rear court were coming banquet odors, though there were no houseboys to be seen, and when we went through the dining room the table was still not set. The houseboys were all on the veranda feverishly passing around filled glasses and collecting empty ones. And everyone now, excepting Sammy, was very plainly drunk.

The brawl did not start until we had been playing for about a half hour. We had started out singing the things we liked, from which repertoire our hosts discovered we had two kinds of songs—"sob" and syncopation. The Barmaid loved the swing and kept asking for more. "No," said the Seaman, "let them play that other one, 'There's no-thing left for me-e-e of days that used to be-e-e.'" He tried singing it himself.

"Shut up," said the Barmaid. The Seaman kept right on yodeling. "Let *them* sing," screamed his wife. And when he did not stop she tottered across the veranda and very calmly gave him a blistering smack on the cheek.

I am not exactly sure about the sequence of what followed, but the next blow was certainly the push our host gave his wife with his fist. Instantly one of the recruiters had rushed over in defense of fair lady and pushed the man, who crashed over onto the German who had been sitting numbly pouring down his drinks. The next thing all four men—the Skipper, the two recruiters, and our host—were swinging into one another.

Sammy had taken only one highball all these hours of waiting for his dinner (which never came), but he was hiccuping convulsively when he got on his crutch and tried to shoo us away from this educational scene. We were up in box seats on the veranda railing (to get out of the way of flying chairs and bottles), and when we happened to glance over to the entrance of the dining room five natives were standing there with their mouths hanging open and their eyes popping. Also behind some palmettos at the far side of the patio was a row of glittering highlights on the eyes of invisible natives. But the Missus was as unreal as any character in a South Sea drama; she was waltzing around, cheering impartially as she grabbed teetering lamps and crashing vases. Every now and then she cleared some piece of furniture back from the arena or gave a behind a kick in passing, not caring, apparently, whose it was.

But the fight was going on in dead earnest. And it was messy. Both recruiters were now pummeling the Skipper on the floor while the Seaman tried to bang them off from above. They were all gasping and sweating and grunting like animals. And then the blood came. That was when we thought we had been educated enough. On the path we looked back at the beautiful house. Brilliant pillows, vases and flowers and bottles and glasses were all over the lovely vine mats, chairs and tables were on their sides, a sofa was turned over, and in the center of this wreckage was a clump of flying fists and legs over which the fat barmaid wife stood screaming, her "permanent" like a Medusa, with a bottle in her hand as if she meant to use it when the right head came up. We passed the row of high-lighted eyes feeling self-conscious and ashamed.

Hours later we were lying on our stretchers, still too stimulated to sleep, when we saw flashlights coming down the path from the house on shore. All five of our late company were walking together, and when they reached the landing the Missus called out to the launch: "Lil' American girls . . . oh, lil' American girls! Come back! *Alo-o-oha . . . alo-o-oha!*" The others joined in singing horribly just the one word "*aloha.*" Then presently three of the white-clad figures descended to the dinghy and started rowing out. The Seaman and his wife stood close together on the wharf with their arms around each other. We could tell by the still-lit flash-

light the way they were swaying. And they must have been teetering right on the edge of the wharf, because suddenly there was a loud splash and the united figures had plopped over into the dark water. "Let 'er drown!" we heard one of the gallant recruiters say. "Every fight in islands s-started by dog or woman." "Ach Gott," said the Skipper at last in agreement, "you iss right." And then, misquoting the island maxim, "Effery dog and woman starts a fight."

For some reason we did not lie over in the Straits that night. The *Nakapo* dropped anchor off Rabaul late on the eighth night.

31

The hook of land on the inner shore of which Rabaul is situated is called Crater Peninsula, the bay formed by the crook being the gigantic crater of an old volcano. In the middle of the bay are some little "beehive" islands which appear and disappear at whim, indicating that something is going on down there in the water, and to the south, still in Blanche Bay, is another island called Vulcan. Rabaul is built on the shore flats, flats which slope off lower and lower toward the south of town, until opposite tiny Matapi Island solid land becomes a huffing and puffing morass of bubbling black sand. The first thing the nose of a sensitive visitor sniffs as he enters the bay, if the wind is right, is the stench of sulphur and brimstone which rises in steam from these safety valves of the volcanic region. At high tide Matapi is an island, but at low one can walk across to it by a wet sand bridge from the mainland. This extension of the island continues the lip of the water-filled crater which is now Blanche Bay. Behind the town, hemming it cozily into the bay circle, is a backdrop of mountain ridges, some of them periodically active volcanoes. But the whole scene from the bay is "intimate," delightful as only a little town of white buildings with plenty of foliage tucked between water and mountains can be.

This picturesque little town and its dramatic surroundings, however, caused Doctor Parkinson to remark (in his *Thirty Years in the South Seas*), "The numerous volcanoes in this uncanny quiet do not inspire a feeling of confidence, and one unconsciously asks himself, when will this district become the theater of a horrible catastrophe?"

The government reports show about twenty healthy earthquakes a year, disturbances violent enough to receive official attention, which means that the tremors one feels every few days are just about normal. However, ever since early German times the seat of government has been shunted from one site to the other seeking a piece of land reasonably certain of not popping His Excellency sky-high one night. At the time of our visit the capital was Rabaul—on the ledge of a volcano crater, surrounded by volcanoes far from extinct, and with bubbling mud in the back yard.

There is no doubt that living in Rabaul is something like living in a reducing vibrator. There is something in "this uncanny quiet," an electrical charge that is not the invigorating kind but rather the tenseness that sometimes makes small boys suddenly take a crack at a glass window with a rock, as much to their surprise as anybody's. As an example: Out from town are "about ninety miles of navigable roads," and Rabaul has "more cars per capita than any town of its size in the world." But what is off the record is that there are more motorcar wrecks per car-owner capita, and more deaths per wreck than any official would admit to anyone who might write about Rabaul. On Saturday afternoon and evening those "more cars per capita" are hooting along those ninety miles, only a few miles of which are navigable at a pace faster than that of a carriage—for which they were originally built. The excuse is to get a breath of air, but it is a form of window-breaking.

If you can imagine, then, in this "uncanny quiet," a town suddenly boomed out of its cradle by the biggest gold discovery of the century (on the mainland of New Guinea), filled with gold prospectors and the merchants who follow such booms, with hundreds of recruited natives from all over the

Territory awaiting employers for the gold fields, with the planters, missionaries, and patrol officers who come in from the hinterlands to shop or spree, and with the scores of village natives who come in every day with vegetables for the native "boom" (market)—if you can imagine all this you will have the transient element which made little Rabaul look to us like Times Square at theater hour.

Actually it would take a lot more people than Rabaul has, both visitors and residents, to fill its roads. The town was laid out by the Germans, so the roads are boulevard-wide and canopied by great old flowering trees that shade the avenues luxuriantly and during the flowering seasons carpet them with fallen petals. The governor general's residence is up on Namanula Hill behind the town, and trailing down from this exclusive site are the hospital, courthouse, and the homes of government officials. The substantial citizenry is made up of these government officers plus a few lawyers, a few doctors and managers of the big shipping companies and stores, all more or less complete with wives. These comprise Society—the portrait clientele, to the Expotition. The residents (semitransient) bunking together in furnished houses around the town itself are the hospital nurses and government and store clerks, many of them girls. Besides the Whites there is a large native constabularly and, of course, several hundred regular native houseboys. Also, behind the town there is a two-block-square Chinatown with the usual prolific population.

For visitors of means there is *the* hotel in the center of Rabaul, and for prospectors, recruiters, adventurers, and Expotitions there is Ah Chee's hotel in Chinatown.

The Territory of New Guinea has only one used gateway and that is the regular steamer from Sydney. There is a freighter that plies between Sydney and the Orient via the Territory and the Philippines, but it sails irregularly and is infrequently used as an entrance. Visitors coming in by the back door as we did are almost unknown unless traveling on their own yacht. So, having cleared at Kieta, we entered Rabaul with no record of it locally. There were many little inconveniences and embarrassments that we probably escaped by this obscurity—such as explaining to a very suspicious customs what two young women might be coming here for when they had so little money and no definite plans (which would make sense to a port official) for supporting themselves. Yet, by not being registered locally, we were practically nonexistent for a while, which had its drawbacks for portrait work.

Our climb to the Residency (and possible portrait orders) on the sacred heights of Namanula Hill can probably be equalled only in some tall "success" story magazine. For quite innocently we started out in Rabaul among the Untouchables at Ah Chee's wonderful hotel. When the *Nakapo* arrived that night Sammy insisted on our going to *the* hotel and sent one of his boys up to engage a room for us. Luckily there was no room available, and we made about ten dollars a day by going to Ah Chee's. Here we got a room with meals at twenty-five dollars a week for both of us. And what is more to the point we met the famous old Chinese owner.

His hotel was not beautiful and it was not even clean, but it was a robust institution. It was a large two-story wooden structure with an outside balcony running all around the second floor and shading the sidewalk below, much like our old southern inns. The balcony was sectioned off by low partitions over which we could see our neighbors scratch their heads. Inside the building was a long, wide, black hall with a big well down to the first floor where, located under the balcony, was the heart of the hotel, the bar. The sleeping rooms were merely partitioned cubicles, the walls of which were not more than eight feet high. The two doorless doorways of our room, one leading to the hall and the other to the balcony, had each a curtain of lap-lap calico hanging in a rope from a sagging string. These curtains were only just wide enough to reach across the doorways when they were stretched down with thumbtacks.

But no guest of Ah Chee's desired privacy. Most of them (and the hotel was brimming) had their curtain tied up in a knot still hanging in the center of the doorway. When one passed down the hall one saw and heard—all sorts of things. They were all masculine.

The other peculiarity of Ah Chee's (which is a peculiarity of most tropical hotels) was that there were no chamber-maids, no porters, no bellhops. Each guest brought his own help. His own boy fixed his wash-wash, served him at table, and made up his room. We might have been embarrassed by our lack if one of the American recruiters had not foreseen this trouble and presented us with a handmaiden. His name was Meru—and of him more anon. He was as mad as a hornet at being transferred to the service of Missus, but he obedi-ently staggered up from the wharf with our cases that could be lifted and, having made our bed, he took up his station sitting on the floor outside the door as did the other personal boys on the floor.

And he had just fallen asleep when we wanted our wash-wash.

Until Meru reported that wash-washhimhestopmissus we busied ourselves in our room as girls will preparing for a bath when they think they are in a room. The curtain had been neatly thumbtacked across the doorway, but it did not reach to within eighteen inches of the floor and through this hiatus we could see all the dozens of feet that thundered up and down the hall; the bare running feet and the ones in shoes with planters' white pants reaching to just above the ankle.

And we noticed that most of these feet lagged as they passed our doorway, while some in shoes even returned after going only a short way beyond. No, there wasn't a hole in the curtain anywhere.

Meru announced wash-wash by planting his feet in front of the curtain, and I went first, Margaret carefully thumbtacking the curtain again behind me. A zipper, or even a door, would have saved a lot of time. When I returned (after the usual ordeal in a pitch-black house wash-wash) I got my reward for pioneering. Margaret had thumbtacked the curtain beautifully all around the edge, but the old calico was just as transparent as a wire screen! In full view of the dimly lit hall stood Margaret, stark naked, with one foot gracefully planted on top of the dresser examining her Shanghai sores under the light above. It was quite an interesting study, something like a Renoir nude.

So everyone at Ah Chee's knew all there was to know about us in our first hour in the madhouse.

They knew, but they did not care; or if they cared they were too preoccupied to do anything about it. In the cubicle next to ours a kind of night-blooming poker game was in progress; and we would not have gone to sleep even if we had been sleepy lest we miss some of it. Every click of chip and clink of bottle might have been heard too if these delicate sounds had not been drowned by the joyous hullabaloo that shook the whole structure. A half-dozen gramophones were screaming and above this were the shouts for *"Boy!"* *"Boy!"* all over the floor, and behind that racket a continuous roar of men's laughter. Somewhere down at the end of the hall there was a thumping and bumping and howling which was caused, we learned later, by the antics of a little German prospector who had once been a circus clown. Past our door thundered a never-ending procession of beer bottles and glasses hurried along by bare feet, and down in the well, whence came a cloud of beer fumes and smoke, was another undying party. Joy, pure unrestrained glee, permeated Ah Chee's, for it was Saturday night.

By Monday a sad quiet had settled over the place. Some of the planters and miners had left, and possibly the presence of women had cast a pall on the gaiety. The poker game next door continued, but now all the jokes and stories we had stayed awake to listen to were told in mumbling undertones and the players choked on their laughter trying to keep it modified. During the day the former clown presented himself to us with a breath and a similarly odoriferous bottle of Japanese perfume, offering the latter an as apology for having caused so much noise. (He had been doing clown tumbling acts.) When we said we wished we had been at the party instead of having been merely shaken by it, the little man was so pleased that he made us an additional present of some small gold-ore nuggets fresh from the mountains of New Guinea.

And it was this man, learning my name, who brought about a quite unusual encounter. That night at dinner he brought to our table another old prospector who shyly asked how I spelled my name. He had once prospected in Alaska and had known a Lewis Mytinger who had come to Juneau with a gold washer, and the two had known one another intimately before the latter was drowned. Lewis Mytinger was my father, whom I had never known. He had invented a gold washer and taken it to Juneau to interest investors. And from this miner here in far-away New Guinea I learned things about the last few months of my father's life and the details of the way he met his death that even my mother did not know. "You look just like your father," the miner said. "I think I would have known you were Lew's daughter even if I had not heard your name—especially meeting you here, at another gold field." And in probably the same kind of hotel.

Our first job, in order to stay in Rabaul and do portraits, was to find inexpensive living quarters. The taboo against white women lifting a hand to do anything for themselves, and our lack of a line of houseboys to lift things for us (natives cannot be indentured for less than two years—and Meru was only a temporary loan) naturally suggested a boardinghouse. And a few boardinghouses there were, but with no vacancies. And there were no more cottages or houses for rent, either furnished or vacant, than is usual in these tropical settlements. There are never enough houses to go around, and often people live for months in the hotels waiting for places to be vacated when their owners go on leave.

It was the American recruiters who, in our ninth hour of despair, steered us to the Ambassador. The name, Ambassador, was entirely humorous for the place was a huge frame building, as spacious as a hangar and looking very much like one, which had been built by the government as the expropriation department to handle the land tangle when the Australians took over during the last war. Offices were partitioned off on both sides of a long hall, and at one end was a big open space, the size of Roseland, which was now the one restaurant in town, run by a former sailor (whom we named Popeye) and his wife. At the time of our tenancy the building was owned by Rabaul's one newspaper, which had its press in an adjoining building; its editor worked and lived in a suite at the far end of the restaurant. Of this editor more hereafter. The offices were being rented out for any length of time and for any reasonably respectable purpose. There was a ship chandler's office down at the far end of the hall, and next to him a new young lawyer; and the rest of the cubbyholes were vacant or occupied by transient miners and recruiters who took them for a day or week at a time. The rooms were so much the size of largish stalls that some humorist had lettered the names of famous race horses on a few doors. There was, of course, no furniture, no running water; the toilet was off the restaurant (through the kitchen), and the wash-

wash houses were in the rear on a court. But the rent was only twenty dollars a month and we expected to furnish our stall with a camp outfit. We could eat one meal a day in the restaurant and lift our hands to help ourselves in private without the aid of a houseboy, or endangering white prestige.

As soon as it became known that we were moving into the Ambassador, furnishings poured in from every direction. Ah Chee, that wonderful old Chinese who has helped so many destitute prospectors and recruiters, promptly offered a big mirror and a bed (we took the box springs and mattress), and such linen and slop bowls and pails and basins as we wanted. He even sent the things down with his boys. The recruiters donated a big mosquito net, and Meru until we were settled. My father's friend produced a beautiful mat from the Admiralty Islands which was fine enough to be a wall hanging, but which he insisted should be a rug. The Editor sent over a small drafting table, and Sammy sent down his love to Margaret from the hospital where he was still holding onto parts of his foot.

When all these things first arrived we did not see how we should get them into the stall, but when our own cases had been stored across the hall in an empty room (the Editor-landlord's suggestion) and the furniture arranged, the room seemed even larger than when it was empty. The street side of it was one big window, so curtains were our first concern. We bought a cheap fish net for window curtains, and a whole bolt of brilliant blue lap-lap calico for the overhangings, to be pulled across at night. And from the same blue we made a cover for the springs and mattress, which had been set up on blocks to look like a hickyah. Ah Chee's pillows, smelling slightly of departed miners, were covered with magenta calico and looked handsome on the blue hickyah. An entrance vestibule-dressing room was created by hanging another full blue curtain across that entire end of the room from the chicken wire which made a burglarproof ceiling, for here, too, the partitions were only eight feet high, while the roof was at least twenty. Then, when amber-colored whisky bottles (with their necks broken off) were set along the window shelf filled with red hibiscus, and a five-gallon gasoline tin containing yellow croton was put on the table, we sat down

at last. We surveyed our handiwork and saw that it was good. The Editor stuck his head in and said, "How jolly!" and the lawyer neighbor passing said, "Why, you're going to be very comfortable . . . Like home, rather!" Then we closed the door and we were alone at last, in our own clean home, with Meru sleeping outside the door.

The way for a woman who is a stranger to tackle the social ladder in any British colonial settlement is a cut-and-dried system. She starts at the top simply by leaving her card at the Residency. This is merely paying one's formal respects, and the card-leaver must, under no circumstances, be seen in the flesh by anyone but a servant. Literally it means, "I have arrived and am ready for recognition." Presumably there are spies who then track one down and report whether one is eligible for (*a*) dinner, (*b*) luncheon, (*c*) tea, or (*d*) total eclipse. There must be some way of finding out about the newcomer other than by a mere name on a card.

The Expotition had no card and it had sore feet and Namanula Hill was an alp which no bicycle we could pedal would go up. And it was also very hot and we had no calling clothes which were fit to be seen even by a servant. The whole business seemed a little strained to an American anyway—to hire a car to climb an alp to deliver a card which we did not have, in order to be followed by spies who would report that we were living in a horse stall.

However, we had to do it if we expected to get any portrait orders.

The first thing, therefore, was to get the card. And that was easy because the Editor dashed off a few on his printing press. The lettering was neat, but the legend was doubtful. The Editor, inspired, had added at the bottom, "American Headhunting Expedition to Melanesia," but had put an exclamation point after it. So he had to dash off a few more, controlling his humor, and while he was up he dashed off a long idiotic account of our headhunting adventures for his newspaper, the Rabaul *Gazette*—all of it invented, which seems to be the failing of journalists.

Then for the clothes, which we should have to get anyway even if we walked no farther abroad than the streets of Rabaul. A sewing machine, easily fifty years old, was borrowed from Ah Chee and brought down swinging on a bamboo pole between the shoulders of Meru and one of the

Chinese's boys. Then we bought lengths of cotton goods (even for dinner frocks) and made them up so simply that even a native boy with his scorching ash-strewing, football-sized charcoal iron could launder them. We featured Fit and Line and that sort of thing, but mostly made pajamas.

We were still sweating and fitting when one afternoon there was a tap at our door. Meru was sleeping, of course, and Margaret was half nude, being fitted, so I went to the door with a mouthful of pins. Outside was a most magnificent native. He was young but he was pompous, and dressed like the local police boys in a brief saw-edged lap-lap, with a uniform cap high on the crest of his big black pompadour. For a minute he examined me from aloft and then he said something. It may have been "Her Majesty approaches" or "Her Excellency is calling" or even "Missushimhestopalongmotorcarcloseuphimhecomealongthisfellaplace." It didn't make any

difference. We glanced out of the window and there was the great shiny car with a crest on it. The wife of the governor general was calling. There was just time for us to wipe the sweat and hair out of our eyes and Margaret to get a bathrobe on. Our usually enchanting room was littered with pins and dress scraps, and hanging from the chicken-wire ceiling were dresses, and more new garments were strewn over the only thing to sit on, the hickyah. Yet, when New Guinea's First Lady entered this sweatshop her first exclamation was, "How charming!" (We are still wondering what she meant.) But she was there to invite us to (a) dinner. And would we mind very much bringing our instruments; she had heard we played

. . . Now where had she heard that! And how did she know we even existed! And why had she overlooked what would not have been forgiven in an Englishwoman—the omission of the calling-card hocus-pocus! In any case, if we had no other engagement the motor would be sent for us at . . .

And that is the way, dear reader, to climb the social ladder in a British colonial settlement. (The secret of this, of course, is "bush telegraph." No one, and especially no woman, can be in these islands as long as we had been and not have it known by everyone, even as far distant from the Solomons as Papua. Word travels via Sydney where the steamer captains meet in the office of the line—when it does not go directly from one group to the next between friends. Captain Voy, bless him, though distant, was still working for his "lasses." Then there was the Rabaul *Gazette* publicity, doubtful social recommendation.)

The logical subject for our first (speculative) portrait in Rabaul was naturally our hostess, and she would have been asked to sit if Margaret, halfway through that enchanting dream-evening of the dinner, had not whispered in my ear that a portrait had been *ordered*. That was nippy work. It was partly Margaret's music, which somehow seemed to make people think my portraits must be equally good, but mostly the dinner. It was perfect: all glistening with candlelight, and savory and fresh and hot or ice-cold. Every time I took a precious forkful I thought of the smeared lap-lap tablecloth on the *Nakapo,* and of our luxury hunger, and I held the bite in my mouth tasting it so that I shouldn't forget. There were twelve guests besides ourselves, some of them the usual government commission-to-investigate-something from Australia and the rest local "substantials." Dinner was early, at eight o'clock, but we had all arrived at sunset—specially invited at that hour for the sunset which is a spectacle looking down across Blanche Bay from the Residency. The cocktails were of American abundance, the wines at dinner varied and copious, and liqueurs quite redundant. The ladies retired to an upstairs sitting room for a full hour after dinner, during which time the flowing bowl continued to pass among the men guests below. It was not surprising therefore that a local dignitary ordered a drawing of himself to send to his mother. He needn't have had a mother for an excuse.

Such a portrait commission, ordered in the flush of the evening, would have been ignored at home. Almost everyone thinks he wants himself painted or drawn when he is feeling glamorous, but has little recollection afterward of making an appointment for a sitting. Margaret, nevertheless, ignored this experience and set a date for the sitting. And, lo and behold, at the appointed time a car arrived to take us to that blessed patron's home where we were to work—and *eat* later.

No time could have been more unfortunate.

For between the dinner and appointment a blight had struck our household. Margaret said it was punishment for having stuffed ourselves at the Residency, but it was dysentery. We had found that lettuce—which looked like lettuce but did not taste like it—and mealy little tomatoes could be bought at the native "boom," and these being the ingredients of the American's beloved salad, we had decided to have them regularly for lunch. We had salad two days and then, whether Meru had not washed the vegetables thoroughly or whether it was his very washing them, with dysentery wogs on his hands, we "took down with misery, terrible." The shells that went up the hill to do the Judge's portrait contained nothing but the spirit of the Expotition. So the portrait drawing was bad. And this was such an important picture; from it we hoped to secure all our other orders. We insisted on doing it over, but the Judge, game soul, declared it was good, much too good to sit for a second drawing.

And when a patron gives one a check and refuses to sit again there is not very much one can do about it.

I was worried about that picture. It did not seem like the kind that would start an epidemic. But then we could tell better when we felt healthier.

32

Before we could start painting natives we had to get around the usual obstacles in a new place, and the first in Rabaul was a domestic crisis. Meru disappeared. We had been appreciating Meru right along, but now that he was gone we were stricken. He was so quiet and well-mannered (when he was awake) and though he must have been scorching inside working for us, there was never a surly answer from him. Actually he was a bona fide aristocrat. He was the son of a chief of Kavieng in the north of New Ireland where (we were told) there were rigid social castes, the slaves being bad men purchased from other villages which did not want them around. And there the sons of chiefs were sent away to get experience in Rabaul, just as the sons of our best bankers are sent to work in European banks and the sons of Oriental aristocrats are sent to the United States. Meru had landed with the American recruiters as personal boy—which must have given him plenty of experience of a certain kind.

But he had the silent, teeth-gritting endurance of the real aristocrat.

The court between the Ambassador and the printing plant was the loafing place of all the boys who worked for the newspaper besides the personal boys of the tenants, and these lads were a savvy lot who had worked off and on for years in the metropolis. They were flash. Their hair was of every conceivable cut and color and their sense of humor that of the Dead End Boys. Meru's hair was a refined black, conservatively cut, and he had nothing but aloof scorn for the gaudy town boys. They retaliated as a gang and hooted at Meru for working for missus. It must have been painful for him because he had to get our drinking and bath water from the same places as the other boys got theirs, and he had to heat the bath pails on the same coconut husk fire as everyone else used in the court. We had often heard the yipping of the gang and wondered how Meru kept his temper.

So we assumed when the boy was absent that first morning that he had run away. And we did not blame him. But life without him was a painful thing. We had thought we scorned prestige, the kind that prevented a white woman doing anything for herself lest the natives see it. But pride balked at getting pails of water where the houseboys got theirs, at being seen loping down the hall with water spilling on our heels. And how could we heat bath water on the court fire with the natives, even if they didn't mind our using their coconut husks. Emptying slop jars was just *out*. We were afraid that gang might even dare to laugh at us, and somehow that seemed to matter, now that we had been entertained at the Residency.

Then we discovered where Meru was—in jail! And the whole sad story illustrates native breeding, when it is there, better than anything else could.

Legally indentured boys cannot be transferred from one employer to another without proper registration of the transfer, and it then devolves upon the new employer to keep the terms of the contract; to feed and shelter the native and pay him. This had not been done in Meru's case because it was understood that he was a very temporary loan. And we had assumed when he continued working for us that the recruiters did not yet need him, and that, when they did, they would certainly pick him up and inform us. We also assumed that Meru was bunking and eating with the recruiters' other boys. And this was where we were wrong.

All the time Meru had been working and suffering for us so uncomplainingly, up to about a week before he was arrested, he had been buffeted around the town picking up what he could to eat and sleeping wherever he could find shelter. For the recruiters had "disappeared." When we found out about the whole business we could not understand why Meru had said nothing to us, unless it *was* stoicism. In any case, eventually he fell in with some boys from his own district who were indentured to one of the big stores, and though their rations were doled out by the pound, they shared with Meru both their rice and their bunks until the day a store official, making the rounds to rout out just such uninvited guests, discovered him and turned him over to the police. It was the sleuth-eared Editor who discovered his whereabouts.

As "employers" we were liable on two counts: the charge of using a boy's services without proper registration; and the second, of neither paying him nor providing bed and board. We had made a "vagrant" of a native. And Rabaul is very diligent about punishing employers who do not provide for their boys. It was Meru's pride that saved us; he refused to admit he was working for missus.

It was lucky for the recruiters that the law located both of them in the hospital. These two had disposed of their Bougainville recruits (having signed them on with employers) and then with the proceeds had gone on a magnificent bust which had landed them in the hospital, sick again. (This was where Meru had missed connections.) The one who had had blackwater in the bush got a recurrence of it, which this time very nearly accomplished the impossible—that of annihilating a Florida real-estate operator. The other one had gone to the hospital voluntarily, deciding that while he was still numb from the binge he would have his broken leg rebroken so that it would set properly. Both these hard-living Americans were on their way back to safer booms in the United

States before we left Rabaul, Meru having long since been restored to their doubtful employ.

And that boy was a rare treasure, as we learned by the contrast to his successors.

For a few days, until we could decide how to strike a balance between prestige and the law which demanded a two-year contract with a houseboy, Sammy lent us Bonga so that we could have a bath. And Bonga was everything that Meru was not; he was a mug, everything that island wives say native houseboys are, besides being surly. For he was a police boy and his dignity was being violated by waiting on women. So we rejoiced when Tombat came into our lives bearing an introductory paper talk-talk. The note was from the Editor:

"Ladies in Distress," it read. "The bearer of this is Tombat, or Falling Rain (because it was raining when he was born). He is a regular Hermes Trismegistus and you should find him useful, as he was my sister's houseboy for two years. He can perform all household duties; wash, iron, cook, wait on table, retail all local scandal, and outbargain a Mulberry Street pedlar—in case you would like him to market at the boom for you. He can also lie like a United States senator, and is the idol of half the black loafers in Rabaul.

"Incidentally, you should feel somewhat impressed by his willingness to take you on as Missus. The rest of my line, Tobonga, Tobuka, Togega, Tomelia, and Tomeria—the To being fellow clansmen, not brothers—refused, one and all, to take work for Missus. (These were the hoodlums who had been ya-ya-ing at Meru.) They just sat in a row showing the whites of their eyes when I called for a volunteer. Buka explained their reluctancy: 'Long 'asterday me lookem eye belong this fella missus on top lik-lik. [The tall one, which was I.] Now he cross man savvy true. [She's a mean one.] Ach! Me no go up now; he fighten me fella.' I was on the point of violating Section 66C of the Native Labor Ordinance of

1912, Papua, by belting one of them over the ear when Tombat volunteered for the job. Three months ago I and these boys had to fight our way out of a village in Warangoi Baining and Tombat ran away. Ever since then he has been anxious to re-establish his reputation for bravery by doing something especially heroic. He regards working for you as his golden opportunity.

"The law won't be on you this time unless Tombat runs away again. He will eat and sleep with the rest of the To, and his wages are nothing. Don't even try to give him tobacco because he will take it, and he is getting his tobacco from the Rabaul *Gazette*."

We looked at this courageous Falling Rain standing up against the blue curtain and saw a great strapping brown boy with a flaring yellow coiffure and a wide silly grin on his face. That grin alone was a recommendation after the sullen Bonga. Tombat was not tall but he was bull-shouldered and virile-looking, with coarse big features, totally different clay from the pale aristocratic Meru. All the To were like him.

And now at last we reached the conversational level of the island Missus; we could talk about nothing but our houseboy. But life with Tombat would not let us think of anything else. The first thing he did to endear himself was to change the color of his hair to match the color scheme of our quarters. We had given him some of the blue curtain material for a lap-lap and the next time we saw him his hair matched the pillows; it was an amazing magenta red and he had tucked in over one ear a frangipani blossom which was the nearest yellow he could get to the croton leaves which were the one odd color accent in the room. One can't *hire* that kind of intelligence in our land.

Our days with Tombat began when we were awakened by a yammering out in the court, after which we followed his progress into the building and down the long hall by a pound-

ing of feet and hilarious exchange of gibes with every boy he
passed. Sometimes he paused to have what sounded like a
wrestling match up the hall, but by and by he had reached
our door which he gave a beating. Then, without waiting to
be bade to enter, he broke in, swept up the heap of clothes
we had worn the day before, and crashed out, still making
sounds with his mouth. By nightfall the garments, all neatly
folded and bearing none of the usual ash smuts and scorched
designs of the iron on them, were lying on the hickyah. "Are
you giving Tombat any soap?" I thought to ask Margaret
one day. No, said Margaret, he hadn't *asked* for soap. But
Tombat was using soap and Margaret knew very well where
he was getting it, not only soap, but tubs and wood for heat-
ing the laundry water, and anything else he thought we
needed. From the Rabaul *Gazette*. Why should Tombat ask
for what he already had? And why should we question him
unnecessarily?

But he did use our iron. Curiously, in this town where
there was electricity (which may have been expensive) the
peck-sized coconut husk or charcoal-heated iron was still
the one in use. For a long time we had been wondering why
we had brought an electric traveling iron to Melanesia; and
now we knew. It was for Tombat to wear as a lavaliere. We
had given it to him to use as an iron but he used it that way
only for its effect on the loafers in the court. They were
consumed with curiosity over this "pickaninny iron" and
Tombat, to oblige them, spent hours running its three square
inches over the huge sheets (using the editor's ironing table),
after which he cooled it by running after the admirers trying
to touch them with it. Finally it was strung around his neck
by the cord where it hung under one arm as a pendent ornament. The connections were so frequently burnt or yanked
out that finally Margaret showed Tombat how to repair
them, and this monkey business with a screw driver never

failed to collect an audience breathlessly silent with interest and hope that the exposed wire ends would cross and "sing."

Meantime, in all this servanted luxury, the Expotition was slowly starving to death. With no portrait orders coming in yet we neither dared afford nor wanted to eat more than one meal a day at Popeye's, the restaurant in the building, for the food there was useless from the point of view of both taste and nourishment. Probably the only thing which did keep us together those days was the dinners we were invited out to. Of course, Tombat was a recommended cook, but we had no kitchen gear or dishes and we thought a meal had to be cooked on a stove. But Tombat heard us talking about it and managed everything with the same riotous efficiency that thumbmarked all his activities.

First of all he went marketing. With our red coin purse (which had in it a little gold elephant to hang onto the last penny) stuck in his arm band as an ornament, and the green palm-leaf dilly bag on his shoulder, Falling Rain went clapping off to outbargain the village Maries at the boom. When all the houseboys were there making their purchases, the two-block-long market was like a cockatoo aviary in the early morning. The village women sat all over the plaza facing in every direction surrounded by their babies, their rumpled-up calico slings, and numerous green palm baskets of fruit and vegetables. They were all women and the house-boys all boys, full of grasshoppers, and the screaming and whooping and laughter at this meeting of the sexes in a womanless town would send the virile Tombat home all but hysterical with success.

He came back with all sorts of luxuries that had cost prac-tically nothing: miniature chickens still alive, tiny eggs (which were not too safe), shell and ordinary fis'—though Tombat would have preferred us to eat tinned meat like proper white folk—huge delicious papayas scented with pepsin seed, ripe pineapples, and custard apples, the consistency and whiteness of heavy cream and sweeter than any other fruit we know. And there were small edible bananas, those we had tried to eat in the villages having been big plantains too coarse and bitter to be eaten raw. And he also brought tomatoes and lettuce salad, swearing that *he* would clean it so that the Missus did not get sore leg along belly.

Then Tombat "produced" (from some place we did not care to question him about) dishes and pots and trays, and with them took full possession of the vacant room across the hall—again without being questioned. Then he brought in a slab of someone's iron roof, put a thick layer of sand over it, added some rocks, camp style, and, when he needed fire, fetched the live coals in a kerosene tin. The smoke he fanned around with a palm frond trusting it to go out through the screen. The smoke that remained in the room made our fellow tenants think the Ambassador was burning down; but then everyone thought it would be fun to see the Ambassador burn down.

Finally, with our trays on the floor, Tombat, squatting on his haunches, excelled his references. The kumara came out of the coals as black and crisp as the coals themselves, but with the soft insides as hot and delicious as any civilized sweet potato. The little chickens roasted in leaves in some rock oven in the mysterious beyond were gamy but as tender and juicy as quail. Tombat never learned to make coffee, possibly because the only coffee we could buy had chicory in it but more probably because he made it like English tea, boiling it until it was black. But the trays were neat and the fruit mountainous, and we never again got dysentery while Tombat fed us.

Instead, we got the already heralded "fis' mouth"—from eating too much fish or else the wrong kind. The curse came in the form of little white bubbles that broke out, not only around the mouth but around the eyes. It was a maddening itch much like poison ivy infection, though luckily it lasted only a few days at a seige. Tombat and the other natives knew no more about it than the local doctor, and we just kept on itching until, having deleted one thing after another from our menu, we discovered it was caused by fish. That threw us back on dead tinned meat, to Tombat's satisfaction.

And so, having lived in abnormal comfort and serenity for a few weeks, we were braced for the Monkey, our next houseboy. All very young houseboys are called "monkey" but none was ever more appropriately named than the one that came to keep us continuously in a malarial fluctuation between crazy fury and rejoicing. He was a small relative of Tombat, and Tombat had received him straight from the arms of the mission fathers with a request that he be placed somewhere to be trained as a houseboy. Tombat thought we were just the missus, soft as old pie and not uselessly neat. The Editor thought so too, because he was missing the services of the efficient Falling Rain. And so, helplessly, we accepted the gift.

Twelve years is the minimum native age for service. The Monkey looked nine, and he was small even for that age, with a wiry little brown body with the jerks and a big round baby head split by an enormous mouth which never closed on two dozen shell-white teeth. Being of the To line the Monkey was virile, but he was also a mission boy with a few extra ideas. He had had only a year of schooling and it was our suspicion that he was offered to any taker for service because Christianity had failed and the fathers saw that the heathen fist was the only hope of salvation. The black eyes of the little boy were buttery with guilelessness, but it was the way he used them that warned us: they "clicked."

Luckily the blow was softened for us by Tombat's undertaking to break the Monkey into training. We could hear the two of them across the hall incessantly at it, To against To. About every third sound was "Wha' name?" the Monkey demanding to know why or what for, like "Baby Snooks." And like her he knew the answers himself. Our own first experience with him was over finances. Tombat had finally allowed him to go to the boom alone with the purse, taking the precaution, however, to tell him that the gold elephant in the purse was there to keep an eye on transactions. It would report to the Missus if any money got out for anything except food.

And with the Monkey buying, meals continued to be served in their usual abundance. Further, every now and then there was some tinned store delicacy, peaches from California, or pineapple from Hawaii, even the delicious gnali nuts that were so precious even to the natives that one could rarely get them. We did not see how the Monkey could manage such things on the little money we allowed him. Then one day Margaret counted up and found too much change in the purse for the number of the day's purchases. A very promising houseboy, we told the Editor that night, and explained why. The Editor looked bewildered for a minute, then grinned and asked to have the Monkey sent in.

One thing we then discovered was that a native does not lie to defend himself—or perhaps he does not feel guilty. The Monkey readily admitted that he had been picking up our groceries where they did not seem to be in use. Some were from the Editor's own stores, some lifted from Popeye's house cook, and odds and ends were picked up at the boom when the Maries were looking the other way.

We thought we handled this crisis with motherly wisdom. We had read a great deal about the native attitude toward food and thought the boy should not be accused of stealing. Food was something that belonged to everyone in the village;

rather, it was a disgrace to all for one to need food, and an even greater disgrace to steal something to eat because that accused those who owned the food of being too stingy to give it—stinginess being the cardinal sin. To buy and sell this prime necessity of life (other than feast pigs) as we do would be unthinkable in the "savage" society, and probably no unsophisticated native would believe that we actually profit on the hunger of our fellowmen and let those who have not the money to buy food starve and die of malnutrition diseases. No, the Monkey's attitude toward food was the exact reverse of ours, for, while he daily saw vegetables being bought and sold at the boom, he probably also saw the silliness of it when he could pick up what we needed without going through the hocus-pocus of handing over our "marks" (shillings) for it. But at length we patiently explained our heathen ways and how the Monkey must *spend* the money in the purse. When we were exhausted the little ape was standing there grinning and clicking his eye. "Yasmissus," he beamed enthusiastically, and whirled out of the room.

He had got away with that.

The next encounter, however, took the scales from our eyes, as Bertie says. All the time the Monkey had been "borrowing" food for us from the town, the money in the purse had not, by any means, remained untouched. There was always less after the daily raids, and now that we had ordered him to spend, the marks began disappearing far in excess of the value of his purchases. Margaret became suspicious and began going to the boom with him, and so stopped that leak. But there was still the store, and for these shopping trips a list was placed in the purse with a request for an itemized receipt, and the money was counted before the purse was given to the boy.

He even tried to get around this watertight arrangement. One day when Margaret had put a pound note in the purse the Monkey returned from the store with neither groceries nor money, nor even the elephant. The elephant had stayed at home for the first time in his life. And sure enough, there he was standing on the window sill—where *we* had not put him. The Monkey said that he had reached the store without dallying and when the clerk had opened the purse there was nothing in it but the list. It was the greatest mystery, because the Monkey had himself lookem Missus put the money along the purse. We could get no other story. So we called again on the long-suffering Editor, and without any hesitation he grabbed the boy by the hair, dug down to the scalp, and extracted the pound note. No one was more astonished than the Monkey himself. "Ach!" he exclaimed, disgustedly, "Marks him-he stop along grass alla same walkabout. Him-he bad fella . . . No savvy 'long Zhezhus." The pound note was a heathen louse to hide in his hair and try to incriminate a lad with the face of a little black cherub.

He looked most like a cherub when we sat down to the evening meal, for then he stood and waited and would not leave until we had said grace. We usually said, "Oh, merciful God, give us strength to see this meal through" (for the Monkey's dishes were seasoned with something that sounded like ground glass), and until we came to the "amen" our treasure stood with his hands folded in prayer, his face still smiling but his eyes sweetly downcast. At the "amen" in which he joined heartily, he would burst out with clicking eyes and flashing teeth to whirl away and get started on some new deviltry he had thought up during grace.

For "borrowing" our last American lipstick and brazenly appearing after siesta with his big mouth "alla same betel nut" he was made to stand in the corner and reflect further on property rights. (He had been given a dose of castor oil to wash away the sin of the pound-note episode.) He stood and yodeled hymns in a falsetto adolescent voice.

The Editor came to us with a wild story that was going the rounds out back about our having told the pickaninny that there were blue and green Americans. We ourselves, in fact, were white like the British missus only because we put a something-nothing on our faces every day, and this magical lotion the Monkey was prepared to supply to the flash boys —at a price, of course. We traced that story by the missing

bottle of mineral oil which we used on our faces in lieu of cold cream, and which the Monkey had "borrowed."

The blue and green Americans needed some digging to get to the bottom of and, omitting that lengthy adventure, the story was somewhat like this: Some time ago we had told the Monkey we were from America. He knew about our country because in mission school America was pointed out as one of the places on the globe where there were black people like himself. He had simply assumed that all Americans were black, and at first could not decide whether we were gamin him (fooling about being Americans) or had done something to get white skins. Patiently we explained—this was during the days when we were still taking our job as missus-to-a-poor-little-cherub seriously—that there *were* black Americans, but there were also white ones, and yellow ones and red ones and brown ones, "almost every color of man there is." And in repeating this astounding information to the To out back the Monkey had simply added the other colors he knew which we had omitted itemizing. But privately he still clung to the notion that we Americans got these differently colored skins by applying them, and that the white skin came out of the bottle.

So we let him sample it—internally. He had quite readily returned the bottle, having discovered it hiding under the building and Tombat was called in to administer the punishment. He would not take it from us. Remembering the effects of the castor oil—and incidentally it is illegal to force a native to take castor oil unless he "needs" it for physical reasons—he stood with his teeth clamped together, still grinning. But Tombat knew how to handle that. He forced the top of the bottle between the pickaninny's teeth, getting his jaws open by pressing on both sides (just as one handles a dog for the same purpose), and then to prevent his spitting out the oil Tombat gave him a sudden slap on the diaphragm. The Monkey gulped and down went the dose. The next minute the little ape was laughing, enjoying the joke as much as anyone.

But he finally got us into civic difficulties. As his guardians we were called into court after he had snatched the lap-lap off a Marie on her way to the boom. She was laden with baskets and babies, both her hands engaged, so the Monkey had yanked at the lap-lap and satisfied his curiosity before the woman could protect herself. By this time we thought a little solitary confinement was just the thing the Monkey needed and were dismayed when the official handed our darling back to us, exacting only a small fine. This was supposed to come out of the Monkey's pay, but even if he had earned this amount so far, to deny him it would have been no corrective. He had seen a Marie and now that that curiosity was satisfied there was not much danger of his repeating that particular offense again. The next time it would be something more horrible, for the Monkey was a genuine anarchist. He had left the laws of the village behind and had not yet learned respect for those of the town.

Denuding a Marie was much more serious than it sounds, for there is a Rabaul law which makes "immodesty" in women punishable. No native woman can enter the town with breast uncovered, and the result is a hideous hip-length blouse which is donned on the outskirts of town and removed on the home trip just as soon as the settlement is left behind. So the Marie whom the pickaninny had attacked was as much frightened by fear of punishment for being seen without a lap-lap as she was outraged at having been exposed. The modesty may be our artificial kind, but it is taken very seriously as far as it goes by these New Britain women. On the way back from the boom to their villages the women bathe in the bay and during the dip change from town clothes back to the faded village lap-lap or grass kilts. And they are so skillful in the shift, removing the good calico as they sink in the water and winding the old piece on as they wade out to shallow beach, that a local resident told us he had stood on the beach for thirty years and had never seen a Marie's behind. The Monkey was, consequently, somewhat of a hero in our parts.

But the town life was getting him, and we decided that he must receive some lesson this time which would bring home to him the rights of others. He must experience shame such as he had inflicted on the burdened Marie. To make him appear in public without his lap-lap, the logical lesson, was of course impossible to put into force. But the Monkey's vanity was enormous and insatiable and that had possibilities. He never passed the mirror without figuratively saying hello, and his hair had changed in color almost daily from the approved red, running the gamut through all the coloring matter that could be borrowed in the building including our paints. Why he had any hair left to primp up after the courses of bleaching and staining can be accounted for only by the steel-wool quality of native grass. He had no scissors but he borrowed ours to trim his hedge and in vain tried to make off with them permanently. When we screamed for scissors they repeatedly came out of the most astonishing places, always having flown there on the wings of a bad fella pigeon. Once they buried themselves, die finish, under the building. But, to the Monkey's credit, they always resurrected themselves when we asked for them, or for anything that was missing. Hair, in any case, was the pickaninny's Achilles heel.

It was very reasonable, we thought: the Monkey had seen a naked Marie—the Maries should see his naked scalp.

We began by explaining at great length the principles of the Golden Rule and exactly why we were about to do what we were. Then, while Margaret laid hold on the Monkey's arms, I whacked off a small hank of his wool from the front center of his coiffure. It was a brief struggle, and then followed the most crushing reaction. The pickaninny stared at the wad of red wool in my hand. His eyes twittered and then tears the size of marbles welled up in them. He was suddenly a tragic little boy. The next instant he had dashed out of the room. And he was swallowed up until the next morning.

Then we met him in court. He had reported *us!*

"Malira" is properly a love spell, but the word is used loosely to cover other kinds of spells including the punishable black magic which causes illness. We were haled into court more or less unofficially to explain a charge of using it on our little houseboy. The Monkey in a very nearly hysterical condition had appeared at the station alone, exhibited his shorn pate, and made a good story of it by claiming we had cut off his hair to give it to a sorcerer. It took but a few minutes to explain our part in it, but none of us could pacify the boy. He was convinced that with that hank of grass missing something dreadful would happen to him.

The sense of justice which primitives have is the one quality even the bitterest of white men concede, and if this boy had been older he would undoubtedly have understood his being subjected to the same treatment as he had given the Marie. But he was a child, and now a frightened one—and we were two of the sorriest jurists who ever meted out punishment. The official finally suggested that we return the hank of hair to the pickaninny. He was very careful to explain, however, that it was not the policy of the court to promote the belief in malira by recognizing any of its parts, but the boy seemed to be in such a condition that he might fret himself into illness before he could be convinced that we meant him no ill.

We were only too happy to return the hair. But there was no hair. We went home and searched through baskets and waste cans, and finally called in the Editor and demanded hair —vermilion hair, the color the Monkey's was currently. The Editor called in his Hermes Trismegistus and demanded red grass, anybody's. We would pay marks for it. Tombat widened his eyes and grinned, disappeared and came back with a hank of yellow hair. Where he had got it he would not tell us, but he was savvy and marks were marks. The lock was dipped in red pigment and delivered to the pickaninny, and the pickaninny was delivered back to the mission for more light.

33

That last chapter does not end, by any means, the story of the Monkey. The cruelest thing we could have done to him was to send him back to the mission after he had had a taste of town. He ran away and returned to Tombat, and Tombat would have returned him to us, but we would have none of him as we did not wish to end up in jail ourselves. And besides, by this time we were being kept uncomfortable by another of Sammy's superior valets. Still under Tombat's protection the Monkey haunted the premises, occupying himself by emptying out our bath water after the boy had heated it, and removing the towels from the house wash-wash between the moment the bath was announced and that when we had got to the coop. He kept himself on our minds as we, apparently, were on his.

One day I was stricken unto death with an abscessed ear. I went to bed with the traveling iron on my head and had waking nightmares in which I was torturing a little black cherub. Margaret said I kept muttering, "Now, off with his head . . . off with his head!" It was my own head I was wishing off for by the third day the pain was so intense that we decided this was not just plain earache but something for a doctor. It was lucky we were in a place where there was a doctor, but foolishly, to save money, I went to the doctor instead of having him come to us. They brought me home on a litter.

This ear trouble, said to be got from sea water, is a common affliction in the islands (which does not, however, make it any less painful); but we doubt very much if it is acquired by going in swimming, for even the Chief Judge, who must be nigh on to seventy, had sieges of it. But it is serious because its aftermath is increasing deafness.[1] At the time I was stricken the doctor had just received some new injection material which he had not yet tried. He explained briefly that he was experimenting on me and then just jabbed. Hence the vapors which struck me out in less than two minutes.

When I was strong enough to sit up and fence again the Editor called. "So he got you after all," he grinned. I felt a little odd for I knew instantly what he meant. He had told us the Monkey was plotting revenge. A ball of my hair combings wrapped in leaves had been found a few weeks before stuffed in a corner of the house cook. Margaret had seen it lying on a cross support and thinking it was a nest of some sort had brought it across to our room to examine. And when we found that the leaves contained my hair we were so amused, suspecting that the Monkey was trying to do a bit of malira on his own, that we told the Editor about it. We thought he was gamin when he wanted to report the pickaninny to the authorities. The best job of bewitching is done by burning the hair, mixing the ashes with ginger and burying the mixture, but it is still not effective unless the person to be cast under the spell knows about it. And this was precisely why, the Editor told us, the hair had been left where we would find it. We did not believe that—not of the Monkey; he was a little hellion, but not cunning.

Yet I must have believed it, subconsciously. During the fever I continually had nightmares about the boy, and I had known altogether too quickly what the Editor meant by his "So he got you after all."

---

[1] For the benefit of those who may get "tropical ear" we have heard that the deafness has been treated successfully with a special arrangement of electrotherapy.

For something does inevitably get you when you have been in a primitive country long enough. It all sounds absurd to hear it in a familiar matter-of-fact environment away from the islands, but illness and death by autosuggestion are not myth but fact and after you have heard enough of it you are convinced. They are a matter of court record. And why, if black magic were not effective, would laws have been passed by hard-headed governments to punish it? The punishment, they claim, is for terrorization, but if terrorization did not have injurious, sometimes fatal, results it would not be punishable.

Of course, I realize I am being commonplace telling one more story about a death caused by black magic, but this one is to illustrate a moral—and to prove incidentally that I am not altogether a jackass-artist with too much imagination, for believing the unbelievable. The story is true, most of it a matter of official record in the New Guinea court, and although we did not witness any of it ourselves, it was told to us by the officer who sat on the case when the principals were finally brought into court.

A sorcerer in a village not far from Rabaul became infatuated with a married woman in the same village to whom he began making "improper advances." The Marie would have nothing to do with him, so he told her he was going to put proper love malira on her. This is generally successful because a woman resisting when knowing she has had a spell put on her usually dies. Most Maries take the line of least resistance, but this wife was evidently more faithful than others because she reported the sorcerer to her husband. Both must have been genuinely frightened at bucking the consequences in resisting the malira; nevertheless the husband went to the sorcerer and threatened him with hellfire if he did not remove the spell. He succeeded in frightening the witch doctor but not in quenching his desires, for while the latter agreed to "wash" the spell away, it was this business that landed him in court on a charge of attempted rape.

The following description of how to wash away a love spell is also in the records of this case. The sorcerer required the girl to closet herself along with him in a hut and then she was made to get down on hands and knees (which is the position for copulation); after that the magician began to bathe the girl, starting at her neck, with the liquid contents of a small bottle. He worked south until he reached the woman's

lap-lap, which he ordered her to remove. And it was her screams at this point in the operation which brought the husband rushing in—and landed him in court on a countercharge of attempted murder.

The sorcerer was given a jail sentence, and Exhibit A, the bottle of malira neutralizer, was tested and found to be merely "dirty water." Then, in the presence of the Marie and her husband, who were still thoroughly frightened because the washing-away of the love magic had not been completed, the bottle was locked in the court safe. But even with both the sorcerer and his dirty water locked up the couple were still so convinced the woman would die that the officer, as a matter of personal curiosity, decided to keep track of the case. The woman was asked to report back periodically for a check on her health, and before she left Rabaul she was given a thorough physical examination at the hospital. She showed no pathological symptoms, though her pulse was slower than normal—the usual result of a native's ordeal in court.

Of course, the girl died. It took a little over six months before her strong young heart ceased to beat simply from the conviction that it must. So long as she was able to make the trips in to Rabaul every test was negative. Yet the pulse became increasingly slower and weaker, and the flesh sloughed away until only bones and sinews were left. But it takes a lot to convince a Scotch barrister that there are fairies, and the minute the woman died he ordered an autopsy. The story of how they got around funeral customs and got the corpse in to the operating table before it began to "spoil" in the heat is not on the official records, for the very good reason that the whole business was decidedly irregular. However, the autopsy revealed nothing the doctor knew about that would have caused death. There were hemorrhoids, unruptured, but no one has ever been known to die just from constipation. Yet the girl was dead, just as she had believed she would be soon.

This case was not unusual except that it was the only one we heard about that had been followed up to its final conclusion and scientifically determined as to whether the death was due to "natural causes." What had the officer to say about it? He did not "know"; undoubtedly there was "something" going on here, logical and all that if we could get to the bottom of it, but it would take time to understand and catalogue it. "Could it be," asked Margaret—who believes in magic and is always looking for proof of it—"that it's simply something we all once understood, and we Whites have forgotten in sophistication?" Perhaps these primitives retain some instinct, some delicate sensibility, that gets things out of the air for them—the sort of elemental "knowing" that makes eels swim across oceans and up strange rivers to search out an ancestral home that they themselves have never known. Hate has powerful vibrations, and even in our extrovert civilization it can wither the sensitive. The death sentence contained in black magic and its effect on its victims might be just another more acute form of the same psychological phenomenon. But how it could work in our behalf if we could recapture fully that elemental conviction primitives have! If conviction alone can kill the tenacious flame of life even in youth and good health, how well could it also work if we believed so earnestly in the goodness of life? And that is my moral. If we could only recapture the primitive's deep capability of believing.

The officer who told us this story of the possessed woman had spent many years in the islands in responsible government posts. I mention this simply to establish him as a crank about repeating tales which might make these islands seem more spectacular than we traveling authors have already made them. Yet the "something-nothing" below the surface in this land had got to even this hard-headed barrister. He admitted it and told us the following experience.

He had a houseboy who had been with him many years, and who fell ill with a diseased heart. The officer was fond of the boy and helped to take care of him, but Bota (the boy) *would* get off and break his strict diet by gorging himself with flying fox or something equally disastrous. Eventually it became clear that the boy had not long to live, and in order to make his last days happier the officer moved him out to Rapindik, about three miles from town where he could be with his father and eat all the flying fox he wanted. "The evening the boy was sent away," the officer said, "I was working late out on the back veranda and I heard someone call out, in exactly his [Bota's] voice. As I knew he was three miles away I guessed it was one of the other boys dreaming. But when I went to their house they were quiet and so soundly asleep I had trouble waking them. I woke them because the thing was so uncanny and I wanted to find out if any of them was dreaming. Still, it must have been one of them though they, of course, insisted that I had heard the voice of Bota. Bota was dying and his spirit had sung out. They were so convinced that Bota had died that I got the wind up and drove out to Rapindik in the morning. Bota *had* died and just about the time, as nearly as I could figure out, that I heard the voice. Curious business . . . but I still think it was one of my boys who had dreamed true, and called out, and it was his voice I heard, not Bota's.

"I took all my boys down to the funeral. The thing upset us a lot. As I left, one of Bota's friends was orating by the graveside much like one of our padres. I heard the opening part, 'Good-bye, Bota. You fella alla same ground now. Maske [never mind], me-fella too by-m-by go finish. Behind [later] all me-fella ground too . . .' But it seemed they weren't talking *at* a dead Bota. They were talking *to* him."

(An afterthought: We know about the argument of materialistic scientists that in the case of death by autosuggestion there is a definite physiological cause: Fear or dread of death releases secretions into the blood stream which may be fatal if prolonged. But this is an argument like saying that it was not the ax of the guillotine which caused La Pompadour's death, but heart failure due to hemorrhage or asphyxiation, or even chagrin at losing her head. The instrument was the ax, we say, and belief is the ax in such native cases as I have illustrated.)

34

The first semiprimitive Negroids I ever saw were Haitians. I once made an overland journey by car from Haiti to Santo Domingo City, leaving Port-au-Prince in the middle of a Friday night. All along the road for miles and miles after we left the city our headlights caught a continuous procession of barefooted black natives, their mules and themselves laden with garden produce, plodding in toward the Port-au-Prince Saturday market. Every now and then there were groups squatting around a little bonfire eating, and as daylight came we saw that all those weary miles the women had been carrying sleeping infants and what produce could not be piled on the already loaded mules. The men strolled along unburdened.

And now here, outside Rabaul, halfway round the world from Haiti, we saw that picture again. Only the Haitian donkeys were missing, for in New Britain the Maries carry to the Rabaul boom all that mules could handle. And the stalwart men who accompany them do not even burden themselves with the little cupid bow and arrows that gave his excuse to the old-man escort of the Guadalcanar garden women. They come along solely to make a killing in town.

The journey from the village begins, like those to the Port-au-Prince market, in the middle of the night, for there are miles to go and the way is slow; and as the sun comes up, the same black groups sit by the wayside nursing their babies and gnawing on chunks of cold roasted yam or sago for breakfast. Finally at the boom, while the men gossip and strut, the women haggle with buyers, and when the sun starts down the western sky they gather up what produce has not been sold and with it trudge the weary miles back to the village, a trip that sometimes extends into another night.

There is usually only one man to four or five pack women, but one early morning on the road to Kokopo we encountered a small family unit: a man and his pet cockatoo, his wife and baby, and "their" market produce. The couple had evidently come some distance, for their legs were covered with gray dust to the knees; and when they stopped, the woman, whose husband gallantly unloaded her, could hardly get her spine straight again. For a minute after she was seated on the ground she remained bent over, looking dumbly at the ground while the already bulging pickaninny dragged at her breast. We thought she must be old, but when at last she brought her head up it was a young face. The baby's white cotton sling was untied from her shoulder and then the child was laid on the ground, for it had begun to doze. Then, while the woman put on her clean town blouse, the husband smeared the dust and coconut oil into each other on his chest and arms and, having got polished for town, proceeded to stoke up his quid of betel nut. His lips were already gory with the juices, and one eye was decorated with a sinister smudge of white lime, literally a sign of the "having the eye out" for no good reason. He had further ornamented himself with a bandolier of split banana leaf, a palm-leaf vanity case worn on the shoulder with his arm thrust through the handle hole, and a screaming white cockatoo tied by the leg to the bandolier. This flash gentleman gave us a brilliant red and white grin when he saw we were not passing on, but the Marie never once looked in our direction. Though by her sullen expression "we knew she knew."

Perhaps this was the reason she started to go. Rather, she began to start to go. First she twisted the ends of the baby's sling around her shoulder—not knotting the calico, however, for the weight of the infant cinched the twists; then she rose to a kneeling position and swung a huge palm-leaf sack of vegetables onto her back with its long handle over her forehead. She kept jerking her head forward while the husband pushed the bag up until it rested on the back of her hips. Then he put a second big sack on top of her back, balanced and resting on the bottom load. All this time the Marie was screaming like a camel being loaded while the man kept on grinning amiably.

Finally the woman was on her feet, having got there without assistance, and when she was bent over to the proper thirty-three-and-a-third degree angle, the husband courteously set about twenty pounds of vegetables on her head. She had to hold onto this top load with her free hand to keep it in balance because as the two got under way the baby, hanging from her neck, began to swing and her other hand, steadying it and holding up its weight to spare the neck as much as possible, was not enough; the swinging wobbled the woman from side to side. She was walking with bent knees, her face down to the earth, and when the two passed us, she stared at us out of the corner of her near eye, her brow pulled up, thinking like an ostrich, I suppose, that being so submerged herself she would not be seen satisfying her curiosity.

But she was to see all she wanted of us before she escaped. We followed the two into town, he dallying before and she staggering after. When we passed the mission grounds he helped himself to a big red hibiscus blossom and carefully tucked it into his yellow grass over one ear. This was a deliberate advertisement that he had not only his white eye but his mind on some Marie. It couldn't have been his wife by any stretch of the imagination, so it must have been some girl he expected to see at the boom. (Flirtations were part of the fun of the boom, but it is very doubtful if they ever passed

beyond the screaming, gamin stage.) After the husband had carefully examined his hair in the mirror from his vanity case, rewrapped his sarong, and tightened his belt, he began to tickle the neck of his cockatoo which raised and lowered its high yellow comb and squawked affectionately. All this time the Marie had been standing in the heat waiting, for all the world like a patient old horse, and when the dazzling husband finally got through primping and playing she fell in behind him as he resumed his junket to town, again like a patient old horse. She was no different from the rest of the Melanesian Maries; patient beyond belief while executing her traditional chores, but volcanic when asked to do anything outside the line of duty.

When we neared the museum in town—a large rambling structure built by the tidy Germans to house the native curios that patrol officers and missionaries and prospectors appropriated from the villagers—we got on our bicycles and bowled on ahead of the couple to get help from the director in capturing this pack Marie for a painting. We were using the north veranda of the museum for a studio and the entire museum staff for ever-obliging interpreters, critics, and model arrangers. But now one and all blanched at the task of getting a Marie to pose. Yet, they did it. It took about an hour of the usual yammering and whining and arm flaying, the director talking in pidgin English to the husband, the husband talking native to his wife, and the wife answering in a muffled scream; while the infant bawled and a crowd of native loafers gathered to snicker at the still-burdened woman for being an ignorant bush Marie. But she was alone now, the only native of her sex present, and without the mob-assistance of her sisters she was almost helpless. Either she could stand there all day and whine, or she could be pushed up against a bank of yellow croton and whine, which would be posing. She was therefore guided over to the croton hedge

and I started the drawing on my canvas without the matter
of her consent ever being settled.

I am positive I suffered more that morning than the Marie
did under her fifty or seventy-five pounds of vegetables. I
blocked in the position and palm bags as fast as I could because I expected the pose to end in a faint at any minute;
but when I ordered a rest, myself nearly fainting from vicari-
ous agony, the woman refused to lay down her burdens.
She wanted to go on to the boom. Margaret gave her a
mark, and that persuaded her to squat, teetering, for a rest,
but she still would not let her husband unload her. Yet she
had to be unloaded because the town blouse had to come off.
That was a scene: getting the jumper off. The woman was
afraid she would be arrested for being seen without a breast
covering, but she was more afraid of the museum director
who was tough with her because he was bored with us. Between him and another mark and a lot more whining and
barking and the crowd being shooed aff, the damned blouse
finally, at long last, came off.

And now the woman refused to be reloaded. And so on and
on through the morning.

To save myself agony I should rather have had the model
sitting on the ground so that I should not have to see her
knees shaking; but she would not sit down when she was
loaded again (a stick of tobacco having accomplished this
miracle) so that there was nothing to do but allow her to
stand, stick a palm leaf up in front of her quivering legs, and
paint, trying to remember that Maries grow up with vegetables on their heads. But that arm holding the basket on her
head! The muscles were trembling, and the sweat oozing out
of the tortured forehead, dropping off nose and chin, must
have been tickling horribly. The woman could not use her
hand to scratch without losing the basket on her head. Two
or three times Margaret went over and put her hand on the

top load and leaned down under the woman's face to show her that she was to swab her face, but the Marie just gazed at her looking like a groundhog on the second of February. Finally she simply stood numb—as I was too by this time— crunched together and enduring like an animal in a bitter storm.

The entire figure including the baby (though not the baskets) was reproduced in about an hour and a half painting time and it was a record more of physical endurance than of painting speed.

There was still the fancy husband to do, but there was no strength left in my skin for him. Yet he too would be gone with the sun, back to the village. "What name belong you-fella?" we inquired, for the man must be asked to come back the next day. "Name belong me-fella Tokobau," he answered. He was one of the To villagers, the same as the virile hoodlums at the Rabaul *Gazette*. In that case (to keep the type consistent with that of the Marie) we could get Tombat to pose as the husband. I revived sufficiently then to make a rough sketch of Tokobau's finery, his painted eye, the bandolier, and cut of his hair, so that Tombat could be tricked out alla same. (The cockatoo we should have to omit.) Then, to the man's disgust we paid him two sticks of tobacco for his posing time and the woman six sticks for ten times as much, and the two, thank goodness, went out of our lives forever, for she was still whining and he still grinning complacently.

But to get Tombat to pose as someone else's husband was not so easy as we thought it would be.

The painting and all of our gear had been left overnight at the museum, as usual, right out on the unguarded veranda where there were enough other precious museum curios to have given a collector a temperature. We asked the Editor to send Tombat up to take a look at the painting so that he could deck himself out in the same fashion. Instead the Editor and the entire To clan went in a body to take that look. They were still snorting when they got back to the Ambassador. The To knew Tokobau and knew his Marie and if the Missus thought that Tombat was going up to that museum and have himself publicly painted into a canvas standing next to Tokobau's woman—ach, what an idea!

In the end we had to move all our painting gear back to the Ambassador and there, in the rear court sheltered behind mats, a single croton branch nailed to the background wall, Tombat posed. But once he had fallen into the mood of the thing he had a hilarious time. He copied the banana fringe bandolier, painted his eye white, and made a palm-leaf vanity bag for his upper arm; while the rest of the To stood on the other side of the mat enclosure screaming with delight as Tombat reported how we were getting on.

Later we overheard an interesting description of how a picture is painted. It was in Tombat's pidgin English and would be unintelligible hash to repeat that way, but some of Tombat's native humor surmounts language differences. Partly interpreted it went something like this: "Missus he stand back a long way. He look as if he will kill Tombat. By and by he come up along picture. He fight him strong fella. Picture he comes, he goes [wobbles]. Missus he say 'ach, goddamn.' Tombat he die. [Tombat freezes into the pose: the audience roars.] By and by Missus he say 'Spello.' *Missus* spello (but) *Tombat* go walkabout. Close up Missus he sing out 'All right.' Tombat die." Tombat freezes into the pose and the audience roars as before. And so on and on and on repeated endlessly and always with the undiminished enjoyment of the audience.

When the figures of the canvas were finished, and the palm baskets had been painted from models we bought at the boom (placed comfortably on the ground, you may be sure) the painting still cried for the cockatoo to make it complete. So Tombat took the Editor's old Ford two-seater and tore out to the country to borrow Tokobau's bird. He came back empty-handed but grinning. Tokobau would not rent his pet. Back went Falling Rain with orders to bring in both bird and owner at any price. Back he came alone. He had told Tokobau that he, Tombat, was along (with) the Marie in the picture, and he had escaped (though not intact) only because he had left the engine of the Ford running. (It was too much trouble to crank.) As it was he had received a coconut on the shoulder with such force that a circle of skin three inches in diameter was missing. It was all To gamin. Tokobau was not mad fella; Tombat was not mad fella. But we still had no cockatoo.

The bird that was eventually painted on the shoulder of the "husband" was a tame resident of Port Moresby, Papua. It posed on the shoulder of a houseboy and for two hours repeated, with intervals of "aw-aw-k," "Jesuschristalmighty-jesuschristalmighty . . ." all the while searching the house-boy's ear for some dainty. The present owner swore the bird had been raised by a missionary.

35

Rabaul is ever like this: I was in the road one day performing the perfectly commonplace task of pumping up a flat bicycle tire—acutely missing the "free air" of our country, and, incidentally, the gallantry of our fair land which needs no formal introduction to a lady with a flat tire—when up behind me came a long line of natives led by a white man in need of a shave and a haircut, which identified him as the recruiter. Every one of those natives—all twenty-six of them, had heads shaped like a gourd! They were Bougainese of the head-binding district. And in the museum was a Chinese lantern initiation hat, so that it took just about three quarters of an hour to lead a young Bougainese to the hat and another fifteen minutes to get smacking into the "Big Buka Brothers."

The canvas that came out of that fortunate encounter stands as the battle site of a bitter war waged between "those who know" and we who saw. We had only *seen* such a lantern hat on an adult native in the bush of Bougainville, but "'they" knew such hats were discarded after the initiation ceremonies of the secret society. The recruiter, with beautiful logic, claimed that such a hat could not be worn by this particular boy because the boy was a recruit and the law did not permit natives wearing the hat to be recruited. When the model himself was asked whether, had he remained in the bush, he would have been wearing such a hat, he said "Yes." But when he was asked if the hats were burned after initiation he said "Yes." Asked if he would be wearing a hat if he were an old man (like the one we had seen in a hat) he said he couldn't because his hair was now cut short and there was nothing to hold the hat on, even if he were old. He sounded like the recruiter.[1]

Another day I was coming in from a ride I had taken alone; I had found a retreat in the Chinese cemetery behind

town to which I went occasionally for the sweet stillness that was nowhere else in Rabaul. Cemeteries and zoos were an indulgence anyway, my interest in the former far from morbid. One could visualize the long-dead Orientals beneath those

[1] The confusion of the "lantern" hats was never satisfactorily solved. If the hats are discarded after initiation, as the authorities firmly claim, then our old man of Bougainville must have been bald, and wearing a hat (of accidentally similar design) not only as protection from the sun, but to safeguard his vanity. Baldness is not common among the Melanesians (and we saw only one head of grizzly gray hair); but there was an old gentleman in Nodup who was bald, and because of it he was almost as much of a village joke as if he had been sitting in bald-head row of our burlesque.

big green mounds, and one was reminded of the precious life still ours—and what to do with it. And I needed stimulus these days. Frankly I was weary. It is all great fun to travel sight-seeing through the tropics, but to work is another matter—when the heat makes one feel drugged, unable to think, and when each siege of malaria leaves one a little more slowly. Then there was the eternal bucking of unexpected obstacles. If they were only the same just twice so that the second time one could get over them easier, we might feel we were making progress. Why, for instance, was Rabaul being unexpectedly so obstinate about ordering portraits! We knew the "dysentery drawing" of the Judge was not the best work technically that the cigarette tin could turn out; but, seen again afterwards in healthier days, it was still not so bad but the likeness was unmistakable. Yet no other resident, having been exposed to the Judge's picture, had wanted himself immortalized. And if this stalemate continued we were doomed as an Expotition. Our limit was the moment when our funds got down to the price of a ticket home, and that was within sight.

But I always came away from the cemetery with my fur smoothed down; the one thing we possessed which was not in that quiet green terminal was breath. And that was something positive.

And so, feeling very positive, although breathless at the moment, I was tearing down the road at a canter trying to beat the chill of the afternoon rain to the sarsaparilla bottle. My steed, one of those sixteen-hand Australian stallions, had a companion piece in the form of a white bull terrier that had a matching personality. The two chased natives. Rather, passing natives fell off their bicycles at our approach and made for the trees, the dog took after them and the horse after the dog. The rider was merely present, for while the horse's head was being pulled acutely to starboard his feet below went to port after the terrier. Progress was on the bias and likely to land one in the side of a hut. Then, when natives were clinging to the trunks of palm trees all along both sides of the road, the stallion waited, posed like a pointer with his tail up, for the terrier to pull the natives down by the feet so that we could eat them.

The only way I could avoid such scenes was to let the horse have his head, which took me soaring over the country-side at such a pace that the bull terrier was too busy and breathless to bite natives. However, if he did pause to tree a boy we were too far ahead to see it, and the one thing this fire-eater horse would not do was go back. In theory the "rides" reduced the malaria-enlarged spleen, in practice they broke down the last solid atom in an already jellied Expoti-tion. But they were a speedy way of getting places to which our chronically sore feet could not take us.

So this day we were soaring down the main stem of Rabaul at our usual thirty miles an hour, and were just heaving past Burns-Philp's big store when the first bullets of rain hit. They struck the roof of formosa and sent showers of petals down into the road, making the bowered tunnel look as if it were raining yellow rain. Natives scuttled from both the rain and the Expotition—all but a long line of almost naked black men approaching up the road. The formation in-dicated newly-arriving recruits, and the usual unshaven bob-haired white man was in the lead. We bore down on them like a machine-gun barrage, and the effects on our target were much the same. Natives sprayed or sprawled in every direc-tion, the terrier after them and the horse after the terrier. And after us a recruiter bellowing with fury.

And that was the beginning of a beautiful friendship. The encounter was even more portentous, for I believe that, in the end, when we had to make up our minds whether the Expotition was going to retreat homeward, or go on west to

Papua and the Dutch Indies to finish the job, the model we painted from this line of recruits decided us.

The model was up a tree when I met him, the bull terrier trying to reach his feet, and the stallion pointing eagerly while the recruiter snorted flames at my leg. I being on the horse was on a level with the treed boy and for the moment I was quite oblivious to the hell going on around me. For the deep-brown back flattened to the tree before me was entirely covered by a magnificent panorama of cicatrice welts. A string of frigate-bird-shaped skin clots started on the upper arm, ran over the shoulders and down the back on both sides of the spine, and in the remaining spaces were rows of large "lozenges." There was barely a whole square inch of skin on that back that had not been slashed open and packed with clay to make the wounds heal in scars.

This was the first skin scarification we had seen in the South Seas. The boy was the first practicing "cannibal" in our lives. He was a Papuan (not a Melanesian) from the Sepik River district of the mainland of New Guinea, and even with his hair shorn and in the lap-lap the recruiter had substituted for the village pants I thought he was the most paintable native we had yet seen. He had what is known as "line." Polynesians are chunkily built all over even when they are not fat. The Melanesians, even the handsome westerners, have disproportionately large features compared to their stature and especially the length of their necks. (An extra development of the lowest cervical vertebrae gives the back of the neck an apelike hunch.) But the Papuan was elegant. In profile there was a fine flying buttress swing to his nose, which was long from root to tip, and the distance from the chin back to the neck was long, and the neck itself was long. The native throughout had this longness, which was not bigness but slenderness, for like most bush people he was emaciated from not having enough to eat.

But for the moment he was not only half starved but terrified to within an inch of his life. He had probably never even heard of any animal the size of an Australian stallion, nor seen a dog as big and nastily aggressive as the bull. And he was not coming down out of his tree. The recruiter had snorted off to round up the rest of his scattered herd; and when he returned to rescue the treed boy, my horse and bull terrier were tied up down the road, but the boy still needed rescuing. *I* was still there. And while the native still clung to his trunk and the rain still pelted down, the dazed recruiter heard that I was just a harmless picture painter, and if he would come to the Ambassador after getting the recruits housed we would like to talk to him about scarified Papuans.

I am not sure that the man did not think I was soliciting, because, come five o'clock, he promptly appeared at our doorway all smiles and sheared to the skin, but, like myself, rattling with the first chills of malaria started by our drenching. Arranging for the boy to pose for us cleared up his mind about the blue and magenta room, but the sundowners we served (for malaria, of course) very nearly undid our progress. They started the fellow off on a recruiter's Rabaul binge from which, so far as we know, he never emerged.

When he left the Ambassador he promised to send the boy over to the museum first thing in the morning, but he apparently went straight to Ah Chee's to continue what we had unwittingly started. It was not surprising, therefore, that no boy appeared at the museum next morning. After making this discovery with a great deal of pain I went back to bed to enjoy malaria, leaving Margaret to find out what had become of the recruiter and boy. This Papuan had to be painted immediately, even though I fried, because we had found that new recruits had a habit of dissolving into thin air in Rabaul. They were there one day and gone the next. Margaret came back with empty hands having traced the recruiter to his point of dissolving; so the Slave (our current houseboy headache) was given a paper talk-talk for the recruiter whom he was to locate or lose his head. In a few hours he was back reporting that the mastah had died. "Not die *finish!*" we asked horrified. No, he had just died. In other words, he was either sick or drunk. And it turned out to be both, though the drunk had the upper hand.

Well, that was fine for my plans, which were to stay in bed until I could stand without reeling. So long as the recruiter remained numb the Papuan could not dissolve, and I earnestly hoped that the recruiter's health was good enough to stand a three-day drunk, as that would give me time to get on my feet. However, as a precaution against the man's getting on his feet himself and transferring the Papuan to an employer, we stationed the Slave at Ah Chee's to watch and report on the progress of the bun.

I look back on that span of malaria as the merriest bit of pain I ever had. Evidently the Slave *never* let the recruiter get out of his sight, and every time the drunk expressed itself in a new form the boy would come tearing back to the Ambassador with the news that head-he-go-round was close up walkabout now—the drunkenness was going away on a walk. I would rise from my bed of pain, dress in pain, and weave down the roads of Rabaul on my bicycle to Ah Chee's. There we would find the recruiter sleeping like a baby. All we had to do in order to ascertain this was to go up to his room and look in.

Margaret explained to the Slave more about the stages of head-he-go-round-belly-he-come-up. When he saw the recruiter walking in a *straight line* and *away* from the bar, not to it, he was to report. So the next time we were routed out was when the recruiter walked in a straight line from the bar to the toilet where he stayed so long that the Slave thought he had lost his man. The recruiter was still incarcerated when we arrived, so we all stationed ourselves outside the toilet to see for ourselves. When the man finally emerged, one look proved that it was safe for me to go back to bed.

In the end I recovered first, and without bothering to get permission we went to the boys' quarters to pick up our Papuan. It was then we discovered that *he* was ill. He had probably never before been far from his village and the trip across from New Guinea had made him landsick. When he was brought out he blanched at the sight of us but was too weak—and probably too frightened—to resist when the Slave headed him into line behind us. On the way over to the museum we were a silly, pathetic, little procession. The Papuan was bewildered or startled by everything; by the chunky little Slave strutting behind him, by the town boys streaking past on their glittering bikes, but mostly fear of the awful fate before him embodied in ourselves who rode fiery horses and kept mad dogs as companions. When a motorcar came snorting up behind us with wings of dust we waited while the Papuan disgorged the rice he needed so badly. It was the first we knew how landsick and frightened he was. The remainder of the trip he followed closely at our heels like a stray dog and for the same reason; not because he loved these strangers or that they would give him anything, but because if he lost them there would be nothing else to anchor to. We should rather have taken him by the hand and led him back to his head-lopping fathers where he knew which dangers were real and how to escape them.

So, to this lad who must have spent his whole life in an isolated Stone Age village and perhaps a five-mile radius of surrounding bush, the museum must have looked like Aladdin's Cave. It was a wonderful and terrible place even to us. All through the three big rooms, on the floor, in cases, covering the walls and hanging from the ceilings, out around the veranda, under the building, and through the grounds were

hundreds of native implements, decorations, and arms. And
not a label in a hundred. It was a treasure house of unidenti-
fied abundance and dreadful confusion. We wanted to use
these things in paintings, but no one knew where they came
from even if we could produce the right models to go with
them. So now we proposed to lead the Papuan through the
jungle and let him identify objects from his own district so
that they could provide a background of local color. Obviously such a heathenishly scarred individual could not be
painted in a lap-lap from Manchester, England.

And so we began. But if we were a silly procession coming
to the museum, going through it we were just as strange. The
boy had received his instructions from the recruiter's interpreter so that he knew what we were up to, but he could not
speak a word of pidgin English and now he found himself
in a roomful of spooks. Faces, luridly colored and threatening,
peered down at us from every conceivable object; from great
masks, wooden figures, drums, and shields, and there were
even a few dried heads, all of which must have had meaning
to the boy. His eyes were wild, his mouth pursed as though
whistling like a chirping ape, and he tottered as he walked.
But then so was I tottering and probably for the same reason;
we were convalescents. And we walked and walked, silently
in single file, waiting for the oracle to speak. When we had
gone through the entire collection slowly for the second time
with still no word we had to conclude that no white man had
ever been to the boy's village before the recruiter to rifle it
of treasures. There was nothing to do but paint just a torso
and head of the model minus village ornaments. And we got
busy on it.

Arranging a pose was always easy, simply because we had
long since given up the idea of getting anything but a comfortable position in a native. Margaret indicated to the boy
that he was to sit down on the veranda and then I waited

about ten minutes to see what position he would settle into, and that was the pose. In the village we drew a line in the dirt around the model's behind or feet so that after rests we could get him back in the same place, but on the veranda we used chalk. And that chalk line going around the boy's seat and folded legs made him jerk. When it was completed, with the lines of the circle joined in front of him, he looked at it all around himself, saw that he was trapped, and went into a rigid trance. It took a half hour before that wore off and I could begin painting a figure relaxed enough to stay that way.

By that time the Papuan seemed to have forgotten about us. He sat facing the gardens of the agriculture experimental station, looking out across the stand of corn, the rows of beans on trellises and, beyond, the fruit trees in neat lines all trimmed to the same height, so orderly and different from a native garden. Growing food was something familiar, and I saw the boy's unblinking eyes glittering back and forth, near and far, observing everything. His head never moved from the position and the bony fingers on his legs were motionless, but the widely spaced toes twitched endlessly as indicators of activity at the other end of the boy. He was *thinking*.

Papuans have been described frequently as the most bestial and stupid of human beings, having not one saving virtue. They eat snakes and ants and dogs, and the tongues and testicles of their enemies, and live in filth and perpetual terror of their neighbors and the malevolent spirits that haunt every rafter and tree and rock. They have shocking sex orgies to promote the fertility of the gardens, and murder and eat even their own infants. But we had read these same things about the Melanesians and, except for their exclusiveness, to which they certainly had a right even though it took noisy, inconvenient forms of expression, we had found them polite and clean, and certainly far from stupid. That we could not understand their kind of intelligence did not prove that it did not exist and was not equal to our own in its own way. Our models had sores and flies, but we had them too, and ants in our pants as well—ourselves having pants, which the natives had probably tried as a garment themselves and discarded generations ago as being ant traps. In any case, we had a very open mind about the "brutish" Papuan before us.

We got the results of the toe-twitching mental disturbance at the end of the second pose, and it had nothing to do with agriculture. At the first rest we had trouble getting the model to take it. We got him to his feet by pulling him up, but then he seemed to think he had to stay inside the chalk circle, until Margaret waved him inside the museum room; when he finally moved, he leaped over the line. During rests I seldom got up these days. I painted sitting on a big mat and when the spello came I simply dropped back, stretched out my numb legs, and usually fell off to sleep for a few minutes; so what Margaret had to do with the magic of the second spello, I missed. I opened my eyes to see the boy standing above me with his lap-lap off and nothing to replace it but a hip string of yellow bones (human vertebrae we found out later). The band had a sort of lavaliere at the back which looked like a bunny tail. Margaret said the boy had picked it out of a case himself and without a word removed his lap-lap and put on the bone belt. That eliminated the Manchester cotton from the picture and allowed me to do the whole lean figure, to everyone's pleasure including the boy's. He was now looking quite human, even smiling once in a wistful eager way.

After the fourth pose—they were about half an hour long —the head was far enough along to look human, so we brought the boy around to see himself. For the moment he reverted to the primitive. He pursed up his lips like an ape, and in his eyes there was no more recognition of this unknown profile than a dog sees when looking at himself in the mirror. Yet after this rest he came back from the museum room with a hat which he indicated was proper for himself by putting it on the back of his head. We haven't the slightest idea how he was thinking around this situation; he didn't recognize himself in the picture, that was certain, and he could not possibly have understood anything about portraiture: if he had even seen any kind of picture in his life we should be surprised. Yet this primitive sensed in some way that he was contributing to the monkey business we were up to. That was intelligence of a sort we could appreciate. As proof that it was intelligence, the minute the boy understood that he was to return to the chalk circle after each rest he went back to it (taking care not to step on the line) and seated himself in exactly the same position, his head posed in the same direction; and he held that pose until he was ordered up again. Margaret had rearranged him just once for the second pose. To some white sitters one can explain this matter of returning to a position until one is blue in the face, and they never understand. Others know without even being told, and this primitive was one of them though he did not know why it was required of him.

The hat was a laboriously constructed piece, a cane foundation with dozens of tiny shells attached in a V with a line of big canine teeth going up the front. It looked more like an arm cuff because it was open at both ends, but the boy was explaining very clearly that his hair should have been long; then it would have been pulled through the cuff to hold the hat on his head. While I painted the hat the model held it in position with his hand; then he came around in back of me to direct the painting of the absent hair. It was when I got it right after many corrections that the boy rewarded us with a long whistle. That whistle was the only native one we heard in Melanesia and it was equal to a first prize at any art exhibition, because it was the only spontaneous compliment any native had given us on our handiwork.

And there were more compliments when we got to the boy's back during the second sitting. He may not have known that it was himself being painted, but the back in the picture was still a rattling good job of scarification. The model squatted before the canvas stabbing his finger at it, chirping and whistling until we could stand it no longer. We went in search of a big enough mirror so that he could get a rear view of the quilting he so much admired. We had a pocket mirror and one of the museum boys had a fairly good-sized shaving glass, but the Papuan's intelligence did not reach to manipulating the two. So far as we know he never found out that he himself owned this wonderful back.

We got more data on the curious hat later. It was an initiation crown like the lantern shakos of the Bougainese, but unlike their hat, once it was put on it stayed on so long as the wearer remained alive and in the village. When the boys were recruited, however, the hats had to come off and the hair with them, because through the years the hat was worn the wiry, kinky wool of the native grew into the cane-and-shell construction so that the two became inseparable. The joker in this hat was that it was not a proper headpiece for our model at all—this is, if one wants to split hairs. The men of the boy's village wore a similar headgear, but the one I painted came from a neighboring district. The Papuan evidently recognized it from having seen it in his vicinity, possibly on heads brought into the village without the natives attached to them. The physical type of the natives, however, does not vary in so few miles as separate these two districts, and the hat was therefore correct in that it was painted on the right type.

But that wonderful raspberry-pink, electric-blue and white shield the boy chose! We had been admiring it ourselves for a long time, wishing we had an excuse to paint it. Then the model brought it to us on one of his rest walkabouts. Silly

with joy, we painted it in the background—turned the wrong way with the designed surface facing in when it should have been out from the boy; but the handle side was plain wood and the color was what we liked. But that was just what the model liked too. It was his only excuse for having brought the piece for us to paint. For it was not even a New Guinea shield, not even Papuan, but a local Nakanai sing-sing "decoration."

After that discovery the only thing we could be sure was authentic in the picture was the hide of the boy himself.

36

Our artistic swan song of the Territory was an attempt to paint a sing-sing, and for even attempting that we deserve some credit. For the inspiration was a supercolossal production of Hollywood dimensions that we tried to re-create on a forty-inch canvas. But that was not the reason why it was a failure; the paint itself lacked all those elements of the senses that make an island spectacle.

There are generally two kinds of sing-sing: the dance and feast and chanting that attend the coming-of-age ceremonies of girls, and betrothals, marriages, and births, which are witnessed by all the villagers; and those other secret dances which have to do with the men's clubs and are not always initiation ceremonies, but may be the whooping up for a raid, or celebration of a successful one. These latter, the native women and outsiders never see.[1]

Another kind of sing-sing has an innocent origin purely social, and may be witnessed by anyone. The theme is some current event. For instance, even the Expotition inspired an embryonic sing-sing which, had the inventors had more time, might have developed into one of "those strange old island chants." When we left a plantation in the Solomon Islands, the native wife of a planter, accompanied by all her female relatives, collected on the veranda to watch us pack. For hours they sat without a word, fascinated by the wealth that went in the trunks. Margaret brought things while I fitted them into their places that I knew so well by this time.

---

[1] Pig is the traditional sing-sing feast dish and the native can find as many excuses for eating his favorite meat as the Italians have found for saint's days. These include everything from first pregnancy and baby's first tooth to circumcision and first menses, besides the other big events like marriage and initiation into the clubs. Pigs are prepared for eating in a different way in each district, but none could have been more—well, interesting, than the one we saw becoming a feast dish. A huge wild boar had been caught in the bush and brought into the village wounded, but still very much alive, trussed to a bamboo pole and carried on the shoulders of four men. The wound had been packed with clay to prevent it from losing blood. The central fire in the clearing was stoked to a blaze and then the pig, still alive, was run over the fire to singe off the bristles and toughen the hide. At this point we had to sit down—because we couldn't stand up. The next stage would have got us down anyway. The pig's squealing mouth was bound shut and then it was upended on the pole and disemboweled by cutting around the anus and, with this as a handle, pulling. That, at least, killed the pig, but without taking its pulse the natives thrust burning wood into the cavity. We are not sure why this was done, but after a while the embers were taken out and, without removing any ashes, a pudding of sago replaced the bonfire. Very little blood was lost in the butchery and what came from the porker's head was caught in a clamshell and poured onto the sago pudding, the opening then being plugged with leaves. For roasting, the pork was placed with tardy reverence on a bed of leaves that lay over the rock oven, and then covered with more leaves, hot sand, and boulders.

There was probably a certain rhythm to the endless business. Finally we came to the clothes trunk and after half-a-dozen garments had been folded down into it one of the women began to hum with her lips closed.

The woman stopped to laugh hysterically with the others and then started humming again, hanging onto the sixth note each time she came to it. Presently another woman joined in, starting on the fourth note, repeating the same melody. Another woman came in and then all were humming. It was a kind of protracted round, like "Three Blind Mice." They hummed for a long time, good straight missionary harmony, and then suddenly the first woman broke into a solo with words, still using only full harmonies of the six notes. "My word," she improvised, "the Missus are going away. They are going . . . going. They put into the box the white dress, the white dress, the white dress. [Three dresses.] They are going away on a launch. They are going away on the steamer. The tall one who makes pictures, the small one who sings with her teeth [that is, whistles]. My word, they go tomorrow."

The music did not come to an end there. The humming continued as an interval and by and by, ever so casually, another woman began her story of our going, going. And so on through the whole afternoon until the lock of the last trunk was snapped. There was one deviation; the woman who had started the sing got up on one occasion and shyly went through an awkward pantomime of bringing things and placing them in a box, her walking back and forth being a business of standing in the same place and coming down on the veranda hard with her heels, which seems to be the universal Melanesian dance step. She was quickly laughed down by her sisters, but this, nevertheless, was the seed of a social sing-sing number. In precisely this way they all start.

These Maries were the only eastern Melanesian women we ever heard sing or saw make any attempt at a "dance," and undoubtedly they did so because they were very familiar with Whites and were not in the village, where they would have probably been laughed down. For the dance seems to be exclusively the pleasure of men. Such dances as I have described, inspired by some current event, are often presented in a concourse to which a number of friendly villages come, each performing the numbers they have devised since their last meet. Popular numbers are traded between villages, the pantomime and stories being taught to the "buyers" just as our dancing teachers pass on their wares.

It all sounds very prosaic when you read about this kind of sing-sing, and the one we witnessed, which inspired our picture, had an even more prosaic theme than that of the Missus-who-can-whistle going away. This was inspired by a missionary going away. The missionary, who had been in the islands twenty-five years, was retiring finally, and the sing concourse was held at the mission station to honor his going.

The station was four miles out of town and we debated for some time whether to make even that short trip on a stifling Saturday afternoon. The missionary flock would probably sit around in clean white shirts with their hair parted and sing "Till We Mee-ee-eet" in a curdling off-key. And we should expire in the heat. Yet we went, and in the Editor's two-seater, with the top down. Even before we left the shaded tunnels of Rabaul we were fried to the seat and breathing pure dust. The Peninsula had had no rain for weeks and the roadbed was under inches of fine white powder which was as buoyant as swan's-down. But as soon as we were out on the road to Kokopo it became apparent that this was going to be a sing-sing worth suffering for. We had never before seen so many natives at one time. On both sides of the road there was an endless procession of town natives going in our direction, dressed to the ears with flowers and beads, their coconut-oiled skins liberally powdered by the fans of dust that we and other cars sprayed over them. And as we drew up to the mission station it was like a fair in a small town— crowds of natives pouring in from all directions, until, in the grounds, we could scarcely move forward among them. There were natives with painted faces and huge head decorations, bodies shining with coconut oil and sweat, and their big mouths yipping. An enormous live pig passed, hanging back down and screaming on a pole carried by two men. The heat and dust closed us all in together as if our own hides were not the precious white. This was the natives' day.

We finally got through to the mission residence and were given seats on a veranda crowded with white visitors. It faced the bay looking out across a wide plaza about the size of a small racecourse. This circular clearing was entirely filled with natives. The first impression was that of a great bowl of confetti, of chunks of color being joggled. The air was full of dust and sunshine, and the bay beyond the fringe of palms on the distant beach was like a slab of washing bluing.

At first the crowd of natives below us was no more than a bewildering mass of feathers and huge headdresses and masks, paint streaked on naked brown skins, in their arm and leg bands streamers of crinkled, colored paper and plumes of big branches of yellow croton and the swordlike leaves of the bush wall—all milling about in the greatest disorder and excitement. I was for charging down into the crowd with my camera but the missionary told me to wait. And presently there was something worth waiting for. A drumming began somewhere down near the beach. The sea of heads turned in that direction and then a wonderful thing happened. The whole mass of natives separated into little groups—as if some god were cutting a pie into little pieces—and the natives of each group began to move in unison with one another. Slowly at first the chanting began, each group with its own chant, each one with its own steps and motions. Some of the men were hopping along, back and forth in single file, others were in formations of two abreast, all going at it in unison like Rockettes. Only one group near the veranda was hemmed into a circle formation by the native spectators, and here the men were doing some kind of solo dance, each one with his own pantomime. Drums were throbbing everywhere, and if these dances had anything to say about a missionary departing the islands it was pretty obscure even when the dancing started. The groups were from all over the Territory and clearly this sing-sing to them was a village sing contest on a scale never before provided them.

The hopping and singing of the groups began mildly enough, but soon the members of each unit, in an effort to make themselves heard above the joggling neighbors, were bawling at the tops of their voices and drumming like mad. The dancing became more violent, the feathers and leaves bobbed frantically, and again the whole acre was a wildly agitated sea of confetti. I was down in it now, pushing my way between the crowding native spectators who hemmed in each group of dancers. They were watching with their mouths open, eyes boggling, and so absorbed that they did not make way for a white woman the way natives usually did. The dancers flaying the air with their arms and hopping back on their heels crashed into their dumb audience, themselves not caring what they struck or how hard. They seemed frantic. Their eyes were bloodshot and the sweat washed the paint on their faces away in streaks. They rattled nuts and shells, pounded on their drums, or waved branches of leaves, while the ribbons of wrinkled paper streaming from their hair and arm bands vibrated like mad. The dust came up in clouds and the air was thick with the odor of coconut oil, hot bodies, and a curiously pungent herb.

I had been trying to take photographs, bodily pushing natives out of the way so that I could get a range, my eyes filled with sweat, and not enough hands to do anything. I suddenly became panicky. Nothing happened to start it. I just found myself suddenly submerged in natives, wild men with great big mouths howling on all sides of me, drums and voices booming. I couldn't breathe. I couldn't escape. Anyone who has been caught in a mob panic knows the feeling. Once, back in another life, I was in a crowded store elevator when a woman's foot got caught in a closing door and the elevator went down with the woman hanging by the foot from the ceiling. Instantly the elevator was filled with unhuman screams, and women fainted still standing upright because there was not room to fall. The cage of humanity was suddenly a cage of beasts, female beasts, clawing and pounding and shrieking. That's mob panic, and I got the same sensation now, hemmed in by these convulsive black men—something here beyond reason or control.

I suppose the vibrations set up had suddenly synchronized with my own personal tempo, like the vibrations of marching men's feet which crash a steel bridge when they reach the right intensity. But one of the unsoothing features of the dances was that the groups never stopped dancing and singing until they were gasping hideously for breath. They went on and on with their faces contorted, inhaling in sobs, until they were bent almost double in pain. And still they danced on. There was something masochistic about it, like self-flagellation. I couldn't get out of the mob fast enough and was almost crying by the time I had fought my way to the veranda.

And this was just a nice social dance by Christian converts with a missionary's departure for a theme. One wonders what the work-up for a headhunting raid would be like.

The British certainly have a gift for paradoxes. When I finally reached the safety of the veranda just in time to save my life and senses, it seemed, someone met me with a cup of tea and a plate of cookies, and at the height of the hysteria raging below us we sat and sipped. I could think of nothing but the old Roman emperors who munched dates while down in the arena lions tore Christians limb from limb. The sun dropped across the bay sending a horizontal pink light over the frenzied mob, the palms on the beach turned a livid green against a strawberry meringue sky. And the Reverend was looking embarrassed.

He looked like a man who has spent twenty-five hard years civilizing and Christianizing savages only to discover on the next-to-the-last day of those years that his flock are still wolves. Below the veranda steps a group of six men, dancing two abreast, were going through a wildly hopping and cackling pantomime. Each was dressed in a Marie's town blouse, and under the blouses they held a stick under each arm which poked the blouse out two points. The illusion of breasts was perfect. This was the only group in the whole sing-sing that provoked laughter in the native spectators. Each dancer had a palm basket with a few hens' eggs in it, and while the Reverend stood on the top step, looking amused in an embarrassed way, the dancers came forward one at a time and put an egg in the basket on the bottom step. If egg laying by the pseudo Maries had any symbolism and the Reverend understood it, it was something he did not care to explain to us.

And so, having seen and smelled and heard and felt a native sing-sing we decided to immortalize in paint this major diversion of primitive life. Not the gigantic spectacle of the mission, for that was far from typical; such crowds of natives never assemble except at the instigation of Whites, and then only once in fifty years or so. Our painting was to be an exclusive little village affair. We began by taking Tombat and the entire To clan up to the museum and letting them deck themselves out in all the seed and shell and bone heirlooms of their district. They were having a high old time, especially since they were all together in the fun and not at their legitimate jobs, and they decorated themselves with white lime and leaves, and posed all over the museum grounds in dance figures while I took photographs of the formations. Tombat was to pose alone for the individual figures later. He also picked out of the museum stock a magnificent mask which he said was a sorcerer's costume used in the men's sing-sings. It was a huge umbrella made of vine pith, the top covered with white pin feathers and the underside painted in a blue and white design. This stood on a complex framework four or five feet above the part that rested on the shoulders of the wearer, who was entirely concealed by a great bulging grass skirt that fell below the knees. Like many of the dance masks it was as cumbersome and unmanageable to wear as an airplane—much like some of those spectacle headdresses of the Follies shows—but Tombat, probably daring the devil, got inside it and, to the howls of the To, did a few ungainly hops about to demonstrate its use. So, though we had not the

least idea of the significance of the mask, nor what kind of song and dance the To were giving us, we went to work on this material.

Unfortunately our canvas was only forty inches wide, which prevented us from painting the panorama that the circle-formed dance called for; it also compelled us to make a perpendicular composition in order to get the tall mask in. I worked three weeks on the thing, and it was a complete dud. I don't know what I expected of paint, but the sing-sing picture was not there. It lacked the dust, the smells, the heat and gasping and frenzy, but most of all it lacked the vibrations that can break a bridge and send a headhunting artist scuttling for safety.

We wondered if this feature of the islands could ever be painted, except possibly in abstractionist symbols. And then what have you? Not a factual record.

37

Before the rains of the southeast monsoon began there was a drought of almost five weeks after an almost rainless dry season, the longest siege anyone could remember. Every bicycle and car that passed our room sent a cloud of white powder dust into it. Rabaul was an inferno. People were beginning to get scratchy. The Judge said his litigation cases were piling up but only as they always did toward the end of the northwest season. Witnesses snarled at each other in court and fought outside. Two men we met when we first arrived in Rabaul were killed two nights apart in motor accidents when they were tearing out through the countryside to get a breath of air. Another acquaintance was found dead on his plantation, and his wife and an assistant overseer were brought into court on a charge of poisoning the husband. Both were finally acquitted, but the overseer later committed suicide. Then the woman's daughter eloped with a man whose legitimate wife removed herself as an obstacle by taking her own life. The unmarried daughter of one of our tennis hostesses, spending her first "winter" at home after graduating from a fashionable girls' school in the South, became pregnant. That was scandal enough even for Rabaul during the changing monsoons, but when another white "virgin" in a neighboring settlement gave birth to a half-caste child the native responsible was nearly lynched with good old Southern enthusiasm.

One sweltering night, when the mosquito net over our bed was making it feel like the inside of a charcoal iron, all hell let loose in the Ambassador. A family, consisting of a man and wife and an infant, had moved into the room adjoining ours, and all through the heat the baby had been ill and was crying incessantly. Husband and wife nagged each other above the wails of the child, not a comma of which but could be plainly heard over the partition that gave us our mutual illusion of privacy. We could even hear them scratching themselves, and Margaret and I took to writing notes to each other and communicating in sign language. We might have moved down the hall a few rooms, but the new tenants were said to be temporary and we thought we could outlive them. Besides, we were feeling rather temporary ourselves at this point; if we moved anywhere it was going to be out of Rabaul.

This particular Saturday night the husband next door, addressing his wife, announced to all of us in the building that he was off to get drunk. His wife tried to keep him at home in the hotbox, and then, when he would not stay, she followed him, leaving the infant alone in the room. Around two o'clock in the morning we were still lying there enduring the heat when the great barnlike building was suddenly filled with screams. They did not come from the room next door, but diagonally from across the hall where a prospector had set up camp. Following the screams there were sounds of choking curses, thrashing and bumping, a terrific struggle going on, and then a woman's voice shrieking, "Don't kill him . . . for God's sake. Don't kill him!" Added to this the baby next door began to scream, and there was a pounding of running feet all through the building. Fists banged on the door across the hall, men shouted, and finally the door was smashed in with a great crash, after which there was more breathless cursing and the gasping and clumping of struggle. There was not a word we could make out that explained the thing, and finally all the clumping and puffing took itself off up the hall.

In the morning we found out that Popeye, the restaurant sailor, had gone on a Saturday night drunk and, thus stimulated, remembered that the miner across from us owed him money from a former visit. He had somehow made his way into the room from the screened wall at the rear of the building and then proceeded to choke the debt out of the miner. It was the sailor's wife who had done the screaming.

But with the removal of that party our Saturday night was not yet over, for an epidemic of real window-smashing had started.

The baby next door was still alone and still wailing pitifully, so we were not asleep when the first shock came. Our bed, propped up on blocks, began to sway ever so gently. Then the whole building suddenly wrenched with a great creak all over the roof. We bolted up. It was an earthquake. And it was an earthquake of official dimensions. While we sat there the entire building began cracking like a matchbox crunched in the fist, and we were rocking back and forth on the bed as if we were in a cradle. Again the feet were thundering over the bare floors and people were shouting as objects began to crash to the floor. The baby was screaming at the top of its lungs and that somehow brought us to life. But it was not soon enough. Before we could get out of bed, the bed had rocked off its blocks and we crashed to the floor muffled in mosquito net. The net was tucked in under the mattress and the drop had broken the strings which held it up. Even in our terror we had to laugh trying to find our way out of that net, each of us pulling in an opposite direction. Lights had been switched on in the rocking building and then suddenly they went off, which seemed to increase the uproar. It sounded as if the roof would fall in. Then the whole building gave a violent terrifying wrench and with it everything that had been hanging or standing crashed. Rabaul seemed to have met its moment of "horrible catastrophe," for outside the road was filled with shouts and the sound of running feet, mostly bare.

The shock lasted for three minutes and was so violent that it made us dizzy. And no sooner were we out of the building than there was another paroxysm almost as long, this one so fierce that the tops of the trees in the road began whipping back and forth. The town was filled with the howls of dogs and the crowing of roosters. We joined some people standing on the corner who were looking up toward the mountains behind town to see if they were in eruption. The horizon above them was clear and blue, but the stench of sulphur rolling up from the flats south of town was a potent reminder that the slim line between being blown up and not being blown up was about as usual.

While we were standing there the mother of the baby next door tore past us screaming with fright. We felt guilty—though the baby's cries had been drowned in the final crashing so that we were not reminded of it in our hysteria to escape from the cracking building. We all followed the woman into the building, for we could be brave now that it had stopped rattling—though not waving.

When we reached the room we saw what must have been one of the narrowest escapes from death any human ever survived. A great heavy wardrobe had fallen forward, evidently when the building nearly split in two, and it had dropped straight over the child's bed. But as it fell the door had swung open, and here it was lying propped half on the door, half on itself over the bed, with the child inside it. The edge of a shelf was not three inches above the child's head. The wardrobe was one that was being stored in the building by the Editor's sister, and if we had borrowed it (as we would have had it not been too heavy to move), it would have been in our room to crash over on our things. As it was we suffered no loss at all.

But on account of the earthquake we made a discovery that was serious. It was the damage done to our Solomon Island canvases by the gases of Rabaul. When we moved into the Ambassador we had unrolled and hung the pictures face to the wall, around the walls of the storeroom so that they would be straight while they finished drying out. And now, as a result of last night's shaking, they were all lying crumpled on the floor. But it was not the wrinkling that had done the damage. It was in picking them up that we saw what Rabaul had done, what the weeks of exposure to the sulphurous atmosphere can do to paint. Every portion that had been painted with lead colors had been affected. White areas had turned golden yellow, but all colors mixed with white had dulled and in most cases turned darker. Some greens had turned black even where the paint had been used pure and, of course, the madder red, which I had not expected to hold up anyway (for the best madders are merely a glaze), had faded out of existence. The change in our pictures and our dismay were about equal.

The canvases would have to be copied immediately or there would be nothing left to copy; but here we faced an impasse. Rabaul could support us no longer. Our stay had profited us nothing. Rather, what provender it had extended had been just enough to pay our expenses to this day, and even that had been mostly a windfall all of a lump. We had been commissioned to do the Chief Justice's portrait for the Rabaul Club, but the check for that picture, instead of solving everything, threw us into new confusion. Until we received it we had been resigned to going home from Rabaul. It was a retreat, though not wholly without honor, for we had the paintings of the Melanesians we had come for. But there were still the Negroid and Mongoloid "ancestors" of the Melanesians, all to the west, to be painted, and to paint them we dared not spend our reserve of passage money home. Then along came the check for the Chief Justice's portrait. There was enough of a balance after we had earmarked some of it for current expenses to start us off in Papua, and ahead there were two moderately large settlements, Samarai and Port Moresby, where we might lop off enough white heads to keep us going until we got to Thursday Island, which is the largest white settlement in northern Queensland. It would be a long chance, and we could not make up our minds to take it.

That debate, however, had nothing to do with the present problem of how to salvage the Melanesian paintings. But one thing was certain, we could not afford to stay in Rabaul to copy them. This was something that could be done properly only with peace of mind and plenty of time. So the next best thing was to try to arrest the deterioration and then get the pictures out of the country as fast as possible.

Ordinary sulphur discoloration on paintings happens in the best of families, right here in our own country, where sulphur dioxide in the air (sulphuric acid united with oxygen in damp air) is created in the cities by coal-burning house and factory furnaces. It is the thing which keeps us busy cleaning table silver and fireplace brass, and turns old paintings a golden yellow. To clean it off, picture restorers charge a great deal of money to run over the paintings with a lump of fresh rye bread, a slice of raw potato or onion. Only don't start cleaning your paintings with any of these vegetables, because if the discoloration has penetrated the varnish to the pigment beneath, the varnish has to be removed, and this is a delicate job for which restorers deserve a great deal of money.

There was nothing in the world that would restore the madder red in our pictures, but the lead colors could be cleaned—perhaps. There was no rye bread, fresh or otherwise, within a thousand miles, and a potato, we found, had no effect on volcanic sulphur discoloration. We borrowed an onion from Government House (eating it afterwards because it was the first onion we had met in moons) and labored with tears in our eyes until we saw that this was no good either. Peroxide, I remembered, was good for something, but the only peroxide we could buy was "flat" from the heat and had no effect. However, the painting we were working on was now wet, so we decided to try soap and water. Boat paint? Why not? We also used a dash of ammonia, to even our horror. The To line stood outside the screen of the house cook and said "ach" and "goddam" admiringly as the colors brightened under the water. The greens never came up to their original brilliance and the red and white leads stayed a little dim, but the ruinous deposit was removed as much as soap could do it. Whatever else it took off we dared not regret.

Afterward the pictures were taken out into the sunny court and the entire To clan dashed bucket after bucket of water over them, to remove the soap lye and ammonia. Then they were spread out in the sun behind the building to dry as much as the tropics would let them. It was the most successful exhibition we ever had. Crowds of town natives, invited by the proud To, came to examine their Solomon Island brothers, to chuckle over their silly village costumes and the "bush" look on their faces. Everyone recognized the Malaita boy-belong-bush instantly by his wild expression.

It was an interesting thing to see the way these boys looked at the pictures. We had heard (and laughed) about the story that the native cannot recognize a portrait snapshot unless he holds it upside down to look at it. These portraits were lying flat on the ground, the natives squatting all around them, and those sitting on the top side of the picture, seeing it upside down, examined it just as interestedly as those who were seeing it from the bottom. They did not skew their heads around the way we do looking at anything inverted. Possibly it was my paintings—making no more sense one way than the other.

The paintings were dried, not only on the paint side, but more thoroughly on the back, and then they were given several coats of good old deck spar varnish. By this time, according to all the laws of the craft, there should have been no paintings left. What paint the sun had not bleached out should have cracked and peeled off, and the canvas should have shrunk and stretched and shrunk again until the pictures were peeling and buckled in ruffles. This probably would have happened if most of the masterpieces had not been painted with century-enduring boat paint on heavy sailcloth. The linen canvases we tacked on the walls to dry. And as an extra precaution against mold rot, after the several coats of varnish with their seasoning of insects, the canvases were put out in the sun again face down to bake from the back. No other easel pictures in the world took such a beating as these.

We now had to decide what to do with the paintings, just as we had to decide what to do with ourselves. And we had to make up our minds quickly, for we were faced with a crisis in a choice of ships and directions. In three weeks the freighter for the Philippines would be going through, but on the day after tomorrow the Sydney steamer would be sailing South, her first port of call being Samarai in Papua. And again, in the harbor was anchored an American scientific expedition schooner and we had been invited to sail on her. This was the cruelest of the choices to have to decide on. The schooner was one we had followed a good part of two years through the South Seas, it having been always a port ahead of us; and its personnel was so familiar to us now by name and reputation that we knew even the individual peculiarities of its members. If we could catch up with that expedition, we had told one another a hundred times, we might be able to thumb a ride since they were going the same way we were. Now the schooner had arrived in Rabaul, and without doing any wangling we had been invited to join her. And she was returning to the Solomons! But our direction, if we stayed in the islands, was west.

So, feeling very feminine and bewildered, we had to decide between retracing our steps (the Solomon Islands) under the ideal conditions of being able to work wherever the expedition schooner anchored, and having it as a permanent base; going on to the unknown in Papua and the Dutch Indies; or going home via the Philippines, with the work unfinished. We made one of those heroic decisions that happen only in fiction. We decided to take a chance—go west. The Papuan model we had had was too good a sample of the type to willfully miss more like him.

The decision to go on to Papua left us just two nights and a day to pack and see our friends before the steamer sailed. It was an overwhelming job in the heat, and the Editor volunteered to take care of the paintings. They were to be rolled together, paint-side out with waxed paper between them, wrapped in mats, and put into a stout box. Then they were to be shipped collect on the Philippines freighter to friends in San Francisco who would be notified to receive them. Being the original work of a citizen of the United States they would be entered duty-free. So far as we could think ahead there were no loopholes in this arrangement.

But this was not allowing for the hazards of Rabaul.

One morning shortly after we left Rabaul an amazed citizenry awakened to find their households, their offices, the hospital, and the barracks of the native constabulary bereft of natives. There was not a native in the entire town! This would be the equivalent of New York waking up one morning to find that every servant and employee, both private and public, had vanished. New York would not be more surprised than Rabaul was. Three thousand house and office boys and two hundred and fifty police had walked out, gone lim-limbur, without a sign of warning, without anyone even suspecting that the move was under foot. Only a week before, the Sepik, Buka, and Manu factions employed in the town had been on the point of murdering one another, and a whole-sale slaughter had been prevented only by the quick action of the government which, incidentally, took no less than four hundred fighting spears from just such amusing light-headed citizens as Tombat and his To relatives. Yet, all this inter-tribal enmity had been swept aside for the combined blow at the white man.

The natives were striking! For higher wages!

Thirty-two hundred natives congregated at Malaguna a few miles out of town and were there, supplied with enough food to withstand a siege until the mastahs came across. Again, the astonishing thing was that this mass move had been planned and executed with such secrecy and co-operation that not one white man in the settlement knew about it until he woke up and found himself roaring for his morning tea in a silent house. Instigation was later traced to some sailors on a visiting vessel "suspected of being Germans."

The "affair was handled successfully," but in such a way that the white element itself split up into two factions. On one side was the conservative government which ran down the native ringleaders of the strike (after all strikers had been put quietly back to work without the wage raise) and gave them jail sentences. On the other side was the usual anti-administration group who wanted to see harsher punishment, in the form of public floggings, for instance, such as the Germans had administered to keep primitives in line. One of the exponents of knocking-off-their-bloody-heads-before-they-do-it-to-us was our erstwhile friend and savior, the Editor. Being an editor he could give air to his opinions in the press, and this evidently kept him so busy for a while that he forgot all about our paintings. The Philippines freighter came and went while our precious pictures still hung, unwrapped, in the storeroom of the Ambassador, accumulating a new coat of rainy season fungus, while the press and government went into the fray with battleaxes.

Months passed.

Meantime we had arrived in Java (the worse for wear) and finally received word from San Francisco that no paintings had turned up. Every exchange of letters took anywhere up to three months, and we finally wrote to the Judge in Rabaul asking him to find out what had become of our pictures. About that time, evidently, the press-government engagement had become serious and when the Judge (government) asked the Editor (anti-) what had happened to our paintings, the Editor found in the pictures an instrument for spite. He refused to tell the government whether or not the paintings had been sent off, and after the Judge's sleuths had discovered that they were still hanging in the Ambassador, he refused to turn them over to him (the Judge) so that they could be shipped to us.

Only the dry season in Rabaul could have made a man act so insanely—and another one was being ushered in by the time this news came to us.

In the end the Rabaul *Gazette* was sued for libel by some outraged local politicians, and the Editor, to save his hide, skipped off to the bush to "hunt gold." He left very hurriedly but apparently his last act, as a vitriolic gesture toward the Judge who he knew would be distressed by not being able to help us, was to hide the paintings. The town was scoured for the missing pictures, and shipping orders for all outgoing boats for months back were searched in an effort to find out whether the paintings were still in Rabaul. Meantime, we in

Java were in despair, for not only were the Solomon Island portraits in the lot, but also everything we had done during those months in Rabaul. The entire collection was just gone; no trace of it could be found.

Rabaul's "horrible catastrophe" which Doctor Parkinson feared so many years ago, occurred on Saturday, September 29, 1937. The business began at three o'clock on Friday night with a succession of "gurias" (tremors) of a violence that had not been felt in the district for years. The tremors continued through the rest of the night and all the next day with intervals of seldom more than a minute between paroxysms. But earthquakes being a more or less normal condition and it being Saturday, everyone went about the week end's recreation much as usual until midafternoon, when a great cloud of multicolored smoke and steam was seen rising out of the bay down in the direction of Vulcan Island. It billowed and rolled and soared in a spectacular way, driving in the general direction of Rabaul.

Then the wind shifted, and what Rabaul saw was the very bowels of the earth rising out of the bay in a column a mile high. Ashes and boulders were being vomited from the column's sides like rockets. Every now and then the great weight of the tremendous geyser seemed to force the bottom out, and the base would expand outwards from the stalk with lightning speed to a diameter of half a mile or more. Across the bay between the spot where Vulcan had been and Matapi Island, south of town, there was a line of eruptions in the water indicating that the undersea fissure extended straight across the bay to Rabaul.

Some of the citizenry, including a few camera cranks, had congregated down at the wharf and were viewing the phenomenon merely as spectators when the wind changed, and brought with it the realization that the eruption was a menace that was likely to involve everyone. A suffocating and blinding dust enveloped the peninsula. Immediately shouts and screams from Chinatown testified that panic had gripped that area—panic caused by fear of the smoke column and by the more substantial threat of a tidal wave. The explosions were occurring in an all but landlocked bay, and Rabaul, on its flat, was a target for high water.

From that moment began the exodus. The road up to the heights of Namanula became a race of speeding cars, bicycles, and running natives. Then the blanket of dust descended in full force, and broad daylight was blacked out into Stygian darkness. One could not see a yard ahead of his feet. Immediately all vehicles came to a standstill and the refugees groped on foot up the hill, frantic, blinded, gagging and screaming, bumping into others in their haste, and falling in the dark. At the same time, blasts of thunder and lightning snapped and roared continuously. Trees crashed with the weight of pumice dust and soon the electricity of Rabaul was put out of action. All night long the ash fell and all night the nine thousand Europeans, Orientals, and natives of Rabaul groped up the hill to the apparent safety of Government House and the hospital. The last to evacuate was the staff of the wireless station, which had become dangerous in the supercharged air. This cut the peninsula off from all outside communications.

In the morning the air had cleared a little, and the master of an American freighter, the *Golden Bear*, lying inside the tortured harbor, turned over the use of his wireless so that the town could establish contact with the *Montoro*, the Sydney steamer, at Kavieng two hundred miles away. The refugees on Namanula Hill were then started over the peninsula to Nodup, on the outside (ocean side) where the *Golden Bear* was to pick them up and take them down the coast to the presumable safety of Kokopo—*if* the *Golden Bear* could make its way out of the harbor, to get around to Nodup. To do this it had to cross the erupting line between the Vulcan geyser and Matapi, and no one knew whether the entrance had been blocked by upheavals in the sea floor. Yet Captain Olsen of the *Golden Bear* never hesitated. His ship was seen heading for the entrance straight toward the geysers. At the doubtful line the smoke of Vulcan rolled over and the little freighter was blotted from sight. An anxious half hour passed;

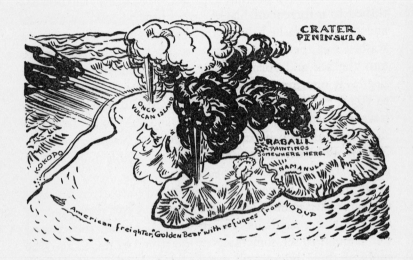

then the pumice clouds lifted and the *Golden Bear* could be seen heading out to sea all safe.

The embarkation of refugees from Nodup went on all Sunday morning, and by noon, with the confidence of increasing daylight, a few doubted the expediency of leaving Rabaul at all. This doubt was dissipated in a flash when at 1:15 the area of Matapi Island on the outskirts of Rabaul blew straight up into the sky with a boom that was heard in Kavieng two hundred miles away.

The explosion of Matapi was a hundred times more violent than that of Vulcan the day before, and it rose its mile in the air with the speed of a torpedo. The geyser was solid black mud, a fountain of mud that rained down on the peninsula. The thunder of its playing was like that of a heavy artillery barrage increased a thousandfold. Between the craters of the volcanoes above the town, above Namanula where the refugees huddled, lightning and fireballs played continuously, the only light in a black world. Then came the cloudburst upon the bedeviled district. The rain of mud from the heavens turned to a torrent of black slush. Hitherto unknown rivers and cataracts slashed down the slopes of the mountains and washed out the road of escape to Nodup. The land swept into the sea and formed banks that grounded the *Golden Bear* as it was attempting to take off refugees. Since Kokopo, to which the refugees were retreating, could not feed such a multitude even for one day, food supplies taken from the stores in Rabaul had been going over the Namanula pass to Nodup; but now the washouts and impassable mud cut off this source of supply.

On Monday, however, the *Montoro* arrived from Kavieng and succeeded in entering the bay; and this fact facilitated the task of getting foodstuffs out of Rabaul. The air had cleared too, enough to see something of the havoc in the town. The roofs of those houses still standing were smothered deep in mud, and many of them had caved in. All vegetation looked as if it had been struck by poison gas. The lovely flowering trees along the road where we had lived were as branchless as trees in no man's land, and their limbs were piled in mud on the road to a depth of fifteen feet. One man, trying to reach his house from the police station, a distance of five hundred yards, plowed for an hour on the journey. In the harbor all light craft had been sunk, including the precious *Nakapo*, and everything remaining above water was under four feet of mud and pumice. Why there was not a disastrous tidal wave is still not understood.

The two major eruptions continued throughout Monday, but the wind was offshore and the mud and pumice were being carried away from Rabaul. Now that the air was cleared, however, something was revealed that caused more anxiety than anything that had gone before. A hitherto quiescent crater on Namanula was sending a fountain of steam into the sky. The bedeviled populace held their breaths. The fountain played for a few minutes, then died down. There had been no ash, but in another minute the geyser shot up again, this time higher than before. It was time for even the government officers who were directing the evacuation to run. But this proved to be unnecessary. The geyser continued to play for twenty minutes and then, like a fountain being shut off, the steam sank lower and lower and finally disappeared. It did not spout again.

"Ach goddam," observed a native police boy, "Kombiu him-he go up, Rabaul him-he buggarup finish for all time."

Our Melanesian paintings escaped the mud bath of the peninsula. They had long since been located by the loyal Judge and were safely in our possession when this district fulfilled its promise of "becoming the theater of some horrible catastrophe." Somehow we have a feeling that in that explosion Matapi and Vulcan were speaking for all of these islands; if they and their natives and vegetation can't push or freeze the white man out, they'll blow him out.

38

On the journey to Papua I had sufficient time to myself to draw up a summary of the Expotition so far. The last of Margaret's Rabaul swains had taken his holiday South specially at this time so that he might have the short trip to Samarai with her alone. Rabaul had been too congested to ask her the thing that was on his mind. He made Number Five. Margaret said that it had become a matter of statistics and ought to be reported with our other findings. If a girl of a certain age spent so much time in Melanesia her chances of marrying some kind of white man were about four to one against those in a cooler climate, even without the Voy to manage things.

I left the two alone; the boy was "suitable," and I thought it would be nice to have Margaret living in New Guinea so that I could make her long visits and paint in comfort. And with that thought I suddenly saw Margaret from a little distance, and was not sure I wanted her to live in New Guinea, even for me. She looked white; not ill, but her skin was curiously transparent. Deficient diet? Lack of ultra-violet rays? Perhaps the steady heat had burned up the red blood corpuscles. She had not got fever, and we laid that to her having faithfully taken quinine; but it was also possible that the pounds of quinine in her system had something to do with her becoming pallor. (Both of us still had all our own teeth despite the threat of losing them.)

As it turned out we do not know whether the daily quinine saved Margaret from malaria. When we finally arrived in

Java, where we were told there was no malaria, Margaret discontinued the preventive. We were on the coast for about three months and then went up to the mountains to live; but we had not been in the colder climate a month before Margaret became desperately ill. Whether it was possible to have carried the malaria wogs over from New Guinea, or whether she had been inoculated by anopheles in Java where there were supposed to be none, is anybody's guess. It is even possible that a quite innocent anopheles, resident of Java, bit me and then Margaret, inoculating her with my malaria, for the mosquito himself must get his wogs from an infected person. What Margaret had might not even have been malaria. The Chinese doctor said it was, but I was not so sure. She was much sicker than I had ever been and for a much longer period. It was when she stopped laughing at herself that I grew worried.

For myself, in summary, I had the conflicting sense of having failed so far in what we had set out to do, and yet of being full of hope. To be sure, we had over thirty portraits of Melanesians and several unfinished studies, as well as anywhere up to a hundred carefully executed drawings. Out of this material, when I recomposed it, I might eventually get ten substantial canvases. But it was not the small amount of work, nor the quality of it in its present state that dismayed me; the work was as thorough as I could make it considering the handicaps. But that was not good enough. There was a certain quality in the subjects I had missed dismally. I knew exactly what it was. It was the absolute "all rightness" of the native in his environment. No other group of people I knew, including ourselves, so fittted into their background that it seemed a cradle made to measure. This was apparent in such simple things as the way brown natives streaked with palm shadows melted into the shadow-streaked earth behind them.

If they were silent one had to peer to be sure they were there. It was apparent in the way the Melanesian man fitted so snugly into his log canoe, and in the familiar ease with which the log slid across the transparent water, as if they were different forms of the same element. But it was mostly in the unpaintable orderliness and admirable social adjustment in the village, the people toward one another, and in their philosophy, sprung from the surrounding bush and ocean. I had painted plenty of background but somehow my figures, in retrospect, were painted on top of it instead of into it. This was perhaps owing to my anxious pursuit of the model himself. But here I felt I had missed most. It is hard to get away from the preconceived idea of cannibals and headhunters as savages, and though we had set out with the very clear intention of painting *not* savages but fellow human beings, the natives had somehow, in spite of us, remained strangers, curiosities—though, naturally, the greater distance we put between ourselves and the subject, the more understandable and likable and altogether human the natives became.

Some of this may have been merely the normal discontent of the artist who almost always feels he could have done it better if he had painted it some other way. Well, we should have a chance now to find that out, and therein was the source of my feeling of hope. For the whole eastern coast of Papua was still Melanesian. Along with all the other things I had omitted painting, I would do a portrait of a banana tree, and a papaya, as well as a sago and a betel-nut palm. I remembered now that I hadn't even painted that everlasting symbol of the islands, a coconut palm. There was still so much to do to get this big picture of Melanesia. I earnestly thanked the good Saint Christopher who had guided us onward instead of homeward, so that we could finish the job—if such a job could ever be really finished.

The white heads we "took" along this stretch could hardly

be regarded as trophies since they brought in no straight revenue. With a few exceptions (in Rabaul) all the portraits that came out of the cigarette tin were those of our hosts, and, in a way, these were revenue because they left those hosts not entirely unrepaid for their generosity in providing us lodgings. So by stretching the metaphor a little it might be said that the magic carpet in the tin had wafted us through the Solomon Islands—by a kind of hind-first action. Certainly the portrait drawings of white heads had taken the Expotition from San Francisco to New Guinea, via the South Pole; and this was a respectable feat for so battered a little tin—even though it had taken it almost two years to do the job.